_2nd edition_

# Reading
# in
# English

_for students of English_
_as a second language_

Dorothy Danielson
Rebecca Hayden
Helen Hinze-Pocher
Daniel Glicksberg

D0043187

Prentice-Hall, Inc. Englewood Cliffs, New Jersey

*Library of Congress Cataloging in Publication Data*

Main entry under title:

Reading in English.

    First ed. (1961) edited by D. Danielson and
R. Hayden.
      Includes bibliographical references and indexes.
      1. English language—Text-books for foreigners.
2. College readers.  I. Danielson, Dorothy.
II. Danielson, Dorothy, ed. Reading in English.
PE1128.D3 1980     428'.6'4     79-20466
ISBN 0-13-753442-6

Editorial/production supervision: Robert Hunter
Cover and interior design: Jayne Conte
Manufacturing buyer: Harry P. Baisley

Printed in the United States of America

10  9  8  7  6  5  4  3  2  1

Prentice-Hall International, Inc., *London*
Prentice-Hall of Australia Pty. Limited, *Sydney*
Prentice-Hall of Canada, Ltd., *Toronto*
Prentice-Hall of India Private Limited, *New Delhi*
Prentice-Hall of Japan, Inc., *Tokyo*
Prentice-Hall of Southeast Asia Pte. Ltd., *Singapore*
Whitehall Books Limited, *Wellington, New Zealand*

*For*
*LARRY DANIELSON*
*LYNN HAYDEN*
*PAUL POCHER*
*EMILY AND NATHAN GLICKSBERG*

# Chapter Opening Illustration Credits

CHAPTER 1 (p. 2):

Illustration by Don Freeman. From *Travels with Charley* by John Steinbeck. Illustration by Don Freeman. Copyright © 1962 by John Steinbeck. Reprinted by permission of Viking Penguin Inc.

CHAPTER 4 (p. 36):

"Romeo and Juliet": Excerpted from *Rommel Drives on Deep into Egypt* by Richard Brautigan. Copyright © 1970 by Richard Brautigan. Reprinted with the permission of Delacorte Press/Seymour Lawrence and The Sterling Lord Agency.

CHAPTER 8 (p. 86):

Illustration by Don Freeman copyright 1938, 1966 by William Saroyan. Reproduced from *My Name Is Aram* by William Saroyan by permission of Harcourt Brace Jovanovich, Inc. and Lawrence Pollinger Limited.

CHAPTER 13 (p. 182):

"The Act": William Carlos Williams, *Collected Later Poems*. Copyright 1948 by William Carlos Williams. Reprinted by permission of New Directions.

CHAPTER 14 (p. 198):

Illustration by Jack Sherman from *Executive* (Vol. 4, No. 3), copyright 1978 Cornell University Graduate School of Business and Public Administration. By permission.

**PHOTO CREDITS:** Chapter 2 (p. 14), Alan Reininger/Leo de Wys, Inc.; Chapter 3 (p. 26), Everett C. Johnson/Leo de Wys, Inc.; Chapter 5 (p. 50), Leo de Wys, Inc.; Chapter 6 (p. 62), Jack Whitaker/Leo de Wys, Inc.; Chapter 7 (p. 74) and Chapter 9 (p. 106), H. Armstrong Roberts; Chapter 10 (p. 138), Wide World Photos, Inc.; Chapter 11 (p. 148), P. Vannucci/Leo de Wys, Inc.; Chapter 12 (p. 168), Bill Mahon/Rapho/Photo Researchers; Chapter 15 (p. 216), Leo de Wys, Inc.

# Copyrights and Acknowledgments

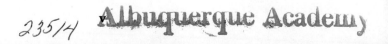

# Preface

This new edition of *Reading in English* is intended for the same group of college and university students as the first edition—advanced ESL/EFL students in reading and composition courses. The content of the present edition is somewhat similar to that found in reading and composition books for native speakers, but the orientation is for ESL, EFL, and bilingual students who need to improve their English to meet the English requirements of academic institutions.

The selections in this edition are by twentieth-century American writers. Our main focus, however, is the development of crosscultural perspectives rather than the teaching of American culture. In the search for material, a primary consideration was the possibility of crosscultural treatment; other factors were topical interest for students and an appropriate level of conceptual and linguistic difficulty.

We have included definitions of some words and occasional cultural notes to help students get on with the reading. The footnoted definitions are for the most part simple and brief. Where a word is used in an unusual sense, we first give the general meaning, followed by the specific meaning. In deciding what to gloss, we referred initially to the first 4,000 words in *The Teacher's Word Book of 30,000 Words* by Edward L. Thorndike and Irving Lorge. We also consulted *The American Heritage*

*Word Frequency Book* by John B. Carroll, Peter Davies, and Barry Richman and *A General Service List of English Words* by Michael West; and we conducted a survey of glossed items to estimate the knowledge and vocabulary level of advanced ESL students and, we hope, applied a generous amount of common sense.

Although we realize that meaning and language cannot be cleanly and neatly separated, we have divided the exercises into two sections: *A Look at the Ideas* and *A Look at the Language*. In both sections we were guided by what we consider to be one of the main objectives of an advanced ESL/EFL course: accurate interpretation and critical interaction with the ideas of the author.

If you are familiar with the first edition of *Reading in English*, you will notice a marked change in the range and types of exercises. Our primary aim has been to get the students involved in the material. In *A Look at the Ideas*, basic comprehension (getting the facts straight) is accomplished by asking students questions that begin "Comment briefly on (a)...; (b)...; (c)..." Students also deal with comprehension on another level by responding to a list of statements, first, from the author's point of view and, then, from their own view. Where concepts are especially difficult or complex, we have tried to open up questions by using a multiple-choice or matching question followed by a series of short questions rather than the conventional "What does the author mean when he says...?"

In *A Look at the Ideas*, we also provide open-ended vocabulary exercises to give students a chance to use vocabulary of their own and from the selection to describe people or situations. There is also ample opportunity for students to discuss and then write reactions to the author's ideas and to apply what insights and information they have gained to their own situations. In some places we give fairly specific suggestions for writing a paper or composition. These suggestions are intended to guide rather than direct or control the writing of students.

In *A Look at the Language*, you will find exercises that focus on vocabulary, the paraphrasing and rewriting of sentences, an examination of the function of words and phrases of a passage, a comparison of registers or communicative styles, an interpretation of the intention of speakers, and an analysis of the organization and style of an author. Here, as in *A Look at the Ideas*, we have tried to offer enough exercises so that teachers and students can select those that will be most interesting and useful for their purposes.

In an Index of Exercise Types, at the end of the book, we have tried to provide a handy reference to major types of exercises. The categories in the index are as follows: Composition and Writing, Crosscultural Comparisons, Interpretation, Organization and Mechanics, Style, and Vocabulary.

We wish to thank the many students whose questions have given us insights and direction. We also thank colleagues and friends who have given us suggestions and support; our colleague James Kohn, who tried out some of the material in its early stages; and students and instructors who participated in the vocabulary survey. We want to pay special tribute to our late colleague Ray L. Grosvenor, who gave us some of his imaginative ideas for exercises. Finally, we are grateful to the following reviewers who offered valuable criticism and encouragement: Dorothy Brown, Berea College, Berea, Kentucky; Betsey Saden, University of Michigan; Rachel Spack Levenson, University of Miami.

# Contents

## 9

## 10

## 11

## 12

## 13

# 14

# 15

*Reading*
*in*
*English*

## John Steinbeck (1902 - 1968)

*John Steinbeck grew up in California and attended Stanford University, where he studied marine biology. He worked at various jobs before gaining fame in the 1930s with his novels—such as* The Grapes of Wrath *(1939)—about farm workers during the Depression. By 1962, the year he was awarded the Nobel Prize for Literature, he had written several novels—including* East of Eden *(1952), dozens of short stories and essays, and other nonfiction work.*

*The following selection is taken from* Travels with Charley: In Search of America *(1962), a collection of essays resulting from a "new discovery" trip Steinbeck took across, and up and down, the United States, accompanied by his French poodle named Charley, in a pick-up truck named Rocinante. At the end he summed up his trip: "From start to finish I found no strangers . . . these are my people and this is my country." His views— after a close examination of the country—reveal a sense of love spiced with criticism.*

# 1

# Travels

# with

# Charley

Niagara Falls[1] is very nice. It's like a large version of the old Bond sign on Times Square.[2] I'm very glad I saw it, because from now on if I am asked whether I have seen Niagara Falls I can say yes, and be telling the truth for once.

When I told my adviser that I was going to Erie, Pennsylvania, I had no idea of going there, but as it turned out, I was. My intention was to creep across the neck of Ontario, bypassing[3] not only Erie but Cleveland and Toledo.

I find out of long experience that I admire all nations and hate all governments, and nowhere is my natural anarchism[4] more aroused than  10 at national borders where patient and efficient public servants carry out their duties in matters of immigration and customs. I have never smuggled[5] anything in my life. Why, then, do I feel an uneasy sense of guilt on approaching a customs barrier?[6] I crossed a high toll bridge and

---

[1]**Niagara Falls:** The famous waterfall serves as a boundary between Canada and the United States. Just below the falls there is a high bridge. To cross the bridge, one must pay a fee (toll).
[2]**version ... Times Square:** It looked like the waterfall on an electric advertising sign in New York City, only bigger.

[3]**bypass(ing):** Go(ing) around.
[4]**anarchism:** A belief or feeling that all forms of government interfere with a person's liberty.
[5]**smuggled:** Brought something into a country without declaring it; that is, illegally.
[6]**barrier:** In this case, a customs checkpoint or point of entry.

negotiated a no man's land[7] and came to the place where the Stars and Stripes[8] stood shoulder to shoulder with the Union Jack.[9] The Canadians were very kind. They asked where I was going and for how long, gave Rocinante a cursory[10] inspection, and came at last to Charley.

"Do you have a certificate of rabies[11] vaccination on the dog?"

20      "No, I haven't. You see he's an old dog. He was vaccinated long ago."

Another official came out. "We advise you not to cross the border with him, then."

"But I'm just crossing a small part of Canada and reentering the U.S."

"We understand," they said kindly. "You can take him into Canada but the U.S. won't let him back."

"But technically I am still in the U.S. and there's no complaint."

"There will be if he crosses the line and tries to get back."

30      "Well, where can I get him vaccinated?"

They didn't know. I would have to retrace my way[12] at least twenty miles, find a vet,[13] have Charley vaccinated, and then return. I was crossing only to save a little time, and this would wipe out[14] the time saved and much more.

"Please understand, it is your own government, not ours. We are simply advising you. It's the rule."

I guess this is why I hate governments, all governments. It is always the rule, the fine print,[15] carried out by fine-print men. There's nothing to fight, no wall to hammer with frustrated fists.[16] I highly

40    approve of vaccination, feel it should be compulsory; rabies is a dreadful thing. And yet I found myself hating the rule and all governments that made rules. It was not the shots but the certificate that was important. And it is usually so with governments—not a fact but a small slip of paper. These were such nice men, friendly and helpful. It was a slow time at the border. They gave me a cup of tea and Charley half a dozen cookies. And they seemed genuinely sorry that I had to go to Erie, Pennsylvania, for the lack of a paper. And so I turned about and pro-

---

[7]**negotiated a no man's land:** In this situation, he crossed the strip of land between the two countries.
[8]**Stars and Stripes:** The flag of the United States.
[9]**Union Jack:** The flag of Great Britain (or, in this case, Canada).
[10]**cursory:** Rapid, hasty.
[11]**rabies:** A serious disease that can be given to people by the bite of an infected animal. It can cause a very painful death.
[12]**retrace my way:** Go back.
[13]**vet:** Veterinarian; a doctor who specializes in the care of animals.

[14]**wipe out:** Take away or cancel.
[15]**fine print:** The rules written in small type that most people never get around to reading. The "fine-print men" are the officials who read them very carefully and see that they are followed exactly.
[16]**frustrated fists:** Prevented from doing or accomplishing something. In this case, useless hands. Steinbeck is angry and ready to fight, but there is no individual to hold responsible or to fight against because governments are impersonal.

ceeded toward the Stars and Stripes and another government. Exiting I
had not been required to stop, but now the barrier was down.

"Are you an American citizen?"                                                    50

"Yes, sir, here's my passport."

"Do you have anything to declare?"

"I haven't been away."

"Have you a rabies vaccination certificate for your dog?"

"He hasn't been away either."

"But you are coming from Canada."

"I have not been in Canada."

I saw the steel[17] come into eyes, the brows lower to a level of
suspicion. Far from saving time, it looked as though I might lose much
more than even Erie, Pennsylvania.                                                60

"Will you step into the office?"

This request had the effect on me a Gestapo knock on the door[18]
might have. It raises panic, anger, and guilty feelings whether or not I
have done wrong. My voice took on the strident tone of virtuous outrage[19] which automatically arouses suspicion.

"Please step into the office."

"I tell you I have not been in Canada. If you were watching, you
would have seen that I turned back."

"Step this way, please, sir."

Then into the telephone: "New York license so-and-so. Yes. Pick-    70
up truck with camper top. Yes—a dog." And to me: "What kind of dog
is it?"

"Poodle."

"Poodle—I said poodle. Light brown."

"Blue," I said.

"Light brown. Okay. Thanks."

I do hope I did not sense a certain sadness at my innocence.[20]

"They say you didn't cross the line."

"That's what I told you."

"May I see your passport?"                                                        80

"Why? I haven't left the country. I'm not about to leave the country." But I handed over my passport just the same. He leafed through[21]
it, pausing at the entry-and-exit stamps of other journeys. He inspected
my photograph, opened the yellow smallpox vaccination certificate

---

[17]**steel:** In this case, hardness.

[18]**Gestapo knock on the door:** Steinbeck has a
feeling of terror similar to that brought about by the
arrival of the Nazi secret police in the time of Hitler.

[19]**strident tone of virtuous outrage:** The
unpleasant tone of voice of one who knows that he
is right and is angry because he is challenged or
questioned.

[20]**I do hope I did not sense a certain sadness at
my innocence:** Steinbeck hopes that the customs
officer is not disappointed because he is innocent.

[21]**leafed through:** Looked rapidly through.

stapled to the back cover. At the bottom of the last page he saw pencilled in a faint set of letters and figures. "What is this?"

"I don't know. Let me see. Oh, that! Why, it's a telephone number."

"What's it doing in your passport?"

90     "I guess I didn't have a slip of paper. I don't even remember whose number it is."

By now he had me on the run and he knew it. "Don't you know it is against the law to deface[22] a passport?"

"I'll erase it."

"You should not write anything in your passport. That's the regulation."

"I won't ever do it again. I promise." And I wanted to promise him I wouldn't lie or steal or associate with persons of loose morals, or covet[23] my neighbor's wife, or anything. He closed my passport firmly

100  and handed it back to me. I'm sure he felt better having found that telephone number. Suppose after all his trouble he hadn't found me guilty of anything, and on a slow day.

"Thank you, sir," I said. "May I proceed now?"

He waved his hand kindly. "Go ahead," he said.

And that's why I went toward Erie, Pennsylvania, and it was Charley's fault. I crossed the high iron bridge and stopped to pay toll. The man leaned out the window. "Go on," he said, "it's on the house."[24]

"How do you mean?"

"I seen you go through the other way a little while ago. I seen the

110  dog. I knew you'd be back."

"Why didn't you tell me?"

"Nobody believes it. Go ahead. You get a free ride one way."

He wasn't government, you see. But government can make you feel so small and mean that it takes some doing to build back a sense of self-importance. Charley and I stayed at the grandest auto court[25] we could find that night, a place only the rich could afford, a pleasure dome of ivory and apes and peacocks,[26] and moreover with a restaurant, and room service. I ordered ice and soda and made a scotch and soda and then another. Then I had a waiter in and bespoke[27] soup and a steak and

120  a pound of raw hamburger for Charley, and I overtipped mercilessly.[28] Before I went to sleep I went over all the things I wished I had said to

---

[22]**deface:** To spoil the surface or appearance of something.
[23]**covet:** Desire; want something very much.
[24]**on the house:** Free; the restaurant, bar, or company will pay the bill.
[25]**auto court:** Motel.

[26]**a pleasure dome of ivory and apes and peacocks:** Like a beautiful, imaginary palace.
[27]**bespoke:** Ordered.
[28]**mercilessly:** Without mercy; in this case, the word is used jokingly, as if the waiter would complain about a large tip.

that immigration man, and some of them were incredibly clever and cutting.[29]

[29]**cutting:** Sarcastic, insulting.

_____ A LOOK AT THE IDEAS _____

1. Describe what happened up to the time that John Steinbeck approached the Canadian border. Tell (a) how he was traveling; (b) who his traveling companion was; (c) what his destination was; (d) why he had to stop at the Canadian customs barrier.

How would you describe Steinbeck's relationship with Charley?

2. Which of the following words would you use to describe how Steinbeck felt as he approached the Canadian customs barrier? Write *S* next to the appropriate words. Explain the reasons for your choices. (This exercise can be done individually or in groups.)

| | | |
|---|---|---|
| 1. ____ excited | 8. ____ happy | 15. ____ mean |
| 2. ____ confused | 9. ____ hostile | 16. ____ angry |
| 3. ____ hurried | 10. ____ stupid | 17. ____ cooperative |
| 4. ____ friendly | 11. ____ suspicious | 18. ____ important |
| 5. ____ fearful | 12. ____ resentful | 19. ____ subversive |
| 6. ____ nervous | 13. ____ defensive | 20. ____ uneasy |
| 7. ____ guilty | 14. ____ aggressive | 21. ____ offensive |

What other words or phrases would you use to describe Steinbeck's feelings and his behavior? Why did he feel this way?

3. The American customs officials said to Steinbeck, "Step this way, please, sir." Someone in another situation might say, "Come here!" When would you use one expression and when would you use the other?

In the following dialogues, we can sense how Steinbeck feels about the Canadian customs officers, the American customs officials, and the bridge toll collector by his choice of words and grammatical structure. Tell how Steinbeck

and the officials feel about each other and why you think
so. For example, would you say that these people act
friendly or unfriendly, seem close or distant, have a positive or a negative attitude?

1. *Steinbeck and the Canadian officers:*

"Do you have a certificate of rabies vaccination on the
dog?"
"No, I haven't. You see he's an old dog. He was vaccinated long ago."
... "We advise you not to cross the border with him,
then."
"But I'm just crossing a small part of Canada and reentering the U.S."
"We understand," they said kindly. "You can take him
into Canada but the U.S. won't let him back."

2. *Steinbeck and the American officials:*

"Are you an American citizen?"
"Yes, sir, here's my passport."
"Do you have anything to declare?"
"I haven't been away."
"Have you a rabies vaccination certificate for your dog?"
"He hasn't been away either."

3. *Steinbeck and the bridge toll collector:*

... "Go on," he said, "it's on the house."
"How do you mean?"
"I seen you go through the other way a little while ago. I
seen the dog. I knew you'd be back."

4. Many people feel that customs officials make everything as
   difficult as possible for travelers and tourists. Does Steinbeck seem to feel this way? Has this been your experience
   or the experience of others you know?

5. When Steinbeck says that he admires all nations and hates
   all governments, what kind of distinction is he making
   between nations and governments? Do you also make this
   distinction?

6. Steinbeck seems to think of rules when he thinks of governments. What kinds of things do you think he might
   associate with nations? What first comes to your mind

when you hear the word "government"? What do you think of when you hear the word "nation"?

7. Check the statement that best reflects your opinion about Steinbeck's attitude toward governments.

    _____ 1. He is too critical of his own government.

    _____ 2. He shouldn't resent rules that are made to protect him.

    _____ 3. He doesn't hate governments as much as he says he does.

    _____ 4. He is understandably frustrated by government rules.

    _____ 5. None of the above expresses my opinion about Steinbeck's attitude.

Give reasons for your choice.

8. When Steinbeck talks about "fine-print men," he is referring to government officials who—

    _____ 1. make rules not to protect people but to restrict their freedom.

    _____ 2. dedicate their lives to the service of their country.

    _____ 3. consider rules more important than the effects of these rules.

Do you think most people react the way Steinbeck did when faced with "fine-print" men and rules?

9. In what areas of government besides customs and immigration do we find "fine-print" people and rules? Outside of government, where else do we find "fine-print" people and rules?

10. Steinbeck remarks that governments can make a person feel small and mean. What did he do to make himself feel better? What would you do (or have you done) in a similar situation?

11. Describe an experience you have had with a government official that either reinforces or contradicts Steinbeck's point of view about rules, governments that make rules, and officials who enforce them.

**12.** Write a brief summary of the behavior and attitudes of the U.S. customs official who questioned Steinbeck. Then discuss the ways in which the official is similar to or different from comparable officials in your country or other countries you have visited.

**13.** In one or two paragraphs, describe an unusual experience you have observed in going through customs.

**14.** Write a composition about Steinbeck's relationship with his dog. Here are some suggestions for writing the composition:

1. You might begin by describing how Steinbeck treats Charley. Would you say that Steinbeck's attitude about dogs, and perhaps other animals, is typically American? Use examples to support your opinion.
2. Next, you might comment on whether Steinbeck's attitude and treatment of Charley would seem strange or would not be understood in another culture you are familiar with. How would such animals generally be treated in that culture?
3. Finally, you might explain which attitude toward dogs and other animals you are comfortable with yourself.

## _____ A LOOK AT THE LANGUAGE _____

1. Below are five sets of sentences. The first sentence in each set is based on the Steinbeck selection; the other three are not. (a) What does the *italicized* word or phrase in the first sentence mean? (b) Does the *italicized* word or phrase have the same meaning in the other sentences? (c) Are all of the sentences in each set idiomatic? Would a native speaker of English be likely to use the word or phrase in this way?

   1. They . . . gave Rocinante a *cursory* inspection.
      I gave the newspaper a *cursory* look.
      It was a *cursory* movie.
      The doctor gave the patient a *cursory* examination.
   2. . . . this would *wipe out* the time saved.
      They're going to *wipe out* the bowl.

They're going to *wipe out* the debt.
They're going to *wipe out* the advantage.

3. ... to hammer with *frustrated* fists.
It was a *frustrated* attempt.
It was a *frustrated* plan.
He was a *frustrated* student.

4. He *leafed through* the passport.
He *leafed through* the book.
He *leafed through* the diary.
He *leafed through* the window.

5. The toll was *on the house.*
The drinks were *on the house.*
The meal was *on the house.*
The chimney was *on the house.*

**2.** Supply the missing letters of the word in each sentence in the right column. The word you produce should result in a sentence opposite in meaning to the one in the left column.

1. He made a careful study.　　He took a _c u r _ _ _ _ _ look.

2. He knew exactly what to do.　　He felt _f r u _ _ _ _ _ _ _ _ because he didn't know what to do.

3. He looked through the book carefully.　　He _l e_ _ _ _ _ _ _ _t h_ _ _ _ _ _ _ _ the book in a hurry.

4. The drinks were paid for by the customer.　　The drinks were _o _ _ _ _ h o_ _ _ _ .

**3.** *Read the following dialogue from the story:*

"Step this way, please, sir."
Then into the telephone: "New York license so-and-so. Yes. Pick-up truck with camper top. Yes—a dog." And to me: "What kind of dog is it?"
"Poodle."

1. In the dialogue above, notice that Steinbeck frequently omits or leaves out parts of sentences to produce a conversational style. Rewrite the conversation, making all sentences complete by adding the parts left out. Does the dialogue still sound like conversation?

2. Now, using the sentences you have just written, write a paragraph in which you report the conversation to a friend who has not read the selection. You might begin your paragraph with: *The customs agent asked Steinbeck to step into the office.*

Compare the effect of your revision with Steinbeck's original.

4. Writers use various devices to relate one idea or part of a passage to another.

1. One device is *omission*, which you have been working with in exercise 3. Here is another example:

"Do you have a certificate of rabies vaccination on the dog?"
"No, I *haven't*. You see he's an old dog. He was vaccinated long ago."

Steinbeck does not add "got a certificate of rabies vaccination on the dog" after *haven't*.

2. Another device is *reference*. Pronoun reference is a common example.

Another official came out. "*We* advise you not to cross the border with *him*, then."

*Him* refers to "an old dog" and "the dog" in the preceding sentences. *We* possibly refers to the two immigration officials, but it is more likely that *we* is generic—that is, the official is speaking for the government or the immigration service when he says "we."

3. Another device is *linking*. Linking signals connect sentences and ideas to one another.

"We advise you not to cross the border with him, *then*."

*Then* relates the official's remark to Steinbeck's preceding remark, "No, I haven't [got a certificate of rabies vaccination on the dog]."

"*But* I'm just crossing a small part of Canada and reentering the U.S."

*But* relates Steinbeck's remark to the preceding remark by the official, "We advise you not to cross the border with him, then."

4. Still another device is *substitution*, or replacement.

"You should not write anything in your passport. That's the regulation."
"I won't ever *do it* again. I promise."

*Do it* replaces or is substituted for "write anything in my passport."

*Directions:* The *italicized* words and phrases indicate devices that link or relate parts of the passages below. Explain what is omitted, referred to, linked, or replaced, and tell how these devices function in relating ideas in the passages.

a) When I told my adviser that I was going to Erie, Pennsylvania, I had no idea of going *there*, but as it turned out, I *was*.

b) I have never smuggled anything in my life. Why, *then*, do I feel an uneasy sense of guilt on approaching a customs barrier?

5. List the main events that occur in "Travels with Charley." Do the events occur in chronological order—that is, in the order in which they actually happen? You might compare your list with the lists of other students to see if your lists are similar. Using your list, write a brief summary of the main events. Words and phrases like *first, then, next, after that,* and *finally* are frequently used as linking signals in a summary of this kind.

# Anais Nin (1903-1977)

*Anais Nin was born in Paris and in her first eleven years traveled extensively with her musician parents. In 1914, her parents separated, and Anais came to New York with her mother and two brothers. It was on the ship crossing the Atlantic that she began her Diary, which later brought her international fame. Early entries in the Diary, first written in French but in English after she was seventeen, contain comments about the strangeness of New York and the cultural differences between Europe and the United States. After she dropped out of school at fifteen, she educated herself by reading widely. In the 1920s and 1930s, she lived and wrote in Paris, returning to the United States only shortly before World War II.*

*During her lifetime she published novels, critical studies, short stories and essays, but the published volumes of the Diary brought her the greatest popularity and critical acclaim. "My Turkish Grandmother" is a segment from her Diary.*

# 2

# My Turkish Grandmother

I was travelling on Air France to New York via[1] Paris when the plane ran into a flock of sea gulls[2] and we had to stop at Athens. At first we sat around and waited for information, looking out now and then at the airplane. Vague news filtered out.[3] Some passengers became anxious, fearing they would miss their connections. Air France treated us to dinner and wine. But after that there was a shortage of seats, so I sat on the floor like a gypsy, together with a charming hippie couple[4] with whom I had made friends during the trip. He was a musician and she was a painter. They were hitchhiking through Europe with backpacks. She was slender and frail-looking,[5] and I was not surprised when he     10 complained that her knapsack[6] was full of vitamins. As we sat talking about books, films, music, a very old lady approached us. She looked like my Spanish grandmother. Dressed completely in black, old but not bent, with a face that seemed carved of wood through which the wrink-

---

[1]**via:** By way of.
[2]**a flock of sea gulls:** A group of white sea birds.
[3]**Vague news filtered out:** Confusing bits of information reached us.
[4]**hippie couple:** Two young people that the author associates with the hippie movement of the 1960s.

Old clothes, long hair, and a lack of interest in the material values of the modern world are frequently associated with the hippie movement.
[5]**frail-looking:** Delicate looking; not strong looking.
[6]**knapsack:** Another name for a backpack.

les appeared more like veins of the wood.[7] She handed me a letter she carried around her neck in a Turkish cloth bag. It was written in exquisite[8] French. It was a request from her daughter to help her Turkish mother in every way possible. The daughter was receiving her doctorate in medicine at the Sorbonne[9] and could not come to fetch[10] her mother

20 for the ceremony, so she had entrusted her to the care of Air France.[11] I read the letter and translated it for my hippie friends. Although we could not talk to the old woman, it was evident that a strong, warm sympathy existed among the four of us. She wanted to sit with us. We made room for her, and she gave me her old wrinkled hand to hold. She was anxious. She did not know what had happened. She realized she would be late for her rendezvous[12] in Paris. We looked for a Turkish passenger who would translate and explain the delay. There was none, but we found an Air France hostess who spoke a little Turkish. We thought the old lady would choose to stay with the hostess, but once the

30 message was conveyed to her, she returned to sit with us. She adopted us. Hours passed. We were told that the plane could not be repaired, that the airline offered us a few hours of sleep in a hotel not too far away, and to be ready for an early flight on another plane. So the four of us were placed in a taxi, which caused my Turkish grandmother such anxiety that she would not let go of my hand; but her anxiety would always recede[13] when she looked at the delicate features and soft eyes of the young woman painter, at the smile and gentleness of the musician's face, at my reassuring words[14] in French, which she did not understand. At the hotel, she would not go into her bedroom alone, so I left our

40 connecting doors open and explained I was right there next to her. She studied this for a while and then finally consented to lie in her bed. A few hours later, we were called and taken to our plane. Because I was changing planes in Paris, I could not take her to the home of her daughter. I had to find someone who would. Questioning the passengers, I found a woman who promised to take her in a taxi to the address in the letter. She held on to my hand until the last minute. Then she kissed me ceremoniously, kissed my hippie friends, and went on her way. Having been in her fishermen's village, I could imagine the little stone house she came from, her fisherman husband, her daughter sent to Paris to study

50 medicine and now achieving the high status of doctor. Did she arrive in

[7]**a face that seemed carved of wood through which the wrinkles appeared more like veins of the wood:** A face that seemed to be made out of wood with a knife (carved) so that the lines (wrinkles) of the woman's face seemed like the natural lines of the wood.
[8]**exquisite:** Excellent.
[9]**Sorbonne:** A well-known university in Paris.

[10]**fetch:** Bring back.
[11]**entrusted her to the care of Air France:** Given her to Air France to take care of.
[12]**rendezvous:** Meeting.
[13]**recede:** Become less.
[14]**reassuring words:** Comforting words; words that remove fear.

time for a ceremony which had to be translated to her? I know she arrived safely. Guarded by universal grandchildren, Turkish grandmothers always travel safely.

## _____ A LOOK AT THE IDEAS _____

1. Describe the situation at the Athens airport up to the time the old Turkish woman approached Anais Nin and her young friends. Explain or give information about the following: (a) the probable origin and the final destination of the flight; (b) the reason for the unscheduled stop; (c) the conduct of the passengers and the provisions made for their comfort.

   Notice that Nin begins with "I" but switches to "we" in lines 2 and 3. What does "we" refer to?

2. Why does Nin refer to the young couple as "hippies"? Is it because (a) they were dirty and badly dressed; (b) they were not wearing conventional clothes; (c) they had long hair; (d) they didn't have much money; (e) they were artistic and sensitive human beings; (f) they liked health food, hiking, and camping out like gypsies?

   Would you call the young couple "hippies"? What does that word mean to you? Do you think your ideas about "hippies" are the same as Nin's?

3. What was the most probable reason for the old Turkish woman approaching and staying with Nin and her young friends?

   _____ 1. They spoke French and she could manage to communicate with them.

   _____ 2. She sensed that they were warm, friendly, and sympathetic people.

   _____ 3. The room was crowded, and it was more comfortable sitting on the floor.

4. Which words or phrases would you use to describe Nin, the hippie couple, and/or the Turkish woman? Write _N_ for Nin, _H_ for the hippie couple, and _T_ for the Turkish woman

next to the appropriate words. (This exercise can be done individually or in groups.)

| | | |
|---|---|---|
| 1. ___ old | 8. ___ delicate | 15. ___ gentle |
| 2. ___ slender | 9. ___ charming | 16. ___ bent with age |
| 3. ___ dirty | 10. ___ odd | 17. ___ simple |
| 4. ___ anxious | 11. ___ understanding | 18. ___ dignified |
| 5. ___ kind | 12. ___ frail | 19. ___ sympathetic |
| 6. ___ sensitive | 13. ___ warm | 20. ___ friendly |
| 7. ___ wrinkled | 14. ___ sophisticated | 21. ___ considerate |

What other words or phrases would you use?

**5.** Summarize the contents of the letter the Turkish woman was carrying in the cloth bag around her neck.

**6.** Describe the Turkish woman's behavior in the taxi and at the hotel. What do her actions tell us about her?

**7.** Describe what took place when the Turkish woman and her new-found friends parted at the airport. Do you think the Turkish woman arrived in time to see her daughter receive her degree in medicine?

**8.** Nin mentions several times that the Turkish woman held her hand:

> . . . and she gave me her old wrinkled hand to hold. (line 24)
> . . . that she would not let go of my hand . . . (line 35)
> . . . held on to my hand until the last minute. (line 46)

In these instances, why does the Turkish woman want to hold hands with Nin? What does this gesture tell us about her and about her feelings toward Nin?

**9.** In the United States, holding hands can imply different things, depending on what the situation is and who is doing the holding. For example, if we see a young couple holding hands, we infer that they are sweethearts or that there is some kind of attraction or romantic attachment. It is not customary in the United States, however, for two adults of the same sex, and about the same age, to hold hands, for there is a strong tendency to interpret this action as evidence of a romantic attachment. This may not be the case in other cultures. Discuss the situations in which people hold hands in your culture or in other cultures that you are familiar with.

10. Why does Nin refer to the old woman she has just met at the airport in Athens as her Turkish grandmother? Why does she say at the end of the selection, "Guarded by universal grandchildren, Turkish grandmothers always travel safely"? What does this statement mean to you?

11. It is customary to point out that family systems and family relationships vary from culture to culture. Are there, however, *universal* children, grandchildren, parents, grandparents, brothers, sisters, aunts, uncles, and cousins? If so, what are the qualities that make them universal?

12. Write a composition in which you compare the relationships of parents and children, grandparents and grandchildren, brothers and sisters, aunts and uncles, cousins, or nieces and nephews in your own social group with a comparable group in another culture. Here are some suggestions:

    1. Write an introductory paragraph in which you state the kind of comparison you are going to make and clearly identify the two groups you are going to compare.
    2. Discuss the ways in which the two groups are similar *and* the ways in which the two groups are different.
    3. Conclude with a summary statement of the comparison you have made.

13. In an airport in Athens, four people of different ages and with different lifestyles and cultural backgrounds were drawn together by a strong, warm bond of sympathy. First, discuss the ways in which their backgrounds and situations were probably different. Then, discuss the nature of the bond that existed among them. What brought them together? What did they have in common?

    In a short composition, describe an experience you have had in which you felt an immediate bond of sympathy toward another person of a very different social and/or

cultural background. You might tell under what circumstances you met the person, what your immediate reaction
was, and in what ways you and the person were seemingly
alike and different.

_____ A LOOK AT THE LANGUAGE _____

1. Below are five sets of sentences. The first sentence in each
   set is based on the Nin selection; the other three are not. (a)
   What does the *italicized* word or phrase in the first sentence
   mean? (b) Does the *italicized* word or phrase have the same
   meaning in the other sentences? (c) Are all of the sentences
   in each set idiomatic? Would a native speaker of English be
   likely to use the word or phrase in this way?

   1. . . . when the plane ran into *a flock of* sea gulls . . .
      We saw *a flock of* sheep in the meadow.
      The cat was chased by *a flock of* dogs.
      There was *a flock of* students in the room.
   2. Vague news *filtered out.*
      The curtains *filtered out* the bright sunlight.
      The people *filtered out* of the plane.
      Her words *filtered out* slowly.
   3. . . . fearing they would miss their *connections.*
      The Wilsons have close *connections* in England.
      These bridges serve as *connections* between the two
      cities.
      We made all of our plane *connections* without difficulty.
   4. . . . and she gave me her old *wrinkled* hand to hold.
      His shirt was dirty and *wrinkled.*
      Their faces were *wrinkled* like old dried fruit.
      The paper was *wrinkled* into four sections.
   5. Did she arrive *in time* for the ceremony?
      We got to the airport *in time* to see them off.
      We will hear from them *in time.*
      Please try to keep *in time* to the music.

2. Change the *italicized* words to *nouns* and insert them in the
   sentences to the right.

1. They were very *charming*.     They had a lot of

   _____ .

2. She was very *anxious*.     She was filled with

   _____ .

3. She responded to their     She responded to their
   *warm* and *sympathetic*     _____ and
   approach.     _____ .

4. We were surprised by his     We were surprised by his
   *gentle* manner.     _____ .

**3.** Supply the missing word in each sentence. The word you
produce should be an antonym, or opposite, of the
*italicized* word.

   1. Once seated in the plane, my anxiety *receded*, but hers
      _____ as we taxied out to the runway
      for the takeoff.
   2. The Turkish woman finally *consented* to lie down on the
      bed and rest, but at first she _____ .
   3. The Air France hostess spoke *fluent* French and English,
      but she spoke only _____ Turkish.
   4. The letter was written in *exquisite* French. One might
      have expected it to have been written in
      _____ French.

**4.** Supply the missing letters for the word in each sentence.

   1. A more general term for a painter is an *a r* _ _ _ _ _ .
      We also refer to a musician as an *a r* _ _ _ _ _ .
   3. A frail-looking person would very likely be very
      *s l e* _ _ _ _ .
   4. An old person usually has many lines in the face, but a
      young person has few, if any, *w r i* _ _ _ _ _ _ .
   5. A more common term for a rendezvous is a
      *m e e* _ _ _ _ .

**5.** The author uses *anxious* and *anxiety* in these places:

   Some passengers became *anxious* . . . (lines 4-5)
   She was *anxious*. (lines 24-25)

... which caused my Turkish grandmother such *anxiety* ... but her *anxiety* would always recede... (lines
34-36)

Why did these people feel *anxious* or suffer *anxiety?* Describe the feelings these words convey to you. In what
situations have you felt or do you usually feel *anxious* or
suffer *anxiety?*

**6.** The *italicized* words and phrases indicate devices that relate
parts of the passage below. Explain what is omitted, referred to, linked, or replaced, and tell how these devices
function in relating ideas in the passage. (For further information on this type of exercise, see Steinbeck, "A Look
at the Language, question 4, page 12.)

At the hotel, she would not go into her bedroom alone, so
I left *our connecting doors* open and explained I was *right
there* next to her. She studied *this* for a while and then
finally consented to lie in her bed.

**7.** In addition to using devices to relate ideas and parts of a
passage, writers make assumptions about the information
they expect their readers to have and the connections they
expect their readers to make. There are many interesting
examples of this in the Nin selection. For instance, in the
first sentence she says "... we had to stop at Athens."
"We" obviously refers to the passengers on the plane;
however, the reader must make this connection, for "we"
does not directly refer to anything that has been said immediately before.

What connections or information does Nin expect the
reader to make or supply in these places?

Line 3: *sat around* (sat around where?)
Line 3: *information* (information about what?)
Line 3: *looking out* (looking out of what?)
Line 4: *filtered out* (filtered out of what?)
Line 5: *connections* (what connections?)
Line 6: *shortage of seats* (shortage of what seats?)
Lines 6-7: *sat on the floor* (sat on what floor?)

Find other examples like these and explain what information or connections Nin expects us to supply or make.

Read these examples aloud, filling in all of the unstated information. What is the effect? Does adding information and supplying the connections change the style of the writer? If so, in what way?

**8.** The following sentences are from the Nin story. (a) First, make short sentences out of each sentence. (b) Then, write one or more sentences of your own that include all the information (but not necessarily all the words) in the short sentences. (c) Finally, compare your sentences with Nin's, and tell how yours and Nin's differ in style and effect. The first is done as an example.

1. Some passengers became anxious, fearing they would miss their connections.

   a. Possible short sentences: *Some passengers became anxious. They feared they would miss their connections.*

   b. Possible new sentence: *Some passengers became anxious because they feared they would miss their connections.*

   c. Comments on style and effect: The connector *because* in the new sentence establishes a direct cause-effect relationship; in Nin's sentence the relationship seems less direct. Do you agree? What else can you say about differences in style and effect?

2. Dressed completely in black, old but not bent, with a face that seemed carved of wood through which the wrinkles appeared more like veins of the wood.

   Notice that Nin's sentence is not a sentence in the conventional sense. The subject (*she*—the old woman) and part of the verb (*was*—was dressed) have been omitted.

3. Questioning the passengers, I found a woman who promised to take her in a taxi to the address in the letter.

4. Having been in her fishermen's village, I could imagine the little stone house she came from, her fisherman husband, her daughter sent to Paris to study medicine and now achieving the high status of doctor.

5. We were told that the plane could not be repaired, that the airline offered us a few hours of sleep in a hotel not too far away, and to be ready for an early flight on another plane.

**9.** Notice that Nin has written this narrative sketch in a single paragraph. We do not know her reason for using this for-

mat, but it is possible that she used it to suggest the close-
ness or intimacy of the group in this situation.

Ordinarily a selection of this length would be broken into
paragraphs. Indicate where you think new paragraphing
might begin. What effect, if any, does paragraphing have
on the narrative?

10. List the main events that occur in "My Turkish Grand-
    mother." Do the events occur in the order in which they
    actually happen? You might compare your list with the
    lists of other students to see if your lists are similar. Using
    your list, write a brief summary of the events that took
    place. Words and phrases like *first, then, after that,* and
    *finally* are frequently used as linking signals in a summary
    of this kind.

# Peter Farb (b. 1929)

*Peter Farb, researcher and writer, has been Curator of American Indian Cultures at the Museum of the American Indian in New York and consultant to the Smithsonian Institution in Washington, D.C. His work and books written with the editors of* Life *in the early 1960s—including* The Forest, The Insects, Ecology, *and* The Land *and Wildlife of North America—prompted Secretary of the Interior Stewart Udall in 1964 to call him "one of the first conservation spokesmen of our period."*

*In* Word Play *(1974), which contains the selection that follows, he returned to an interest in languages, developed as an undergraduate at Vanderbilt University and later as a graduate student at Columbia University. Students of foreign languages may recall humorous and painful experiences as they read Farb's comments on the problems of translating from one language to another.*

# 3

# How to
# Talk about
# the World

Most people assume that a text in one language can be accurately translated into another language, so long as the translator uses a good bilingual dictionary. But that is not so, because words that are familiar in one language may have no equivalent usage in another. The word *home*, for example, has special meaning for English speakers, particularly those who live in the British Isles. To an Englishman, a *home* is more than the physical structure in which he resides;[1] it is his castle, no matter how humble, the place of his origins, fondly remembered, as well as his present environment of happy family relationships. *This is my home* says the Englishman, and he thereby[2] points not only to a structure but also    10
to a way of life. The same feeling, though, cannot be expressed even in a language whose history is as closely intertwined with English as is French. The closest a Frenchman can come is *Voilá ma maison* or *Voilá mon logis*—words equivalent to the English *house* but certainly not to the English *home*.

Mark Twain humorously demonstrated the problems of translation when he published the results of his experiment with French. He printed the original version[3] of his well-known story "The Celebrated

---

[1]**resides:** Lives.
[2]**thereby:** By means of that; thus.

[3]**original version:** In this case, the original story written in English.

Jumping Frog of Calaveras County," followed by a Frenchman's translation of it, and then a literal translation[4] from the French back into English. Here are a few sentences from each version:

*Twain's Original Version:* "Well, there was a feller here once by the name of Jim Smiley, in the winter of '49—or maybe it was the spring of '50—I don't recollect exactly, somehow though what makes me think it was one or the other is because I remember the big flume[5] wasn't finished when he first come to the camp."

*French Version:* "Il y avait une fois ici un individu connu sous le nomme de Jim Smiley: c'etait dans l'hiver de 49, peut-être bien au printemps de 50, je ne me rappelle pas exactement. Ce qui me fait croire que c'était l'un ou l'autre, c'est que je me souviens que le grand bief n'était pas achevé lorsqu'il arriva au camp pour le première fois."

*Literal Retranslation into English:* "It there was one time here an individual known under the name of Jim Smiley; it was in the winter of '49, possibly well at the spring of '50, I no me recollect exactly. That which makes me to believe that it was one or the other, it is that I shall remember that the grand flume was no achieved when he arrives at the camp for the first time."

Twain, of course, exaggerated his example of bizarre[6] translation—but sometimes such ineptness[7] can have disastrous[8] consequences. At the end of July 1945, Germany and Italy had surrendered and the Allies issued an ultimatum[9] to Japan to surrender also. Japan's premier called a press conference at which he stated that his country would *mokusatsu* the Allied ultimatum. The word *mokusatsu* was an extremely unfortunate choice. The premier apparently intended it to mean that the cabinet would "consider" the ultimatum. But the word has another meaning, "take no notice of," and that was the one the English-language translators at Domei, Japan's overseas broadcasting agency, used. The world heard that Japan had rejected the ultimatum—instead of that Japan was still considering it. Domei's mistranslation led the United States to send B-29s, laden[10] with atomic bombs, over Hiroshima and Nagasaki. Apparently, if *mokusatsu* had been correctly translated, the atomic bomb need never have been dropped.

---

[4]**literal translation:** An exact, word-for-word translation.
[5]**flume:** In a gold-mining camp, an artificial channel or open pipe through which water passes.
[6]**bizarre:** Very strange.

[7]**ineptness:** Foolishness or a poor performance.
[8]**disastrous:** Terrible.
[9]**ultimatum:** Statement of final condition not open for discussion.
[10]**laden:** Loaded with; carrying.

Such anecdotes[11] about failures in translation do not get at the heart of the problem, because they concern only isolated words and not the resistance of an entire language system to translation.[12] For example, all languages have obligatory categories of grammar[13] that may be lacking in other languages. Russian—like many languages but not like    60
English—has an obligatory category for gender which demands that a noun, and often a pronoun, specify whether it is masculine, feminine, or neuter. Another obligatory category, similarly lacking in English, makes a verb state whether or not an action has been completed. Therefore, a Russian finds it impossible to translate accurately the English sentence *I hired a worker* without having much more information. He would have to know whether the *I* who was speaking was a man or a woman, whether the action of *hired* had a completive or noncompletive aspect[14] ("already hired" as opposed to "was in the process of hiring"), and whether the *worker* was a man or a woman.                                           70

Or imagine the difficulty of translating into English a Chinese story in which a character identified as a *piaomei* appears. The obligatory categories to which this word belongs require that it tell whether it refers to a male or a female, whether the character is older or younger than the speaker, and whether the character belongs to the family of the speaker's father or mother. *Piaomei* therefore can be translated into English only by the unwieldy statement "a female cousin on my mother's side and younger than myself." Of course, the translator might simply establish these facts about the character the first time she appears and thereafter render[15] the word as "cousin," but that would ignore the    80
significance in Chinese culture of the repetition of these obligatory categories.

The Russian and Chinese examples illustrate the basic problem in any translation. No matter how skilled the translator is, he cannot rip[16] language out of the speech community that uses it. Translation obviously is not a simple two-way street between two languages. Rather, it is a busy intersection at which at least five thoroughfares[17] meet—the two languages with all their eccentricities,[18] the cultures of the two speech communities, and the speech situation in which the statement was uttered.                                                                       90

---

[11]**anecdotes:** Short stories (most often amusing).
[12]**resistance of an entire language system to translation:** The difficulty of translating.
[13]**obligatory categories of grammar:** Required grammatical classes of words.
[14]**aspect:** A verb form, especially related to sense of time.

[15]**render:** Translate.
[16]**rip:** Tear.
[17]**thoroughfares:** Roads or streets (usually busy).
[18]**eccentricities:** Peculiarities; strangeness.

1. Discuss the connotations or associations of the word "home" (a) to an Englishman and (b) to a Frenchman, based on the opening paragraph in Peter Farb's essay. What connotations does the word "home" have in your native language?

2. Describe the experiment Mark Twain made to demonstrate the problems in translating from one language to another. Compare Twain's original version with the literal retranslation. What is wrong with the retranslation? Why does Farb say that Twain's example is exaggerated?

3. Translate Twain's original passage from "The Jumping Frog" into another language. List the main problems you had in doing the translation. Then, without looking at the original Twain passage, retranslate your version into English. Compare your translation with the original.

4. What example does Farb use to show that inaccurate translation can have very serious consequences? What does he mean when he says that stories about "failures in translation do not get at the heart of the problem"?

5. In order to translate "I hired a worker" into Russian, what would the translator have to know? What would you have to know to translate that sentence into another language?

6. Would any of the *italicized* words or phrases in the following sentences be difficult to translate into your native language or another foreign language? Why?

   1. I feel very much *at home* here.
   2. I have many *good friends* here.
   3. There are many *interesting things* to see and do.
   4. Whenever I'm *blue,* I go for a walk.

7. The author points out that translating a Chinese story with a character identified as a "piaomei" into English would present problems. Why? What solution does he propose? Is that solution satisfactory?

8. What is the author illustrating with the Russian and Chinese examples?

_____ 1. The basic difficulty and complexity of those languages

_____ 2. The amount of skill required to translate those languages into English

_____ 3. The problems a translator faces in translating from one language to another

9. Explain what Farb means when he says that translation is more like a five-way intersection than a two-way street. List and give examples of the five things the author says are involved in translation.

10. As Farb points out, cultures as well as languages are difficult to equate. Attitudes as well as patterns of behavior may differ from one culture to another.

Write an essay in which you discuss a behavior pattern of a particular social group in another culture that would seem unusual to someone from a similar social group in the United States. For instance, you might select something like dating patterns in your own social group or the position of women in your social class. Here are some suggestions for organizing your essay:

1. Begin by making a few general statements about the behavior pattern you have selected.
2. Then use three or four concrete examples that illustrate the particular pattern you are describing.
3. Conclude by briefly restating the major features of the cultural pattern you have been discussing.

## A LOOK AT THE LANGUAGE

1. Supply the missing letters for the synonyms of the words below the blanks. (Most of the synonyms in this exercise are explained in the footnotes.)

Let me tell you a short _a n e _ _ _ _ _ about an
                              story

_e c c _ _ _ _ _ _ _ man who
        strange

r e s _____ in an old house at the
   lived

i n t _____ of two
    corner

t h o _____ . He never paid any
   busy streets

attention to his e n v _____ , and he
              surroundings

was famous for his i n e _____ . He would
          poor performance

walk down the middle of the street l a _____ with
                loaded

books. He would r i ___ out pages as he walked and
       tear

throw them into the air. Because of him, there were some

d i s a _____ accidents. Perhaps you
   terrible

think I am e x a _____ but I am
         stretching the truth

not; his actions were certainly very b i z _____ .
                        strange

2. The following sentences are from the Farb selection. (a) Explain the function or use of the *italicized* word or phrase in the sentence. (b) Decide how many of the items in parentheses you could substitute for the *italicized* word or phrase; and comment on the effect of the substitution. The first item is done for you.

1. Twain, *of course* (certainly, obviously, preferably, without a doubt), exaggerated his example of bizarre translation...

   a. *Of course* is a qualifier. The writer is saying "I grant or admit that Twain's example is exaggerated."

   b. All but *preferably* could be substituted for *of course*. The sentences with *certainly, obviously, without a doubt* would have essentially the same meaning as the original sentence; *without a doubt* is perhaps closest in meaning to *of course*.

   Do you agree with these comments? What else would you like to say about the substitutions?

2. ... *but* (however, for, since, nevertheless) sometimes such ineptness can have disastrous consequences.

3. Japan's premier called a press conference *at which*

(where, there, at that time, that) he stated that his country would "mokusatsu" the Allied ultimatum.

4. *No matter* (it makes no difference, it doesn't matter, it matters not, regardless) how skilled the translator is, he cannot rip language out of the speech community *that* (in which, which, where, at which) uses it.

5. Translation obviously is not a simple two-way street between two languages. *Rather* (instead of that, on the contrary, preferably, however), it is a busy intersection *at which* (where, in which, that, on which) at least five thoroughfares meet—the two languages with all their eccentricities, the cultures of the two speech communities, and the speech situation *in which* (at which, that, where, on which) the statement was uttered.

3. The *italicized* words and phrases indicate devices that relate parts of the passage below. Explain what is omitted, referred to, linked, or replaced, and tell how these devices function in relating ideas in the passage. (For further information on this type of exercise, see Steinbeck, "A Look at the Language," question 4, page 12.)

> Most people assume that a text in one language can be accurately translated into another language, so long as the translator uses a good bilingual dictionary. *But that* is not *so,* because words that are familiar in one language may have no equivalent usage in *another.* The word "home," *for example,* has special meaning for English speakers, particularly those who live in the British Isles. To an Englishman, a "home" is more than the physical structure in which he resides; *it* is his castle, no matter *how humble, the place* of his origins, *fondly remembered,* as well as *his* present environment of happy family relationships. "This is my home" says the Englishman, and he *thereby* points not only to a structure but also to a way of life. *The same feeling, though,* cannot be expressed even in a language whose history is as closely intertwined with English *as is French.*

4. Reread the first paragraph of the essay. Select the correct phrase to complete each of the following statements; write the appropriate letter in the blanks.

_____ 1. The main idea of this paragraph is presented (a) in the first sentence, (b) in the second sentence, (c) in the last sentence.

_____ 2. The second sentence (a) agrees with the first sentence, (b) contradicts the first sentence.

_____ 3. The paragraph develops (a) by giving a list of *reasons* that support the main idea, (b) by giving several different examples to support the main idea, (c) by discussing one well-chosen example.

_____ 4. The paragraph finishes (a) by restating the main idea, (b) by introducing a new idea, (c) by completing the discussion of the example.

5. Now write a paragraph with the same type of organization used in the paragraph you have just examined in exercise 4. Begin with one of the following ideas or choose one of your own:

1. *Some people think it is easy to translate from* _____ *into English. But I* . . .

2. *Some people think that the word "home"* (or another word of your choice) *is the same in English as it is in* _____. *But I believe* . . .

# Kurt Vonnegut, Jr. (b. 1922)

Kurt Vonnegut, Jr., was born in Indianapolis, Indiana. After graduating from high school there, he went to Cornell University to study biochemistry. Two years later, Vonnegut transferred to the Carnegie Institute of Technology, but his studies were interrupted by his induction into the armed services. After World War II ended in 1945, he returned to the United States, married his childhood sweetheart, and enrolled at the University of Chicago, where he studied anthropology but did not take a degree.

Since 1950, he has been a free-lance writer and has lived on the East Coast with his family. Two of his children, Edith and Mark, are also published authors. Vonnegut's published work includes several novels, two plays, and over a hundred short stories. "Long Walk to Forever," presented here, appeared in the collection of short stories Welcome to the Monkey House (1968). Like many of his stories and novels, this story contains a humorous but serious commentary on modern life. Here, we see the roles a young man and a young woman play in a post World War II courtship in the United States.

---

### Romeo and Juliet

*If you will die for me,*
*I will die for you*

*and our graves will*
*be like two lovers washing*
*their clothes together*
*in a laundromat.*

*If you will bring the soap,*
*I will bring the bleach.*

*—Richard Brautigan*

# 4

## Long Walk

## to

## Forever

They had grown up next door to each other, on the fringe of a city,[1] near fields and woods and orchards, within sight of a lovely bell tower that belonged to a school for the blind.

Now they were twenty, had not seen each other for nearly a year. There had always been playful, comfortable warmth between them, but never any talk of love.

His name was Newt. Her name was Catharine. In the early afternoon, Newt knocked on Catharine's front door.

Catharine came to the door. She was carrying a fat, glossy magazine[2] she had been reading. The magazine was devoted entirely to    10 brides. "Newt!" she said. She was surprised to see him.

"Could you come for a walk?" he said. He was a shy person, even with Catharine. He covered his shyness by speaking absently, as though he were a secret agent pausing briefly on a mission between beautiful, distant, and sinister[3] points. This manner of speaking had always been Newt's style, even in matters that concerned him desperately.

---

[1]**fringe of a city:** The outer edge (limit) of a city; in this case, near where the countryside begins.
[2]**glossy magazine:** A phrase referring to a popular magazine with many pictures, usually printed on shiny paper.
[3]**sinister:** Evil; bad; in this case, dangerous.

"A walk?" said Catharine.

"One foot in front of the other," said Newt, "through leaves, over bridges—"

20          "I had no idea you were in town," she said.

"Just this minute got in," he said.

"Still in the Army, I see," she said.

"Seven more months to go," he said. He was a private[4] first class in the Artillery. His uniform was rumpled.[5] His shoes were dusty. He needed a shave. He held out his hand for the magazine. "Let's see the pretty book," he said.

She gave it to him. "I'm getting married, Newt," she said.

"I know," he said. "Let's go for a walk."

"I'm awfully busy, Newt," she said. "The wedding is only a week

30    away."

"If we go for a walk," he said, "it will make you rosy. It will make you a rosy bride." He turned the pages of the magazine. "A rosy bride like her—like her—like her," he said, showing her rosy brides.

Catharine turned rosy, thinking about rosy brides.

"That will be my present to Henry Stewart Chasens," said Newt. "By taking you for a walk, I'll be giving him a rosy bride."

"You know his name?" said Catharine.

"Mother wrote," he said. "From Pittsburgh?"

"Yes," she said. "You'd like him."

40          "Maybe," he said.

"Can—can you come to the wedding, Newt?" she said.

"That I doubt," he said.

"Your furlough[6] isn't for long enough?" she said.

"Furlough?" said Newt. He was studying a two-page ad for flat silver.[7] "I'm not on furlough," he said.

"Oh?" she said.

"I'm what they call A.W.O.L.,"[8] said Newt.

"Oh, Newt! You're not!" she said.

"Sure I am," he said, still looking at the magazine.

50          "Why, Newt?" she said.

"I had to find out what your silver pattern is," he said. He read names of silver patterns from the magazine. "Albermarle? Heather?" he said. "Legend? Rambler Rose?" He looked up, smiled. "I plan to give you and your husband a spoon," he said.

"Newt, Newt—tell me really," she said.

"I want to go for a walk," he said.

---

[4]**private:** The lowest rank or title in the U.S. Army.    [7]**flat silver:** Silverware (knives, forks, spoons).
[5]**rumpled:** Wrinkled; crushed.    [8]**A.W.O.L.:** Absent *without* *leave* (permission).
[6]**furlough:** An official army vacation time.

She wrung her hands in sisterly anguish.[9] "Oh, Newt—you're fooling me about being A.W.O.L.," she said.

Newt imitated a police siren softly, raised his eyebrows.

"Where—where from?" she said.                    60

"Fort Bragg," he said.

"North Carolina?" she said.

"That's right," he said. "Near Fayetteville—where Scarlett O'Hara[10] went to school."

"How did you get here, Newt?" she said.

He raised his thumb, jerked it in a hitchhike gesture.[11] "Two days," he said.

"Does your mother know?" she said.

"I didn't come to see my mother," he told her.

"Who did you come to see?" she said.                    70

"You," he said.

"Why me?" she said.

"Because I love you," he said. "Now can we take a walk?" he said. "One foot in front of the other—through leaves, over bridges—"

They were taking the walk now, were in a woods with a brown-leaf floor.

Catharine was angry and rattled,[12] close to tears. "Newt," she said, "this is absolutely crazy."

"How so?" said Newt.

"What a crazy time to tell me you love me," she said. "You never    80 talked that way before." She stopped walking.

"Let's keep walking," he said.

"No," she said. "So far, no farther. I shouldn't have come out with you at all," she said.

"You did," he said.

"To get you out of the house," she said. "If somebody walked in and heard you talking to me that way, a week before the wedding—"

"What would they think?" he said.

"They'd think you were crazy," she said.

"Why?" he said.                    90

Catharine took a deep breath, made a speech. "Let me say that I'm deeply honored by this crazy thing you've done," she said. "I can't

---

[9]**She wrung her hands in sisterly anguish:** She was worried or concerned as a sister would be. (Literally, she rubbed or twisted her hands together; a gesture used by some people when they are upset or worried.)
[10]**Scarlet O'Hara:** The woman who is the central character in Margaret Mitchell's *Gone with the*

*Wind*, a famous novel about the South at the time of the Civil War.
[11]**He raised his thumb, jerked it in a hitchhike gesture:** He signaled to drivers in passing cars that he wanted a ride.
[12]**rattled:** In this case, confused.

believe you're really A.W.O.L., but maybe you are. I can't believe you
really love me, but maybe you do. But—''

"I do," said Newt.

"Well, I'm deeply honored," said Catharine, "and I'm very fond of
you as a friend, Newt, extremely fond—but it's just too late." She took a
step away from him. "You've never even kissed me," she said, and she
protected herself with her hands. "I don't mean you should do it now. I
just mean this is all so unexpected. I haven't got the remotest idea[13] of
how to respond."

"Just walk some more," he said. "Have a nice time."

They started walking again.

"How did you expect me to react?" she said.

"How would I know what to expect?" he said. "I've never done
anything like this before."

"Did you think I would throw myself into your arms?" she said.

"Maybe," he said.

"I'm sorry to disappoint you," she said.

"I'm not disappointed," he said. "I wasn't counting on it. This is
very nice, just walking."

Catharine stopped again. "You know what happens next?" she
said.

"Nope," he said.

"We shake hands," she said. "We shake hands and part friends,"
she said. "That's what happens next."

Newt nodded. "All right," he said. "Remember me from time to
time. Remember how much I loved you."

Involuntarily,[14] Catharine burst into tears. She turned her back to
Newt, looked into the infinite colonnade of the woods.[15]

"What does that mean?" said Newt.

"Rage!" said Catharine. She clenched[16] her hands. "You have no
right—''

"I had to find out," he said.

"If I'd loved you," she said, "I would have let you know before
now."

"You would?" he said.

"Yes," she said. She faced him, looked up at him, her face quite
red. "You would have known," she said.

"How?" he said.

---

[13]**not the remotest idea:** No idea at all.       [16]**clenched:** Tightened.
[14]**involuntarily:** Unable to control her feelings.
[15]**infinite colonnade of the woods:** A long row of
trees without an end in sight.

"You would have seen it," she said. "Women aren't very clever at hiding it."

Newt looked closely at Catharine's face now. To her consternation,[17] she realized that what she had said was true, that a woman couldn't hide love.

Newt was seeing love now.

And he did what he had to do. He kissed her.

"You're hell to get along with!" she said when Newt let her go.

"I am?" said Newt.

"You shouldn't have done that," she said.                                    140

"You didn't like it?" he said.

"What did you expect," she said—"wild, abandoned passion?"[18]

"I keep telling you," he said, "I never know what's going to happen next."

"We say good-by," she said.

He frowned slightly. "All right," he said.

She made another speech. "I'm not sorry we kissed," she said. "That was sweet. We should have kissed, we've been so close. I'll always remember you, Newt, and good luck."

"You too," he said.                                                          150

"Thank you, Newt," she said.

"Thirty days," he said.

"What?" she said.

"Thirty days in the stockade,"[19] he said—"that's what one kiss will cost me."

"I—I'm sorry," she said, "but I didn't ask you to go A.W.O.L."

"I know," he said.

"You certainly don't deserve any hero's reward for doing something as foolish as that," she said.

"Must be nice to be a hero," said Newt. "Is Henry Stewart Chasens   160 a hero?"

"He might be, if he got the chance," said Catharine. She noted uneasily that they had begun to walk again. The farewell had been forgotten.

"You really love him?" he said.

"Certainly I love him!" she said hotly. "I wouldn't marry him if I didn't love him!"

"What's good about him?" said Newt.

---

[17]**consternation:** Confused amazement.          [19]**stockade:** Army prison.
[18]**wild, abandoned passion:** Uncontrolled passion.

"Honestly!" she cried, stopping again. "Do you have any idea how
170    offensive you're being? Many, many, many things are good about
Henry! Yes," she said, "and many, many, many things are probably bad
too. But that isn't any of your business. I love Henry, and I don't have to
argue his merits[20] with you!"

"Sorry," said Newt.

"Honestly!" said Catharine.

Newt kissed her again. He kissed her again because she wanted
him to.

They were now in a large orchard.

"How did we get so far from home, Newt?" said Catharine.
180    "One foot in front of the other—through leaves, over bridges,"
said Newt.

"They add up—the steps," she said.

Bells rang in the tower of the school for the blind nearby.

"School for the blind," said Newt.

"School for the blind," said Catharine. She shook her head in
drowsy[21] wonder. "I've got to go back now," she said.

"Say good-by," said Newt.

"Every time I do," said Catharine, "I seem to get kissed."

Newt sat down on the close-cropped grass[22] under an apple tree.
190    "Sit down," he said.

"No," she said.

"I won't touch you," he said.

"I don't believe you," she said.

She sat down under another tree, twenty feet away from him. She
closed her eyes.

"Dream of Henry Stewart Chasens," he said.

"What?" she said.

"Dream of your wonderful husband-to-be," he said.

"All right, I will," she said. She closed her eyes tighter, caught
200    glimpses of her husband-to-be.

Newt yawned.[23]

The bees were humming in the trees, and Catharine almost fell
asleep. When she opened her eyes she saw that Newt really was asleep.

He began to snore softly.

Catharine let Newt sleep for an hour, and while he slept she
adored him with all her heart.

---

[20]**argue his merits:** Discuss his good points.
[21]**drowsy:** Sleepy.
[22]**close-cropped grass:** Grass that is cut very
short.

[23]**yawned:** Opened his mouth wide and slowly took
in a deep breath, showing he was relaxed and
sleepy.

The shadows of the apple trees grew to the east. The bells in the tower of the school for the blind rang again.

"*Chick-a-dee-dee-dee*,"[24] went a chickadee.

Somewhere far away an automobile starter nagged and failed,[25] nagged and failed, fell still.                    210

Catharine came out from under her tree, knelt by Newt.

"Newt?" she said.

"H'm?" he said. He opened his eyes.

"Late," she said.

"Hello, Catharine," he said.

"Hello, Newt," she said.

"I love you," he said.

"I know," she said.

"Too late," he said.                    220

"Too late," she said.

He stood, stretched groaningly. "A very nice walk," he said.

"I thought so," she said.

"Part company here?" he said.

"Where will you go?" she said.

"Hitch into town, turn myself in,"[26] he said.

"Good luck," she said.

"You, too," he said. "Marry me, Catharine?"

"No," she said.

He smiled, stared at her hard for a moment, then walked away    230 quickly.

Catharine watched him grow smaller in the long perspective of shadows and trees,[27] knew that if he stopped and turned now, if he called to her, she would run to him. She would have no choice.

Newt did stop. He did turn. He did call. "Catharine," he called.

She ran to him, put her arms around him, could not speak.

[24]**"Chick-a-dee-dee-dee":** The sound the chickadee bird makes.
[25]**. . . an automobile started, nagged and failed:** The motor would not start.
[26]**turn myself in:** Surrender to the military police.

[27]**Catharine watched him grow smaller in the long perspective of shadows and trees:** He looked smaller to her as he walked farther and farther away.

## A LOOK AT THE IDEAS

1. Describe the situation at the beginning of the story. Tell (a) when and where Catharine and Newt first met; (b) how old they are now; (c) how long it has been since they last saw each other; (d) what kind of community they grew up

in; (e) why Newt is visiting Catharine at this time; and (f) how he got to her house.

2. The author tells us that Newt and Catharine had grown up next door to one another. What do the following sentences tell us about their relationship?

   1. There had always been playful, comfortable warmth between them, but never any talk of love. (lines 5-6)

   2. "Can—can you come to the wedding, Newt?" she said. (line 41)

   3. She wrung her hands in sisterly anguish. (line 57)

   4. "Does your mother know?" she said. (line 68)

   5. "What a crazy time to tell me you love me," she said. "You never talked that way before." (lines 80-81)

   6. "You've never even kissed me," she said... "I don't mean you should do it now. I just mean this is all so unexpected. I haven't got the remotest idea of how to respond." (lines 98-101)

   Find other sentences in the story that tell about their relationship and feeling for one another.

3. Which words would you use to describe Catharine and/or Newt? Write *C* for Catharine and *N* for Newt next to the appropriate words. (This exercise can be done individually or in groups.)

   |     |     |     |     |     |     |
   |-----|-----|-----|-----|-----|-----|
   | 1. ___ young | 8. ___ rattled | 15. ___ clever |
   | 2. ___ conventional | 9. ___ romantic | 16. ___ blind |
   | 3. ___ imaginative | 10. ___ attractive | 17. ___ happy |
   | 4. ___ liberated | 11. ___ silly | 18. ___ crazy |
   | 5. ___ desperate | 12. ___ remote | 19. ___ shy |
   | 6. ___ reckless | 13. ___ immoral | 20. ___ daring |
   | 7. ___ childish | 14. ___ glossy | 21. ___ mature |

   What other words or phrases would you use to describe Catharine and Newt?

   Write a short physical description of Catharine or Newt from the details the author gives us and from the picture you have of them in your mind.

4. How many times does Newt urge Catharine to go for a walk? How many times does he say, "One foot in front of

the other..."? What is the effect of this repetition? What does it tell about Newt's character and his understanding of Catharine? How do you feel about Newt and his style of talking?

5. Find the sentences in the story where Vonnegut mentions the bell tower and the school for the blind. Why do you think the author mentions the school and its bell tower so often? How do you react to the statement that Newt and Catharine grew up within sight of a lovely bell tower that belonged to a school for the blind? What do these symbols suggest?

6. In the middle of the story, Catharine says that women can't hide their love. Is this statement true in her case? Has she been trying to hide her love? If so, why? Has she been successful?

To what extent do you believe Catharine's generalization about women is true? Can men hide their love as well as or better than women? Are the behavior patterns different from culture to culture? In other cultures, do men or women tend to hide their love?

7. The author tells us that Newt saw love in Catharine's face and that she adored him "with all her heart" as she sat under the tree watching him sleep. Yet she said "No" when he asked her to marry him. Check the reasons that you think best explain her behavior.

    _____ 1. Henry Stewart Chasens would make a better husband.

    _____ 2. The marriage had already been arranged and the invitations had been sent off.

    _____ 3. Her parents would have been embarrassed and angry if she didn't marry Henry.

    _____ 4. She didn't know how to react to Newt's sudden proposal of marriage.

    _____ 5. Newt wouldn't be able to support her.

    _____ 6. She loved Newt but wasn't sure she understood him.

    _____ 7. Her wedding the following week was important to her.

_____ 8. She didn't want Newt to think she was too eager to marry him.

_____ 9. Her parents would not let her break her engagement to Henry.

_____ 10. She didn't have time to sort out her feelings about Newt.

What other reasons can you think of for her refusal?

When Catharine lets Newt go, do you think she is sure he will turn back and call to her again? If you were Catharine, would you send Newt away? If you were Newt, what would you do?

8. The theme or main idea of a short story usually gives us some understanding of the author's views about people and life. Write a paragraph in which you explain the theme of a "Long Walk to Forever." Discuss the sentences, phrases, and words in the story or in the title that you think reveal the theme or make it more obvious to the reader. You might begin your paragraph like this: *The theme of "Long Walk to Forever" by Kurt Vonnegut is . . .*

9. According to your perception of the young couple, check which of the following you think are likely to happen to Catharine and/or Newt:

_____ 1. Newt will get a new job at the school for the blind.

_____ 2. They will have five children, three boys and two girls.

_____ 3. They will have only one daughter.

_____ 4. Newt will have a difficult time keeping a job.

_____ 5. Newt will become the manager of a large factory.

_____ 6. Catharine will become very active in the women's liberation movement.

_____ 7. Newt will become an army officer.

_____ 8. Catharine will be an excellent wife and mother.

_____ 9. They will live in Austria for five years.

_____ 10. The couple will eventually get a divorce.

What other things can you think of that might happen to them?

10. Write a composition in which you describe the kind of life you think Catharine and Newt will have together. You might, for example, focus on one or more of the following: Newt's job, the kind of house they live in, their relationship with each other as well as with their parents and children, their political beliefs, their activities in the community.

11. What would happen to Newt and Catharine if they were a young couple from your own social group? Write a composition in which you discuss the problems they might have. What do you think would be the most likely outcome of their situation in your culture?

12. Young romantic lovers are often referred to as Shakespeare's characters, Romeo and Juliet. In the Brautigan poem preceding the Vonnegut story (page 36), what seems to be the speaker's view of romantic love? Do Newt and/or Catharine have this same view? What is your idea of romantic love?

## _____ A LOOK AT THE LANGUAGE _____

1. Substitute other words or expressions with the same meaning for the *italicized* words in these sentences:
   1. She lived near the *fringe* of the city.
   2. He had been travelling all night and his clothes were *rumpled*.
   3. The sight of him got her all *rattled*.
   4. She didn't know how to *respond* to his suggestion.
   5. To her *consternation*, he just seemed to be drowsy.

2. Vonnegut continually omits words and phrases to tie the dialogue together and make the conversations seem more natural. For example, Catharine says, "A walk?" If there were no omission, she might say, "Did you say that you wanted me to go for a walk with you?"

   Rewrite the following dialogue, adding words and phrases that have been omitted. Use appropriate punctuation.

"A walk?" said Catharine.

"One foot in front of the other," said Newt, "through leaves, over bridges—"

"I had no idea you were in town," she said.

"Just this minute got in," he said.

"Still in the Army, I see," she said.

"Seven more months to go," he said.

Now compare what you have written to Vonnegut's original. How do they differ? Does your version seem like natural speech? Does the relationship between Catharine and Newt seem the same? If not, how does it differ?

3. Report the conversation between Newt and Catharine to a friend who hasn't read the story. Change your expanded sentences from question 2 above to reported speech. You might begin: *Catharine asked Newt if he wanted her to go for a walk with him. Newt said . . .*

4. The following sentences are from the Vonnegut story. (a) First, write a paraphrase of each sentence, using as many sentences as you need. (b) Then compare your paraphrase with Vonnegut's sentence and tell how yours differs in style and effect. The first is done as an example.

1. To her consternation, she realized that what she had said was true, that a woman couldn't hide her love.

(a) Possible paraphrase: *She had said that a woman couldn't hide her love. She was amazed and confused when she realized that what she had said was true.*

(b) Comments on style and effect: The first sentence clearly identifies what she had said. The second sentence establishes a direct relationship between what she said and her reaction to her own statement afterward.

In Vonnegut's sentence, the reason for her consternation is more indirect because the reference to what she said comes at the end. In addition, Vonnegut is more subtle about letting the reader infer that she realizes that her general statement about women actually applies to herself. He is also more indirect in suggesting that she is amazed and confused because she suddenly realizes she has not been able to hide her love. In neither the paraphrase nor Vonnegut's sentence are we told whom she loves. The following sentence would, perhaps, be closer to the idea conveyed by Vonnegut: *When she suddenly realized that, like other women, she couldn't hide her love, she was amazed and con-*

*fused*. Vonnegut's sentence is, however, more compact and therefore seems more in keeping with his style.

Do you agree with these observations? What else can you say about differences in style and effect?

2. He covered his shyness by speaking absently, as though he were a secret agent pausing briefly on a mission between beautiful, distant, and sinister points.

3. Catharine watched him grow smaller in the long perspective of shadows and trees, knew that if he stopped and turned now, if he called to her, she would run to him.

4. Somewhere far away an automobile starter nagged and failed, nagged and failed, fell still.

5. Is this story told from the point of view of a character in the story or an observer outside the story? In what way would the story be different if it were told by Newt or Catharine? What insights and information can the observer give us that a character in the story could not?

6. List the main events or happenings in the story. Do the events occur in the order in which they actually happen? You might compare your list with the lists of other students to see if your lists are similar. Using your list, write a brief summary of the plot or main events of the story. Would someone who has not read the story know what it is about after reading your summary? What would the person miss?

# Richard Hagopian (1914 - 1976)

*Richard Hagopian was born near Boston in Revere, Massachusetts, where he grew up in an Armenian-Italian neighborhood. Gifted with a fine tenor voice, he first planned a career as a singer and studied at the New England Conservatory of Music. While on a concert tour, he met the poet Robert P. Tristram Coffin and showed him some of his short stories, and Coffin encouraged him to complete a book of stories.*

*"Wonderful People"—included in Hagopian's early collection of stories,* The Dove Brings Peace *(1944)—is a love story, very briefly sketched, with which almost anyone can identify. In telling the story, the author speculates on the potential of human beings for change and growth.*

# 5

# Wonderful

# People

I saw her and liked her because she was not beautiful. Her chin was not just right and something about her nose fell short of perfection. And when she stood up, well, there wasn't much to see but her tallness, the length from her hips to her feet, and the length from her hips to her shoulders. She was a tall girl and that was all. She was the first tall girl I had ever liked, perhaps because I had never watched a tall girl get up from a table before; that is, get up the way she did, everything in her rising to the art of getting up, combining to make the act look beautiful and not like just another casual movement, an ordinary life motion.

Maybe I liked her because when I talked to her for the first time I    10 found that she had tall ideas too, ideas which like her chin and nose did not seem just right to me, but like her getting up were beautiful. They hung together.[1] They were tall ideas, about life and people, morals and ethics. At first they seemed shockingly loose[2] to me, but when I saw them all moving together, like her body, they hung together. They looked naturally beautiful. They had the same kind of pulled-out poetry[3] that sometimes defies[4] the extra-long line and hangs together;

[1]**hung together:** Fitted; harmonized.
[2]**shockingly loose:** Disturbingly or surprisingly (shockingly); undisciplined or unprincipled (loose).
[3]**pulled-out poetry:** Free-style poetry.
[4]**defies:** Challenges.

hangs together when you see the whole thing finished, when you've scanned it up and down[5] and seen all the line endings melt into a
20    curious kind of unity, which makes strange music—strange because everything is long yet compact.[6] She was music. I see it now, her getting up impressed me at the time because for the first time I felt poetry in a person rising—music in body parts moving in natural rhythms. I liked the tall girl.

By stature[7] I was not tall. I was built almost too close to the ground. Perhaps that is why I had old-fashioned ideas, ideas as simple and as pure as the good soil. Maybe my eyes saw more in the ground than other people's because I was closer to it. I was what you might call compact. Everything was knitted together strongly,[8] like my ideas about
30    life, morals and ethics, all squeezed together, rhyming[9] easily, making music of a strong, dominant[10] sort. Call it smugness[11] if you wish. But I really couldn't move far without taking along everything I had. My ideas were like that too. I could take a radical fling[12] once in a while, but sooner or later, mostly sooner, the rest of me ganged up[13] and compressed[14] the wild motion with one easy squeeze.

We were a funny pair, the tall girl and I, funny because we were so different in everything. She was a slow walker and I had to hold back. She talked in long lines and I used the short one. She ate easily and I ate hard and fast. We were different.
40    The tall girl and I fell in love with each other. Why, I do not know. We just did, that's all. We did crazy things: tall things and compact things, like running madly up and down a beach laughing and feeling loose and free, or like sitting down and knitting our minds together[15] to feel after a piece of music or a problem. Something made us agree. We couldn't figure out what, but we agreed. And after looking at each other and seeing our bodies and the stuff behind them, we couldn't quite understand, but we accepted our good luck and we called ourselves wonderful people.

After a while we talked about marriage, children, and a home. For
50    a few months we didn't agree on a couple of things, but, as I said, we were wonderful people, and one day we decided to get married.

But the tall girl and I didn't get married. For one moment somewhere I think we stopped being wonderful people, and she must have felt her tallness for the first time, and maybe the ground came up too

---

[5]**scanned it up and down:** Looked it over; examined it closely.
[6]**compact:** Packed together tightly or closely.
[7]**by stature:** From the standpoint of height.
[8]**knitted together strongly:** Put together tightly.
[9]**rhyming:** In poetry, the repeating of sounds.
[10]**dominant:** Controlling; strong.

[11]**smugness:** Self-satisfaction.
[12]**a radical fling:** A wild departure from the traditional or customary.
[13]**ganged up:** Got together against.
[14]**compressed:** Pressed closely together.
[15]**knitting our minds together:** Putting our minds together.

close to my face. But that was all; it was the end. Something had come between the tall girl and me. I don't know what it was, but something died and with it went all the funny music and poetry in people.

Many years have passed and sometimes I get a strange feeling—I mean about walking and getting up. I don't seem to hang together as I used to. Only last week my best friend told me to pull myself together.  60 And when I looked around, I'll be damned if I wasn't just all pieces and parts, going this way and that, down and . . . up. Up! That was it. I felt taller. And I felt good. I liked the freedom. I could reach for an idea now without straining[16] everything in me to hold it; and I didn't care about the rest of me. What music there was left in me, what music I heard in others, was the strange kind one finds in long-line poetry.[17] It made me happy.

Sometimes I think of the tall girl; but she doesn't seem tall any more. She just seems natural—arms, legs, ideas, and everything. I wonder what I thought was *tall*? Sometimes I wonder if she is the same  70 girl I first saw rising from a table. I don't know. But people grow taller, I know that. Perhaps they grow shorter and more compact too. Maybe that's what makes us wonderful people.

[16]**straining:** Forcing; stretching; putting great pressure on.

[17]**long-line poetry:** Poetry with long sentences (lines) that give a smooth, flowing effect.

## _____ A LOOK AT THE IDEAS _____

1. Explain (a) why the young man liked the tall girl when he first saw her; (b) what features of the girl were not beautiful; (c) why the young man was impressed by the way she got up from the table; (d) the kinds of ideas the girl had; and (e) the kinds of poetry and music her ideas were like.

2. Describe (a) the young man's physical appearance; (b) the kinds of ideas he had; and (c) the kinds of poetry and music his ideas were like.

3. The young man and the tall girl called themselves "wonderful people." Why?

    _____ 1. They enjoyed telling one another about the different kinds of problems they had.

_____ 2. They experienced feelings of harmony and delight despite their differences.

_____ 3. They weren't afraid to do wonderful, crazy things that other people didn't do.

Do you agree they were "wonderful people"? What makes people wonderful from your point of view? If someone said to you, "Carol and Bob are such wonderful people," how would you picture them or how would you interpret the statement?

4. Why didn't the young man and the girl get married? What came between them? How did the young man feel about the end of the romance? What happened as the years passed? Why didn't the girl seem tall any longer?

5. Select the words that describe one or the other of the main characters in the early part of the story. (a) Write *M* for the man and *W* for the woman (the "tall girl") in the space to the left of the word. (b) Next, put a plus (+) or a minus (−) sign in the blank to the right of the word to indicate whether your reaction is *positive* or *negative*. For example, if you associate mostly positive or favorable things with the word "tall," put a "+" to the right of the word. If your associations are mostly negative or unpleasant, put a "−" to the right of the word. (This exercise can be done individually or in groups.)

| (+ *or* −) | (+ *or* −) | (+ *or* −) |
|---|---|---|
| 1. ___ tall ___ | 7. ___ conservative ___ | 13. ___ dominant ___ |
| 2. ___ impulsive ___ | 8. ___ poetic ___ | 14. ___ imaginative ___ |
| 3. ___ analytical ___ | 9. ___ tense ___ | 15. ___ undisciplined ___ |
| 4. ___ sturdy ___ | 10. ___ practical ___ | 16. ___ radical ___ |
| 5. ___ reliable ___ | 11. ___ loose ___ | 17. ___ compact ___ |
| 6. ___ short ___ | 12. ___ old-fashioned ___ | 18. ___ orderly ___ |

What other words would you use to describe the young man and/or the tall girl?

In general, what characteristics do you associate with "tallness" and "shortness"? List the characteristics and rate each as positive (+) or negative (−). Which kind of person do you tend to like better?

Do you consider yourself to be fundamentally a tall person or a short one? Explain.

**6.** Decide whether the young man, the young woman, and you yourself would agree or disagree with the statements below. In each column, mark *A* for agree, *D* for disagree, and *U* if you are uncertain. Explain the reasons for your choices.

|  | Young Man | Young Woman | You |
|---|---|---|---|
| 1. Things that are beautiful are more important than things that are useful. | ——— | ——— | ——— |
| 2. Tradition is important and should be respected. | ——— | ——— | ——— |
| 3. Concrete goals should be carefully evaluated in a logical, orderly way. | ——— | ——— | ——— |
| 4. Doing things that make you feel good is better than doing things you have to do. | ——— | ——— | ——— |
| 5. Proper rules of behavior are important. | ——— | ——— | ——— |
| 6. If you work hard, you will be rewarded. | ——— | ——— | ——— |
| 7. Feelings are more important than ideas. | ——— | ——— | ——— |
| 8. Experience can change people's personalities. | ——— | ——— | ——— |
| 9. People who are separated become markedly different. | ——— | ——— | ——— |
| 10. Absence makes the heart grow fonder. | ——— | ——— | ——— |

On the basis of the items you checked, do you seem to be more like the "tall girl" or the "short man"?

**7.** Describe someone you know who is either "tall" or "short." Illustrate what you mean by using concrete details. You might begin: *Like Hagopian, I also have known a tall person . . .*; or: *Like Hagopian, I also have known a short person . . .*

8. The theme or main idea of a short story gives us some understanding of the author's views about people and life. Write a paragraph in which you explain the theme of "Wonderful People." Point out sentences, phrases, and words in the story or title that you think reveal the theme or make it more obvious to the reader. Do you agree or disagree with Hagopian's view about people and life? Illustrate your own view with examples from your own experience and observation. Here is a suggestion for a beginning sentence: *The theme of "Wonderful People" by Richard Hagopian is . . .*

9. Both this story and the Vonnegut story are about young people in love. Would you describe either the young man or the young woman in "Long Walk to Forever" as a "tall" or a "short" person? In what ways are the characters similar and in what ways are they different? Write a composition in which you compare the four characters. Consider using this four-paragraph organization:

   1. You might begin by briefly explaining what "tallness" and "shortness" mean in Hagopian's "Wonderful People."

   2. Then write an analysis of Catharine, the young woman in Vonnegut's "Long Walk to Forever." Discuss the qualities that make Catharine seem "tall" or "short" to you. In what ways is she similar to or different from both the woman and the man in Hagopian's story?

   3. Continue by discussing Newt, the young man in the Vonnegut story, using the same pattern outlined in 2 above.

   4. Conclude by emphasizing briefly your main reasons for considering the two Vonnegut characters "tall" or "short" *or* by summarizing briefly your main ideas about the similarities and differences among the four characters in the two stories.

## A LOOK AT THE LANGUAGE

1. Below are three sets of sentences. The first sentence in each set is from the story; the others that follow are not. (a) Explain what the *italicized* word in the first sentence means;

(b) fill in the blanks in the other sentences with the appropriate grammatical form of the *italicized* word; (c) tell whether the words you have inserted have the same meaning as the *italicized* word in the first sentence.

1. ... like my ideas about life, morals and ethics, all squeezed together, rhyming easily, making music of a strong *dominant* sort.

   a) He gave _____ negative

   responses.

   b) She _____ the conversation
      (verb—simple past tense)
   completely.

   c) The desire for _____ is often a more
      (noun)
   powerful motivation than the desire for money.

   d) He was completely _____ by his
      (adjective—past participle)
   older brother.

   e) He was never a _____ person.
      (adjective)

2. I could take a *radical* fling once in a while...

   a) Something is _____ wrong with that
      (adverb)
   idea.

   b) Her _____ behavior shocked
      (adjective)
   everyone.

   c) Politically, he was a _____.
      (adjective—used as a noun)

   d) His _____ was an embarrassment to
      (noun)
   his family.

   e) Living in an expensive hotel was a _____
      (adjective)
   departure from his usual lifestyle.

3. I was what you might call *compact*.

   a) He doesn't want a big car; he wants a

   _____ model.
           (adjective)

   b) She opened her _____ and pow-
                        (noun)

   dered her nose.

   c) The strawberries were arranged

   _____ in the box.
          (adverb)

   d) She liked the _____ of the kitchen.
                  (noun)

   e) They made a _____ to discuss the
                  (noun)

   problem thoroughly before taking any action.

**2.** Comment on the paradox (contradictory statement or un-usual combination of words or ideas) in this sentence from the story: "I saw her and liked her because she was not beautiful."

Rewrite the sentence changing *because* to *although*. Compare your sentence with Hagopian's sentence. Is the effect different? Find other examples of unusual combinations of words or contradictory statements in the story. What is the effect of the paradox in the examples you have found?

**3.** The *italicized* words and phrases indicate devices that relate parts of the passage below. Explain what is omitted, referred to, linked, or replaced, and tell how these devices function in relating ideas in the passage. (For further information on this type of exercise, see Steinbeck, "A Look at the Language," question 4, page 12.)

   Sometimes I think of the tall girl; but *she* doesn't seem tall any more. *She* just seems natural—arms, legs, ideas, and everything. I wonder what I thought was tall? Sometimes I wonder if *she* is the same girl I first saw rising from a table. I don't *know*. But people grow taller, I know *that*. Perhaps they grow shorter and more compact *too*. Maybe that's what makes *us* wonderful people.

**4.** In "Wonderful People," Hagopian repeats "tall" and "hang together" a number of times. He also uses other words and phrases that have a meaning similar to these phrases. Skillful repetition of this kind serves to reinforce and emphasize ideas and to link different parts of an essay, story, or passage.

In order to see how repetition of words and phrases works, select an item from the list below and count the number of times it occurs in each of the seven paragraphs of "Wonderful People." Count all the forms. In other words, count *tallness* as well as *tall*. Also list other words and phrases that express a similar meaning.

1. tall and tallness

   *Example: Paragraph #1: tall* occurs four times; *tallness* occurs once. Also, "the length from her hips to her feet, and the length from her hips to her shoulders" is related to the idea of tallness. (Continue looking for *tall* and *tallness* in the remaining paragraphs, or select another phrase and begin with paragraph 1.)

2. hang (hung) together
3. compact
4. poetry and/or music
5. rising or getting up
6. wonderful people.

**5.** The following sentences are from the Hagopian story. (a) First, make short sentences out of each sentence. (b) Then, write one or more sentences of your own that include all the information (but not necessarily all of the words) in the short sentences. (c) Finally, compare your sentences with Hagopian's, and tell how yours and Hagopian's differ in style and effect. The first is done as an example.

1. We were a funny pair, the tall girl and I, funny because we were so different in everything.

   a) Possible short sentences: *We were a funny pair. The tall girl and I were a funny pair. We were funny. We were so different in everything.*

   b) Possible new sentence: *The tall girl and I were a funny pair because we were so different in everything.*

   c) Comments on style and effect: The new sentence is similar to the original, but it lacks the emphasis Hagopian puts on the word *funny* because the repetition is eliminated. The following sentence would, perhaps, be closer in meaning to the idea conveyed by Hagopian: *The tall girl and I were a funny pair. We were a funny pair because we were so different.*

Do you agree with these observations? What else can you say about differences in style and effect?

2. Everything was knitted together strongly, like my ideas about life, morals and ethics, all squeezed together, rhyming easily, making music of a strong, dominant sort.

3. My ideas were like that too. I could take a radical fling once in a while, but sooner or later, mostly sooner, the rest of me ganged up and compressed the wild motion with one easy squeeze.

4. We did crazy things: tall things and compact things, like running madly up and down a beach laughing and feeling loose and free, or like sitting down and knitting our minds together to feel after a piece of music or a problem.

6. This story contains abstractions or words that are difficult to understand because they do not refer to specific objects or concrete reality. Phrases like *fifty foot tree* or *one inch blade of grass* are fairly specific and concrete. *Tallness* or *lack of tallness*, on the other hand, are general and abstract. Arrange the items in columns *A* and *B* from the most abstract to the most specific. Number 1, which is marked in each column, is the most abstract; the highest number in each column will be the most specific.

| A | B |
|---|---|
| ____ tall people | __1__ literature |
| ____ a tall girl | ____ short stories |
| ____ tall girls | ____ a short story |
| ____ Virgie Rezian, who is 5′ 10″ tall | ____ fiction |
| __1__ tallness | ____ Hagopian's short story, "Wonderful People" |
| ____ the tall girl | ____ Hagopian's short stories |
| ____ a girl 5′ 10″ tall | ____ a seven-paragraph Hagopian short story |
| ____ the girl who is 5′ 10″ tall | |
| ____ Virgie, who is 5′ 10″ tall | |

7. In this story, Hagopian uses a number of comparisons.* For example, when he says "She *was* music," he is comparing the girl to music. When he says ". . . ideas *as* simple and pure as the good soil," he is comparing simple and pure ideas with good, clean, plain soil or earth.
   Find other comparisons in the story and tell what is being compared.

8. List the main events or happenings in the story. Does the narrator tell the story in the order in which the events actually happen? You might compare your list with the lists of other students to see if your lists are similar. Using your list, write a brief summary of the plot or main events. Would someone who has not read the story know what it is about after reading your summary? What would that person miss?

---

*Comparisons of this kind are called metaphors and similes, which differ only in grammatical structure. A simile contains the word *like* or *as*, as in ". . . ideas *as* simple and pure *as* . . ." A metaphor is a direct or straight comparison—"She *was* music."

# Marya Mannes (b. 1904)

Marya Mannes, a native New Yorker, daughter of musicians, grew up in a home atmosphere that encouraged creativity and humanity. Although she did not attend a university, she received a disciplined education in a New York private school and a broad education from living, working, reading, and traveling. Over the years she has been a prolific writer of essays, published in many different magazines and newspapers. Her books include More in Anger (1958) and Last Rights (1973), which are collections of her essays; They (1968), a novel; and Out of My Time (1971), the author's autobiography.

Mannes has her own ideas about everything from politics to art, and some of them are expressed in More in Anger, in which "Wasteland" appears. She wrote this book in the angry mood of one willing to stand up and say what she thought about heedless waste in the United States. What she says is lively and, as one reviewer put it, hers is "not a gloomy but a sparkling anger."

# 6

# Wasteland

Cans. Beer cans. Glinting[1] on the verges[2] of a million miles of roadways, lying in scrub, grass, dirt, leaves, sand, mud, but never hidden. Piels, Rheingold, Ballantine, Schaefer, Schlitz,[3] shining in the sun or picked by moon or the beams of headlights at night; washed by rain or flattened by wheels, but never dulled, never buried, never destroyed. Here is the mark of savages, the testament[4] of wasters, the stain of prosperity.

Who are these men who defile the grassy borders of our roads and lanes, who pollute[5] our ponds, who spoil the purity of our ocean beaches with the empty vessels of their thirst? Who are the men who    10 make these vessels in millions and then say, "Drink—and discard"? What society is this that can afford to cast away[6] a million tons of metal and to make of wild and fruitful land a garbage heap?[7]

What manner of men and women need thirty feet of steel and two hundred horsepower to take them, singly, to their small destinations?

[1]**glinting:** Shining.
[2]**verges:** Edges.
[3]**Piels ... Schlitz:** Names of different brands or kinds of beer.
[4]**testament:** Statement of how property should be distributed after death; in this case, what wasters leave behind them to be remembered by.
[5]**pollute:** Make dirty.
[6]**cast away:** Throw away.
[7]**garbage heap:** Pile of garbage or waste material.

Who demand that what they eat is wrapped so that forests are cut down to make the paper that is thrown away, and what they smoke and chew is sealed so that the sealers can be tossed in gutters[8] and caught in twigs and grass?

20     What kind of men can afford to make the streets of their towns and cities hideous[9] with neon[10] at night, and their roadways hideous with signs by day, wasting beauty; who leave the carcasses[11] of cars to rot[12] in heaps; who spill their trash into ravines[13] and make smoking mountains of refuse[14] for the town's rats? What manner of men choke off the life in rivers, streams and lakes with the waste of their produce, making poison of water?

    Who is as rich as that? Slowly the wasters and despoilers[15] are impoverishing[16] our land, our nature, and our beauty, so that there will not be one beach, one hill, one lane, one meadow, one forest free from the debris[17] of man and the stigma[18] of his improvidence.[19]

30     Who is so rich that he can squander[20] forever the wealth of earth and water for the trivial[21] needs of vanity or the compulsive demands[22] of greed;[23] or so prosperous in land that he can sacrifice nature for unnatural desires? The earth we abuse and the living things we kill will, in the end, take their revenge; for in exploiting[24] their presence we are diminishing our future.

    And what will we leave behind us when we are long dead? Temples? Amphora?[25] Sunken treasure?

    Or mountains of twisted, rusted steel,[26] canyons of plastic containers, and a million miles of shores garlanded,[27] not with the lovely
40 wrack[28] of the sea, but with the cans and bottles and light-bulbs and boxes of a people who conserved their convenience at the expense of their heritage, and whose ephemeral[29] prosperity was built on waste.

---

[8]**gutters:** Channels or troughs, located along the sides of streets next to sidewalks, that carry away water after it rains.
[9]**hideous:** Very ugly; frighteningly ugly.
[10]**neon:** Type of lighted glass tubes used in advertising signs.
[11]**carcasses:** Dead bodies (usually animals).
[12]**rot:** Decay; become spoiled.
[13]**ravines:** Narrow valleys.
[14]**refuse:** Waste; garbage.
[15]**despoilers:** People who spoil or ruin.
[16]**impoverishing:** Making poor; ruining.
[17]**debris:** Waste.
[18]**stigma:** Mark of shame.
[19]**improvidence:** Wastefulness.
[20]**squander:** Waste.

[21]**trivial:** Of little value; unimportant.
[22]**compulsive demands:** Compelling demands that one cannot control or stop.
[23]**greed:** Very strong, unreasonable desire for wealth or material possessions.
[24]**exploiting:** Using selfishly.
[25]**amphora:** Ancient Greek or Roman jars or containers used to hold wine or oil.
[26]**rusted steel:** Steel covered with a reddish-brown material, usually the result of water or dampness, that ruins the steel.
[27]**garlanded:** Decorated (usually with circles of flowers or leaves).
[28]**wrack:** Seaweed; sea plants.
[29]**ephemeral:** Short-lived.

1. The title "Wasteland" refers to—

    _____ 1. a land that is wasted

    _____ 2. a land covered by waste

    _____ 3. a land inhabited by wasters

    _____ 4. all of the above

    _____ 5. none of the above

   Explain the reason for your choice. Also, comment on the appropriateness of the title.

2. In the last sentence of the first paragraph, Marya Mannes says, "Here is the mark of savages, the testament of wasters, the stain of prosperity." (lines 6-7) In this sentence, the best replacement for *here* would be—

    _____ 1. along millions of miles of roads and highways

    _____ 2. the presence of beer cans along our roads and highways

    _____ 3. failure to hide, bury, or destroy beer cans

    _____ 4. none of the above

   Who are the savages and the wasters? Do you agree that piles of empty beer cans are a negative sign of prosperity?

3. All paragraphs except the first and last begin with questions. Does Mannes expect the reader to answer these questions? Why does she ask questions rather than make statements? How do you react to the series of questions? Why do you think she uses "these men," "the men," "kind of men," and "manner of men" rather than "people" or "men and women" in the questions in the second and fourth paragraphs?

   How many questions can you find that ask essentially this question: Is there any society with such unlimited wealth that it can go on forever wasting and destroying the beauty and resources of the earth?

**4.** In "Wasteland" Mannes's main purpose is—

_____ 1. to find out who is responsible for the destruction and pollution of the earth

_____ 2. to let people know that she thinks they are savages and wasters

_____ 3. to make people realize the consequences of exploitation of the earth

_____ 4. none of the above

Give reasons for your choice.

**5.** Write *A* before the statement if you think Mannes would be likely to agree with it; write *D* if you think she would be likely to disagree with it. Then tell how you feel about each statement.

_____ 1. We don't have to worry about using up our natural resources because scientists can produce satisfactory substitutes.

_____ 2. Only uncivilized and unthinking people would waste nature's beauty and resources.

_____ 3. In the future, everyone who wants to work should be able to have a comfortable, healthy life.

_____ 4. What we hand down to future generations will be mountains of garbage and trash.

_____ 5. More laws against littering—throwing or dumping garbage and trash on roads and beaches and in lakes, rivers, and oceans—should be passed and rigidly enforced.

**6.** In what part of the essay does Mannes state her position about the senseless waste and destruction of the earth's beauty and resources? Does the following restatement of Mannes's position seem accurate to you?

> *Our continuous exploitation of the earth for our convenience means that future generations will inherit a world of very limited natural beauty and resources.*

Restate her position in your own words. Be as accurate as possible in presenting her view.

**7.** Write a composition in which you express agreement or disagreement with Mannes's views about the exploitation of the earth. Here are some suggestions:

    1. In the first paragraph, sum up Marya Mannes's main ideas. You might begin with a sentence like this: *In "Wasteland," Marya Mannes maintains that . . .* At the end of this paragraph, state your own position. Your sentence might begin: *I agree (disagree) for the most part with Marya Mannes because . . .*

    2. In the next paragraph or paragraphs, give your reasons for agreeing or disagreeing with Mannes.

    3. Conclude with a summary statement of your own position and your main arguments to support it.

**8.** Read the following passage and tell how the Indians felt about the white man's treatment of the land. Would Mannes be likely to agree or disagree with the Indians? Would she say that it is only the white people who are exploiting the earth? What are your views?

> The White people never cared for land or deer or bear. When we Indians kill meat, we eat it all up. When we dig roots we make little holes. When we build houses, we make little holes. When we burn grass for grasshoppers, we don't ruin things. We shake down acorns and pinenuts. We don't chop down the trees. We only use dead wood. But the White people plow up the ground, pull down the trees, kill everything. The tree says, "Don't. I am sore. Don't hurt me." But they chop it down and cut it up. The spirit of the land hates them. They blast out trees and stir it up to its depths. They saw up the trees. That hurts them. The Indians never hurt anything, but the White people destroy all. They blast rocks and scatter them on the ground. The rock says, "Don't. You are hurting me." But the White people pay no attention. When the Indians use rocks, they take little round ones for their cooking. . . . How can the spirit of the earth like the White man? . . . Everywhere the White man has touched it, it is sore.*

---

*From Dorothy D. Lee, "Anthropology" in *Religious Perspectives in College Teaching,* ed. by Hoxie N. Fairchild et al. Copyright 1952 The Ronald Press Company, New York.

9. Write a composition in which you compare Mannes's views about the treatment of the earth with the views of the Indians. Here are some suggestions:

1. In the first paragraph, summarize the Indians' views.

2. If you think Mannes would agree with the Indians, begin your second paragraph with a sentence similar to this one: *Marya Mannes would, in general, agree with the Indians.* If you think she would not agree, you could write: *On the other hand, Marya Mannes believes . . .* If you think she would both agree and disagree, you could say: *Marya Mannes would probably agree with some of the ideas of the Indians but not with others.* Continue this paragraph and as many others as you need to discuss how the views of Mannes and the Indians are similar and/or different.

3. Conclude with a brief paragraph in which you summarize your main arguments and restate your position.

## _____ A LOOK AT THE LANGUAGE _____

1. Rather than repeat the same word several times in the essay, Marya Mannes often uses synonyms—different words with the same general meaning. For example, she uses several verbs that mean *to get rid of* or *dispose* of something, several verbs that mean to *ruin something* or *make it dirty,* and a number of nouns to designate *worthless material that is disposed of.* Make lists of the words in the essay with these meanings. The first letter of each word is given. If you find or think of other words with the same general meaning, add them to the list.

   1. *Verb:* to dispose of; to get rid of

      <u>d e s _ _ _ _ _</u>   <u>c a s _ _ a w _ _</u>
      <u>t h r _ _ _ a w _ _</u>

   2. *Verb:* to make dirty or ruin

      <u>d e f _ _ _ _</u>   <u>p o l _ _ _ _ _</u>   <u>s p o _</u>

   3. *Noun:* worthless or useless material to be disposed of

      <u>g a r _ _ _ _ _</u>   <u>t r a _ _</u>
      <u>r e f _ _ _ _</u>   <u>w a s _ _</u>   <u>d e b _ _ _</u>

For which of these phrases does *tossed* mean to throw away or get rid of? What do the others mean? (a) *tossed* the paper in the street; (b) *tossed* the ball in the air; (c) *tossed* the salad in a big wooden bowl; (d) *tossed* the letter in a drawer; (e) *tossed* in bed all night long; (f) *tossed* the envelope in the wastebasket.

2. While Mannes often uses a synonym rather than repeat a word, she also chooses to repeat the same word from time to time. For example, she begins her essay, "Cans. Beer cans." Why do you think she repeats *cans*? Why do you think she repeats *never* in lines 2-3 and 5? ("never hidden," "never dulled, never buried, never destroyed") What is the effect of the repetition? Find other examples in the essay where she repeats the same word or words and comment on the reason for and the effect of the repetition.

3. In the papers you write, is it generally considered better style to use synonyms rather than to repeat the same word several times? In what situations or kinds of papers might you want to repeat the same word or phrases as Mannes does?

4. Mannes's style, which is very vigorous and personal, differs in many respects from the style of typical academic writing. For example, Mannes's first four sentences are not traditional sentences with subjects and predicates. Do academic papers typically begin with sentences like these? Do you usually begin compositions or papers that you write for courses with sentences like these?

Revise the first four sentences in Mannes's essay so that all sentences in the paragraph have a subject and a predicate. "Beer cans," for example, can be the subject of the first revised sentence: *Beer cans, glinting on the verges of a million miles of roadway, lie in scrub . . .* How else might you rewrite the first sentence?

Compare your revised sentences with Mannes's four sentences. Which sentences are more likely to capture the attention and interest of the reader? In what kind of writing or situation might the revised sentences seem more appropriate?

5. Would you agree that Mannes's rich, colorful language is not particularly characteristic of academic writing? Compare the paragraph below, written in a style more or less characteristic of academic papers, with Mannes's first paragraph and comment on the differences in style and effect. Which paragraph would probably be more successful in making people see what they are doing to their land? Which paragraph is more matter of fact and objective?

> *Beer cans are scattered along a million miles of roadway. Cans with an assortment of brand names shine in the sunlight and become visible at night when singled out by moonbeams or car headlights. These cans may be washed by rain and flattened by the wheels of cars, but they are always there. They are rarely collected, carted away, and destroyed. Their presence is a sign of a prosperous society, apparently more concerned with its convenience than with conservation of the beauty of nature and natural resources.*

6. Rewrite the following phrases from "Wasteland" in a style similar to the paragraph in question 5 above. In other words, be more direct and neutral in phrasing and choice of words.

   Line 10:       empty vessels of their thirst

   Lines 12-13:   to cast away a million tons of metal and to make of wild and fruitful land a garbage heap

   Lines 14-15:   thirty feet of steel and two hundred horsepower to take them, singly, to their small destinations

   Lines 28-29:   free from the debris of man and the stigma of his improvidence

   Lines 39-40:   a million miles of shores garlanded, not with the lovely wrack of the sea

7. Would you be likely to use as many questions as Mannes does in writing a summary of this essay or in writing papers for your academic courses? Have you noticed extensive use of questions in other essays in this book? In what kinds of situations might you want to use a number of questions?

Select a subject you think is suitable and write a paragraph in which you mainly use questions. What effect do you want to create? Is your paragraph typical of your other academic writing?

8. Many academic essays have a thesis statement (a statement of purpose or position to be supported by argument and/or evidence) at or near the beginning of the essay. Often the thesis statement is contained in a single sentence, though some writers use two or more sentences to make their thesis clear. Mannes may not have written the type of thesis statement one usually finds in an academic paper, but she does state her position about the senseless waste and destruction of the earth's beauty and resources. Check the sentence or sentences below that you think state or reveal her position and might be called her thesis.

_____ 1. Here is the mark of savages, the testament of wasters, the stain of prosperity. (lines 6-7)

_____ 2. Slowly the wasters and despoilers are impoverishing our land, our nature, and our beauty, so that there will not be one beach, one hill, one lane, one meadow, one forest tree free from the debris of man and the stigma of his improvidence. (lines 26-29)

_____ 3. The earth we abuse and the living things we kill will, in the end, take their revenge; for in exploiting their presence we are diminishing our future. (lines 33-35)

_____ 4. And what will we leave behind us when we are long dead? Temples? Amphora? Sunken treasure? (lines 36-37)

_____ 5. Or mountains of twisted, rusted steel, canyons of plastic containers, and a million miles of shores garlanded, not with the lovely wrack of the sea, but with the cans and bottles and light-bulbs and boxes of a people who conserved their convenience at the expense of their heritage, and whose ephemeral prosperity was built on waste. (lines 38-42)

_____ 6. None of the above

Restate Mannes's main point in the form of a thesis statement one might expect to find in a typical academic essay.
Compare your restatement to the one you wrote for question 6, "A Look at the Ideas." Are they the same or different?

9. Comment on any other differences you have observed in
Mannes's style and the style of typical academic writing
besides those pointed out in questions 4, 5, 6, 7, and 8.

10. Mannes's topic is timely and could be discussed in a
number of different ways, depending on the purpose.
Write an essay on the same topic in an academic style—the
style you might use in writing a paper for a college or
university course or seminar. Consider your purpose.
How does your purpose differ from Mannes's purpose?

If you like, you can use Mannes's general thesis or main
point, and the arguments and/or evidence she uses to support it, but write the essay in your own words. In your
essay, use the typical organization found in academic
papers—the deductive rather than the inductive mode.
(When you use the deductive mode, you state the thesis or
main point at or near the beginning of the essay, then
present and discuss arguments and/or evidence to support
the thesis, and conclude by summing up the thesis and
arguments. When you use the inductive mode, as Mannes
does in "Wasteland," you lead or build up to your thesis
and then make your concluding remarks. When writers
use the inductive mode, they often do not state their thesis
or main point in one sentence. Sometimes they use two or
even three sentences to make the point, and sometimes
they do not state their thesis explicitly. The reader must
infer it.)

Here are some suggestions for writing your paper:

1. Use the restatement of Mannes's thesis you prepared in
question 8 or write another one. Then make a list of the
evidence Mannes uses to support her thesis.

2. Now write an introductory paragraph and put the thesis statement at the end of the paragraph.

3. In the next paragraph or paragraphs, present the evidence and/or arguments to support your thesis.

4. Conclude with a summary statement of the thesis and supporting evidence.

# Carl Sagan (b. 1934)

*Carl Sagan (pronounced "say-gun") is Professor of Astronomy and Space Sciences and Director of the Laboratory for Planetary Studies at Cornell University. He is also the author of a number of successful books including* The Cosmic Connection *(1973), the Pulitzer Prize-winning* The Dragons of Eden *(1977), and* Broca's Brain *(1979).*

*Sagan, who has said that he enjoys writing because it forces him to think clearly and to come forth with new ideas, has written more than 350 papers for scientific journals and magazines and newspapers; and he has produced radio and television scripts for the Voice of America, the British Broadcasting Corporation, and the Public Broadcasting Service. In this excerpt from* The Cosmic Connection, *he speculates on the fate of the Earth. Will it in time become a frozen mass or a fiery cauldron?*

# 7

# The Ice Age

# and

# the Cauldron

On our tiny planet, spinning in an almost circular orbit[1] at a nearly constant distance from our star, the climate varies, sometimes radically,[2] from place to place. The Sahara is different from the Antarctic. The Sun's rays fall directly on the Sahara and obliquely[3] on the Antarctic, producing a sizable temperature difference. Hot air rises near the equator, cold air sinks near the poles—producing atmospheric circulation. The motion of the resulting air current is deflected by Earth's rotation.[4]

There is water in the atmosphere, but when it condenses, forming rain or snow, heat is released into the atmosphere, which in turn changes the motion of the air.

Ground covered by freshly fallen snow reflects more sunlight back to space than when it is snow-free. The ground becomes colder yet.

When more water vapor or carbon dioxide is put into the atmosphere, infrared[5] emission[6] from the surface of the Earth is increasingly

10

[1]**circular orbit:** Circular path of a planet or star.
[2]**radically:** Extremely; completely.
[3]**obliquely:** At an angle from.
[4]**rotation:** Turning, especially around a center point.

[5]**infrared:** Part of light that cannot be seen by the human eye. Infrared rays give off heat.
[6]**emission:** Radiation; giving off or sending out.

blocked. Heat radiation cannot escape from this atmospheric green-house,[7] and the Earth's temperature rises.

There is topography[8] on Earth. When wind currents flow over mountains or down into valleys, the circulation changes.

20     At one point in time on one tiny planet, the weather, as we all know, is complex. The climate, at least to some degree, is unpredictable.[9] In the past there were more violent climatic fluctuations.[10] Whole species, genera, classes, and families of plants and animals were extinguished,[11] probably because of climatic fluctuations. One of the most likely explanations of the extinction[12] of the dinosaurs is that they were large animals with poor thermoregulatory systems;[13] they were unable to burrow,[14] and, therefore, unable to accommodate to a global decline in temperature.

The early evolution of man[15] is closely connected with the emer-
30 gence of the Earth from the vast Pleistocene glaciation.[16] There is an as yet unexplained connection between reversals of the Earth's magnetic field[17] and the extinction of large numbers of small aquatic[18] animals.

The reason for these climatic changes is still under serious debate. It may be that the amount of light and heat put out by the Sun is variable on time scales of tens of thousands or more years. It may be that climatic change is caused by the slowly changing direction between the tilt[19] of the Earth's rotational axis[20] and its orbit. There may be instabilities connected with the amount of pack ice in the Arctic and Antarctic. It may be that volcanoes, pumping large amounts of dust into the atmosphere,
40 darken the sky and cool the Earth. It may be that chemical reactions reduced the amount of carbon dioxide and other greenhouse molecules in the atmosphere, and the Earth cooled.

There are, in fact, some fifty or sixty different and, for the most part, mutually exclusive theories[21] of the ice ages and other major climatic changes on Earth. It is a problem of substantial intellectual interest. But it is more than that. An understanding of climatic change may have

---

[7]**atmospheric greenhouse:** The idea that the atmosphere—the layer of air around the earth—acts like the glass walls of a greenhouse, keeping the heat from escaping.
[8]**topography:** Geographic shape of the land.
[9]**unpredictable:** Cannot be told or understood in advance.
[10]**fluctuations:** Movements, especially up and down or irregular.
[11]**extinguished:** Put out (usually for a fire, candle, or light); in this case, killed off.
[12]**extinction:** Killing or dying off.
[13]**thermoregulatory systems:** Systems to regulate or control temperature; in this case, body temperature.
[14]**burrow:** Make a hole in the ground to act as a shelter or protection against weather changes.

[15]**evolution of man:** Development of man from lower or simpler kinds of animals.
[16]**Pleistocene glaciation:** A period of time about a million years ago when the Earth was covered by glaciers—huge masses of ice and snow.
[17]**magnetic field:** Pattern of magnetic or electric current around the earth.
[18]**aquatic:** Growing or living in or near water.
[19]**tilt:** Positioning at an angle rather than level; slant.
[20]**axis:** The imaginary center line through the earth about which the earth rotates once every twenty-four hours.
[21]**mutually exclusive theories:** Theories of such a nature that if one is correct, other theories must be incorrect.

profound[22] practical consequences—because Man is influencing the environment of the Earth, often in ways poorly thought-out, ill-understood, and for short-term economic profit and individual convenience, rather than for the long-term benefit of the inhabitants of the    50
planet.

Industrial pollution is churning[23] enormous quantities of foreign particulate matter[24] into the atmosphere, where they are carried around the globe. The smallest particles, injected[25] into the stratosphere, take years to fall out. These particles increase the albedo or reflectivity of Earth and diminish the amount of sunlight that falls on the surface. On the other hand, the burning of fossil fuels, such as coal and oil and gasoline, increases the amount of carbon dioxide in the Earth's atmosphere which, because of its significant infrared absorption, can increase the temperature of the Earth.                                                60

There is a range of effects pushing and pulling the climate in opposite directions. No one fully understands these interactions. While it seems unlikely that the amount of pollution currently deemed acceptable can produce a major climatic change on Earth, we cannot be absolutely sure. It is a topic worth serious and concerted[26] international investigation.

Space exploration plays an interesting role in testing out theories of climatic change. On Mars, for example, there are periodic massive injections of fine dust particles into the atmosphere; they take weeks and sometimes months to fall out. We know from the *Mariner 9* experience    70
that the temperature structure and climate of Mars are severely changed during such dust storms. By studying Mars, we may better understand the effects of industrial pollution on Earth.

Likewise for Venus. Here is a planet that appears to have undergone a runaway[27] greenhouse effect. A massive quantity of carbon dioxide and water vapor has been put into its atmosphere, so cloaking the surface as to permit little infrared thermal emission to escape into space. The greenhouse effect has heated the surface to 900 degrees F or more. How did this greenhouse-overkill happen on Venus? How do we avoid its happening here?                                                  80

Study of our neighboring planets not only helps us to generalize the study of our own, but it has the most practical hints and cautionary tales[28] for us to read—if only we are wise enough to understand them.

---

[22]**profound:** Deep; in this case, very great.
[23]**churning:** Moving violently about.
[24]**particulate matter:** matter or substance made out of small bits or particles.
[25]**Injected:** Forced or driven as through a tube (or, in the case of medicine, through a needle).

[26]**concerted:** Planned or performed together.
[27]**runaway:** Out of control.
[28]**cautionary tales:** Stories that contain a warning of danger.

1. In the first five paragraphs, Carl Sagan advances several reasons for the wide variation in climate from place to place on this planet. Explain how the following factors affect climate: (a) the sun's rays; (b) the water in the atmosphere; (c) snow-covered ground; (d) water vapor and carbon dioxide; (e) the topography of the Earth.

2. What explanation does Sagan give for the extinction of the dinosaurs? What other examples does he give to illustrate the impact of violent climatic changes in the past on life on this planet?

3. Sagan says there are some fifty or sixty different theories of the ice age and other major climatic changes on this planet. What does he mean when he says that these theories are, for the most part, mutually exclusive?

   _____ 1. If one theory is true, the others cannot be true.

   _____ 2. These theories are understood by only a few people.

   _____ 3. All of these theories are equally probable.

4. Sagan mentions several reasons that could account for the radical climatic changes in the past. Explain the reasons connected with (a) the Sun's output; (b) the Earth's rotational axis and orbit; (c) the Arctic and Antarctic ice pack; (d) the eruption of volcanoes; (e) chemical reactions.

5. Sagan says that understanding theories about past major climatic changes is important on a practical as well as an intellectual level. What reasons does he give? How can industrial pollution affect the Earth's temperature? What conclusions does Sagan make about the consequences of man's influence on the environment?

6. What information about Mars did scientists obtain from the *Mariner 9* experience? How can this information be useful to us? What possible lesson can we learn from the greenhouse effect on Venus?

7. Which of the following is the main point of this essay?

_____ 1. Radical climatic changes in the past produced drastic changes in life on this planet.

_____ 2. Space exploration has made it possible for scientists to test a number of their theories about the reasons for climatic change.

_____ 3. Man's influence on the environment has made study of climatic change on other planets of practical as well as intellectual interest.

_____ 4. Depending on which theory one accepts, the Earth is destined to become either a land of ice and snow or a fiery cauldron.

Give reasons for your choice. Is the main idea connected to the warning in the concluding paragraph of the essay?

8. Sagan states: "... Man is influencing the environment of the Earth, often in ways poorly thought-out, ill-understood, and for short-term economic profit and individual convenience, rather than for the long-term benefit of the inhabitants of the planet" (lines 47-51). Does his point of view seem similar to that of Marya Mannes in "Wasteland"? Does he, like Mannes, seem to write in anger and indignation at man's short-sightedness? Is Sagan's purpose, like Mannes's, to shake people up, make them react, perhaps make them angry, *or* to inform and caution them about possible consequences of industrial pollution? Find sentences and phrases in the essay that reveal or illustrate Sagan's approach and intention.

9. To what extent do you think the policies of governments and industries will be influenced by the warnings of scientists like Sagan? Do you think it technically possible at this time to control industrial pollution? Is it economically desirable to control pollution? How much do you think rigid control of industrial pollution would change our present lifestyle.

10. Write a composition in which you discuss Sagan's ideas about pollution and climatic change. Here are some suggestions:

1. First, summarize Sagan's main points about the possible effects of industrial pollution on climatic change.

2. Then, discuss the likelihood of scientists like Sagan influencing the policies of governments and industries in
   controlling pollution.

3. Next, give your own estimate of the probable outcome
   of the problem of pollution and climatic change.

4. Finally, sum up Sagan's views and your own assess-
   ment of society's response to the warnings of scientists.

11. Sagan says that scientists do not yet fully understand the
    "range of effects pushing and pulling the climate in oppo-
    site directions." On a more immediate level, do changes in
    the climate or the weather push and pull you in opposite
    directions? Write a composition in which you discuss how
    the climate or the weather influences your behavior and
    feelings. Are you bored, depressed, or moody when it is
    cold, foggy, or rainy? Do your spirits rise with the temper-
    ature? What do you do when the weather turns cold? What
    happens to you when it is unbearably hot? Do you prefer
    to live in a warm, cold, or mild climate? Given the option
    of freeze or burn, ski or swim, sit by the fire or lie in the
    sun, what would you choose? You can develop your point
    of view by generalizing from typical examples or by focus-
    ing on an individual experience.

## ——————— A LOOK AT THE LANGUAGE ———————

1. Fill in the blanks with the appropriate form of the *italicized*
   word. This form of the word is used in the essay.

   1. The study of *climate* is important because
      _____ conditions may have a great influ-
      ence on life.

   2. The planets *rotate* in orbit around the Sun. The
      _____ of the Earth is faster than that of
      Saturn

   3. The *atmosphere* surrounds the earth.
      _____ conditions determine the cli-
      mate.

   4. The climate has *fluctuated* violently in the past. These
      _____ have caused great changes in life
      on Earth.

5. Weather patterns have great *complexity*. Most people do not know how _____ they really are.

6. Do you think that pollution will *profoundly* influence life on Earth? Will pollution have a _____ effect on our climate?

7. It is important that the nations of the world work in *concert* to fight pollution; only with _____ action can we improve the air we breathe.

**2.** The *italicized* words and phrases indicate devices that relate parts of the passage below. Explain what is omitted, referred to, linked, or replaced, and tell how these devices function in relating ideas in the passage. (For further information on this type of exercise, see Steinbeck, "A Look at the Language," question 4, page 12.)

> The smallest particles, injected into the atmosphere, take years to *fall out*. *These* particles increase the albedo or reflectivity of Earth and diminish the amount of sunlight that falls *on the surface*. *On the other hand*, the burning of fossil fuels, such as coal and oil and gasoline, increases the amount of carbon dioxide in the Earth's atmosphere which, because of *its* significant infrared absorption, can increase the temperature of the Earth.

**3.** Sagan assumes that the reader of his essay already has certain information. For example, what information does he expect the reader to supply when he says "on our tiny planet" (line 1), "from our star" (line 2), "The Sahara is different from the Antarctic" (lines 3-4), "on one tiny planet" (line 20)?

Find other examples where Sagan assumes that the reader has background information.

**4.** Here are some things to keep in mind in using quotations in the papers you write.

1. Put quotation marks around the words or sentences you are quoting.

> In "The Ice Age and the Cauldron," Sagan says, "The climate, at least to some degree, is unpredictable." (lines 21-22)

Notice that there are two sets of quotation marks. The second set encloses the quoted statement. What is the function of the first set?

2. In American English, it is customary to place commas and periods inside quotation marks, as in the example in 1 above. Question marks are placed inside quotation marks if they are part of the quotation; otherwise, they are placed outside. Compare:

a) What does Carl Sagan mean when he says, "Man is influencing the environment of the Earth..."? (lines 47-48)

b) Marya Mannes asks, "Who are the men who make these vessels in millions and then say, 'Drink—and discard'?"

Single rather than double marks are used when the material quoted contains quotation marks, as in the example above ('Drink—and discard').

3. Be sure the quotation is accurate. You must use the exact words of the author you are quoting. Check the accuracy of the following quotation by comparing it with the statement in "The Ice Age and the Cauldron."

Carl Sagan points out that "In the past, there were more violent fluctuations in climate." (line 22)

4. Use three dots (...) to indicate words, phrases, or clauses omitted from a quotation. If the omission follows a period, keep the period and add the three dots. Compare these quotations from "The Ice Age and the Cauldron":

a) Carl Sagan says, "On our tiny planet... the climate varies, sometimes radically, from place to place." (lines 1-3)

b) He also points out that "Space exploration plays an interesting role in testing out theories of climatic change.... By studying Mars, we may better understand the effects of industrial pollution on Earth." (lines 67-73)

What has been omitted from each of these quotations? Does the omission affect the accuracy of the quotation?

5. When you incorporate a quotation in a sentence, as in examples 1, 2, 3, and 4 above, be sure that your incorporating sentence has a subject and a predicate. Also, when you omit information from a statement you are quoting, make sure that the remaining part of the quoted statement has a subject and a predicate. For example, what are the subjects and predicates of the quoted state-

ments in 4 (a) and (b)? What are the subjects and predicates of the incorporating sentences in 4 (a) and (b)?

5. Check the following quotations from "The Ice Age and the Cauldron" for accuracy in wording and punctuation. Also, make sure that both incorporating sentences and quoted statements have a subject and a predicate. *Make whatever corrections are necessary.*

   1. In explaining some of the reasons for climatic variations, Sagan says, "The rays of the Sun fall directly on the Sahara and obliquely on the Antarctic, producing a sizable difference in temperature." (lines 4-5)

   2. Sagan points out that "It may be that volcanoes, pumping . . . the sky and cool the Earth." (lines 38-40)

   3. In discussing space exploration, Sagan says, "By studying Mars we may better understand the effects of industrial pollution." (lines 72-73)

6. When you report rather than quote what someone has said, you do not use quotation marks, but the statement should be reported as accurately as possible in your own words. Read the quotation below and the two reports that follow. Which report is more accurate? How would you report the quotation?

   | | |
   |---|---|
   | *Quoted Statement:* | Carl Sagan says, "On our tiny planet . . . the climate varies, sometimes radically, from place to place." |
   | *Report A:* | Carl Sagan says that the changes in climate from place to place on our planet Earth are sometimes extreme. |
   | *Report B:* | Carl Sagan says that the climate changes from one part of our small planet Earth to another. |

7. Choose three important statements from the essay. First, copy the quotation; then, write a sentence in which you quote the statement; finally, report the information in the statement in your own words. Be as accurate as possible in quoting and reporting the statement. Here is an example:

   1. Quoted statement: "On our tiny planet . . . the climate varies, sometimes radically, from place to place."

2. Sentence containing the quoted statement: *In "The Ice Age and the Cauldron," Carl Sagan points out that "On our tiny planet . . . the climate varies, sometimes radically, from place to place."*

3. Report of the statement: *In "The Ice Age and the Cauldron," Carl Sagan points out that the changes in climate from one part of our small planet to another are sometimes extreme.*

8. Indicate the order in which Sagan presents his ideas in the essay by marking the items below from 1 (first) to 7 (last).

_____ Points out the contribution of space exploration to our understanding of our own planet

_____ Strongly suggests that studies of other planets will not only help us understand our own planet but also provide us with information useful for our survival

_____ Mentions that some great climatic changes have taken place in the past

_____ Discusses the influence of man on the environment and some possible consequences

_____ Speculates on some reasons for violent climatic changes in the past

_____ Gives reasons for climatic variation from place to place on our planet

In what part of the essay does Sagan present his main point or thesis? Restate his thesis in your own words, and compare it with the statement you chose as the main point of the essay in question 7, "A Look at the Ideas," (page 79).

Does Sagan use a deductive mode or an inductive mode in writing his essay? (Does he proceed deductively and present his main idea or thesis at or near the beginning of the essay, as is commonly done in academic writing, or does he proceed inductively and build up to his thesis or main point later in the essay?)

9. Write a summary of the main points in "The Ice Age and the Cauldron" using the inductive mode. Then write another summary using the deductive mode. Here are some suggestions:

1. Make a list of the main points of the essay in the order in which Sagan presents them. This order should corre-

spond to the order you decided on for question 8 above. Then write a summary of the main ideas using this order. Will the summary be in the inductive or the deductive mode?

2. Reorganize the list of main points you prepared in 1 so that the thesis or main point of the essay comes first and the other points follow in logical or reasonable order. Did you use the deductive or the inductive mode in writing this summary?

3. Compare the two summaries. Which one do you prefer? Which one did you find easier to write? Do you generally feel more comfortable writing in the deductive or the inductive mode?

# William Saroyan (b. 1908)

William Saroyan's parents and relatives were Armenian immigrants who settled in the farm area around Fresno, California. At fifteen, Saroyan dropped out of school and earned his living by doing different kinds of jobs. He also read widely and began writing in his distinctive natural style. By the late 1930s his many short stories, novels, and plays had established him as a writer. In 1940, his play The Time of Your Life won a Pulitzer Prize, and it is still performed today. Over the years Saroyan has continued to delight his readers with his stories and memoirs.

Many of Saroyan's stories stem from his experience in the Armenian community around Fresno. He writes in a simple, flowing style about warm-hearted, life-loving people—sometimes, as in "The Pomegranate Trees," carried away by fantastic dreams of glory. This story first appeared in a collection of stories entitled My Name Is Aram (1940).

# 8

## The

## Pomegranate

## Trees

My uncle Melik was just about the worst farmer that ever lived. He was too imaginative and poetic for his own good. What he wanted was beauty. He wanted to plant it and see it grow. I myself planted over one hundred pomegranate trees[1] for my uncle one year back there in the good old days[2] of poetry and youth in the world. I drove a John Deere[3] tractor too, and so did my uncle. It was all pure esthetics,[4] not agriculture. My uncle just liked the idea of planting trees and watching them grow.

Only they wouldn't grow. It was on account of the soil. The soil was desert soil. It was dry. My uncle waved at the six hundred and eighty acres of desert he had bought and he said in the most poetic Armenian anybody ever heard, Here in this awful desolation[5] a garden shall flower, fountains of cold water shall bubble out of the earth, and all things of beauty shall come into being.[6]

10

---

[1]**pomegranate trees:** Small trees that yield a fruit with a tough skin, usually red, covering many small seeds.
[2]**one year back there in the good old days:** A year in my childhood with its many fond memories.
[3]**John Deere:** Brand name of a tractor.

[4]**esthetics:** The philosophic study of beauty; in this case, the enjoyment of beauty.
[5]**awful desolation:** Terrible, uninhabited, lonely, barren land.
[6]**shall come into being:** Will grow.

Yes, sir, I said.

I was the first and only relative to see the land he had bought. He knew I was a poet at heart, and he believed I would understand the magnificent impulse[7] that was driving him to glorious ruin.[8] I did. I knew as well as he that what he had purchased was worthless desert
20  land. It was away over to hell and gone,[9] at the foot of the Sierra Nevada Mountains.[10] It was full of every kind of desert plant that ever sprang out of dry hot earth. It was overrun with[11] prairie dogs, squirrels, horned toads, snakes, and a variety of smaller forms of life. The space over this land knew only the presence of hawks, eagles, and buzzards. It was a region of loneliness, emptiness, truth, and dignity. It was nature at its proudest, dryest, loneliest, and loveliest.

My uncle and I got out of the Ford roadster[12] in the middle of his land and began to walk over the dry earth.

This land, he said, is my land.
30  He walked slowly, kicking into the dry soil. A horned toad scrambled[13] over the earth at my uncle's feet. My uncle clutched[14] my shoulder and came to a pious halt.[15]

What is that animal? he said.

That little tiny lizard? I said.

That mouse with horns, my uncle said. What is it?

I don't know for sure, I said. We call them horny toads.

The horned toad came to a halt about three feet away and turned its head.

My uncle looked down at the small animal.
40  Is it poison? he said.

To eat? I said. Or if it bites you?

Either way, my uncle said.

I don't think it's good to eat, I said. I think it's harmless. I've caught many of them. They grow sad in captivity,[16] but never bite. Shall I catch this one?

Please do, my uncle said.

I sneaked up on[17] the horned toad, then sprang on it while my uncle looked on.

Careful, he said. Are you sure it isn't poison?
50  I've caught many of them, I said.

I took the horned toad to my uncle. He tried not to seem afraid.

---

[7]**impulse:** An inner urge or push toward action.
[8]**glorious ruin:** Complete but magnificent downfall or loss.
[9]**away over to hell and gone:** Far out, away from civilization.
[10]**Sierra Nevada Mountains:** A mountain range in eastern California.
[11]**overrun (with):** Completely occupied (by).

[12]**roadster:** An open car with a single seat that was common in the 1930s.
[13]**scrambled:** Went hurriedly; crawled quickly.
[14]**clutched:** Grabbed, grasped, seized.
[15]**pious halt:** A stop (halt) that looked as if it were filled with religious feeling.
[16]**captivity:** Kept as in prison.
[17]**sneaked up on:** Moved quietly toward.

A lovely little thing, isn't it? he said. His voice was unsteady.

Would you like to hold it? I said.

No, my uncle said. You hold it. I have never before been so close to such a thing as this. I see it has eyes. I suppose it can see us.

I suppose it can, I said. It's looking up at you now.

My uncle looked the horned toad straight in the eye. The horned toad looked my uncle straight in the eye. For fully half a minute they looked one another straight in the eye and then the horned toad turned its head aside and looked down at the ground. My uncle sighed with relief.          60

A thousand of them, he said, could kill a man, I suppose.

They never travel in great numbers, I said. You hardly ever see more than one at a time.

A big one, my uncle said, could probably bite a man to death.

They don't grow big, I said. This is as big as they grow.

They seem to have an awful eye for such small creatures, my uncle said. Are you sure they don't mind being picked up?

I suppose they forget all about it the minute you put them down, I said.          70

Do you really think so? my uncle said.

I don't think they have very good memories, I said.

My uncle straightened up, breathing deeply.

Put the little creature down, he said. Let us not be cruel to the innocent creations of Almighty God. If it is not poison and grows no larger than a mouse and does not travel in great numbers and has no memory to speak of, let the timid[18] little thing return to the earth. Let us be gentle toward these small things which live on the earth with us.

Yes, sir, I said.

I placed the horned toad on the ground.          80

Gently now, my uncle said. Let no harm come to this strange dweller on my land.[19]

The horned toad scrambled away.

These little things, I said, have been living on soil of this kind for centuries.

Centuries? my uncle said. Are you sure?

I'm not sure, I said, but I imagine they have. They're still here, anyway.

My uncle looked around at his land, at the cactus and brush[20] growing out of it, at the sky overhead.          90

What have they been eating all this time? he shouted.

---

[18]**timid:** Shy; easily frightened.
[19]**dweller on my land:** Animal that dwells or lives on my land; inhabitant.

[20]**cactus and brush:** Desert plants and ground covering, usually brown and dry.

I don't know, I said.

What would you say they've been eating? he said.

Insects, I guess.

Insects? my uncle shouted. What sort of insects?

Little bugs, most likely, I said. I don't know their names. I can find out tomorrow at school.

We continued to walk over the dry land. When we came to some holes in the earth my uncle stood over them and said, What lives down
100   there?

Prairie dogs, I said.

What are *they*? he said.

Well, I said, they're something like rats. They belong to the rodent family.

What are all these things doing on my land? my uncle said.

They don't know it's your land, I said. They've been living here a long while.

I don't suppose that horny toad ever looked a man in the eye before, my uncle said.
110   I don't think so, I said.

Do you think I scared it or anything? my uncle said.

I don't know for sure, I said.

If I did, my uncle said, I didn't mean to. I'm going to build a house here some day.

I didn't know that, I said.

Of course, my uncle said. I'm going to build a magnificent house.

It's pretty far away, I said.

It's only an hour from town, my uncle said.

If you go fifty miles an hour, I said.
120   It's not fifty miles to town, my uncle said. It's thirty-seven.

Well, you've got to take a little time out for rough roads, I said.

I'll build me the finest house in the world, my uncle said. What else lives on this land?

Well, I said, there are three or four kinds of snakes.

Poison or non-poison? my uncle said.

Mostly non-poison, I said. The rattlesnake is poison, though.

Do you mean to tell me there are *rattlesnakes* on this land? my uncle said.

This is the kind of land rattlesnakes usually live on, I said.
130   How many? my uncle said.

Per acre? I said. Or on the whole six hundred and eighty acres?

Per acre, my uncle said.

Well, I said, I'd say there are about three per acre, conservatively.[21]

Three per acre? my uncle shouted. Conservatively?

Maybe only two, I said.

How many is that to the whole place? my uncle said.

Well, let's see, I said. Two per acre. Six hundred and eighty acres. About fifteen hundred of them.

Fifteen hundred of them? my uncle said.

An acre is pretty big, I said. Two rattlesnakes per acre isn't many.  140 You don't often see them.

What else have we got around here that's poison? my uncle said.

I don't know of anything else, I said. All the other things are harmless. The rattlesnakes are pretty harmless too, unless you step on them.

All right, my uncle said. You walk ahead and watch where you're going. If you see a rattlesnake, don't step on it. I don't want you to die at the age of eleven.

Yes, sir, I said. I'll watch carefully.


We turned around and walked back to the Ford. I didn't see any  150 rattlesnakes on the way back. We got into the car and my uncle lighted a cigarette.

I'm going to make a garden of this awful desolation, he said.

Yes, sir, I said.

I know what my problems are, my uncle said, and I know how to solve them.

How? I said.

Do you mean the horny toads or the rattlesnakes? my uncle said.

I mean the problems, I said.

Well, my uncle said, the first thing I'm going to do is hire some  160 Mexicans[22] and put them to work.

Doing what? I said.

Clearing the land, my uncle said. Then I'm going to have them dig for water.

Dig where? I said.

Straight down, my uncle said. After we get water, I'm going to have them plow the land and then I'm going to plant.

What are you going to plant? I said. Wheat?

Wheat? my uncle shouted. What do I want with wheat? Bread is five cents a loaf. I'm going to plant pomegranate trees.                      170

---

[21]**conservatively:** Estimating carefully.
[22]**Mexicans:** In this case, farm workers from
Mexico or of Mexican background.

How much are pomegranates? I said.

Pomegranates, my uncle said, are practically unknown in this country.

Is that all you're going to plant? I said.

I have in mind, my uncle said, planting several other kinds of trees.

Peach trees? I said.

About ten acres, my uncle said.

How about apricots? I said.

180 By all means, my uncle said. The apricot is a lovely fruit. Lovely in shape, with a glorious flavor and a most delightful pit.[23] I shall plant about twenty acres of apricot trees.

I hope the Mexicans don't have any trouble finding water, I said. Is there water under this land?

Of course, my uncle said. The important thing is to get started. I shall instruct the men to watch out for rattlesnakes. Pomegranates, he said. Peaches. Apricots. What else?

Figs? I said.

Thirty acres of figs, my uncle said.

How about mulberries? I said. The mulberry tree is a very nice
190 looking tree.

Mulberries, my uncle said. He moved his tongue around in his mouth. A nice tree, he said. A tree I knew well in the old country. How many acres would you suggest?

About ten, I said.

All right, he said. What else?

Olive trees are nice, I said.

Yes, they are, my uncle said. One of the nicest. About ten acres of olive trees. What else?

Well, I said, I don't suppose apple trees would grow on this kind of
200 land.

I suppose not, my uncle said. I don't like apples anyway.

He started the car and we drove off the dry land on to the dry road. The car bounced about slowly[24] until we reached the road and then we began to travel at a higher rate of speed.

One thing, my uncle said. When we get home I would rather you didn't mention this *farm* to the folks.

Yes, sir, I said. (*Farm?* I thought. *What farm?*)

I want to surprise them, my uncle said. You know how your grandmother is. I'll go ahead with my plans and when everything is in
210 order I'll take the whole family out to the farm and surprise them.

[23]**pit:** Hard center, much like a stone.
[24]**bounced about slowly:** Moved up and down slowly like a bouncing ball.

Yes, sir, I said.

Not a word to a living soul, my uncle said.

Yes, sir, I said.

Well, the Mexicans went to work and cleared the land. They cleared about ten acres of it in about two months. There were seven of them. They worked with shovels and hoes. They didn't understand anything about anything. It all seemed very strange, but they never complained. They were being paid and that was the thing that counted.[25] They were two brothers and their sons. One day the older brother, Diego, very politely asked my uncle what it was they were    220 supposed to be doing.

Señor, he said, please forgive me. Why are we cutting down cactus?

I'm going to farm this land, my uncle said.

The other Mexicans asked Diego in Mexican[26] what my uncle had said and Diego told them.

They didn't believe it was worth the trouble to tell my uncle he couldn't do it. They just went on cutting down the cactus.

The cactus, however, stayed down only for a short while. The land which had been first cleared was already rich again with fresh cactus and    230 brush. My uncle made this observation with considerable amazement.

It takes deep plowing to get rid of cactus, I said. You've got to plow it out.

My uncle talked the matter over with Ryan, who had a farm-implement business.[27] Ryan told him not to fool with horses.[28] The modern thing to do was to turn a good tractor loose[29] on the land and do a year's work in a day.

So my uncle bought a John Deere tractor. It was beautiful. A mechanic from Ryan's taught Diego how to operate the tractor, and the next day when my uncle and I reached the land we could see the tractor    240 away out in the desolation and we could hear it booming in the awful emptiness of the desert. It sounded pretty awful. It *was* awful. My uncle thought it was wonderful.

Progress, he said. There's the modern age for you. Ten thousand years ago, he said, it would have taken a hundred men a week to do what the tractor's done today.

Ten thousand years ago? I said. You mean yesterday.

---

[25]**that was the thing that counted:** That was what was important.

[26]**in Mexican:** In Spanish or Mexican Spanish (similar to "He speaks American"—meaning American English).

[27]**farm-implement business:** Farm machinery or tool business.

[28]**not to fool with horses:** Not to bother with horses.

[29]**to turn a good tractor loose:** To put a tractor to work.

Anyway, my uncle said, there's nothing like these modern conveniences.

250      The tractor isn't a convenience, I said.

What is it, then? my uncle said. Doesn't the driver sit?

He couldn't very well stand, I said.

Any time they let you sit, my uncle said, it's a convenience. Can you whistle?

Yes, sir, I said. What sort of a song would you like to hear?

Song? my uncle said. I don't want to hear any song. I want you to whistle at that Mexican on the tractor.

What for? I said.

Never mind what for, my uncle said. Just whistle. I want him to
260   know we are here and that we are pleased with his work. He's probably plowed twenty acres.

Yes, sir, I said.

I put the second and third fingers of each hand into my mouth and blew with all my might. It was good and loud. Nevertheless, it didn't seem as if Diego had heard me. He was pretty far away. We were walking toward him anyway, so I couldn't figure out why my uncle wanted me to whistle at him.

Once again, he said.

I whistled once again, but Diego didn't hear.

270      Louder, my uncle said.

This next time I gave it all I had,[30] and my uncle put his hands over his ears. My face got very red, too. The Mexican on the tractor heard the whistle this time. He slowed the tractor down, turned it around, and began plowing straight across the field toward us.

Do you want him to do that? I said.

It doesn't matter, my uncle said.

In less than a minute and a half the tractor and the Mexican arrived. The Mexican seemed very delighted. He wiped dirt and perspiration off his face and got down from the tractor.

280      Señor, he said, this is wonderful.

I'm glad you like it, my uncle said.

Would you like a ride? the Mexican asked my uncle.

My uncle didn't know for sure. He looked at me.

Go ahead, he said. Hop on. Have a little ride.

Diego got on the tractor and helped me on. He sat on the metal seat and I stood behind him, holding him. The tractor began to shake, then jumped, and then began to move. It moved swiftly and made a good

---

[30]**gave it all I had:** Whistled as long and as loud as
possible until my breath gave out; put all my energy
into it.

deal of noise. The Mexican drove around in a big circle and brought the tractor back to my uncle. I jumped off.

All right, my uncle said to the Mexican. Go back to your work.        290
The Mexican drove the tractor back to where he was plowing.

My uncle didn't get water out of the land until many months later. He had wells dug all over the place, but no water came out of the wells. Of course he had motor pumps too, but even then no water came out. A water specialist named Roy came out from Texas with his two younger brothers and they began investigating the land. They told my uncle they'd get water for him. It took them three months and the water was muddy and there wasn't much of it. There was a trickle[31] of muddy water. The specialist told my uncle matters would improve with time and went back to Texas.                                          300

Now half the land was cleared and plowed and there was water, so the time had come to plant.

We planted pomegranate trees. They were of the finest quality and very expensive. We planted about seven hundred of them. I myself planted a hundred. My uncle planted quite a few. We had a twenty-acre orchard of pomegranate trees away over to hell and gone in the strangest desolation anybody ever saw. It was the loveliest-looking absurdity[32] imaginable and my uncle was crazy about it. The only trouble was, his money was giving out. Instead of going ahead and trying to make a garden of the whole six hundred and eighty acres, he decided to devote   310
all his time and energy and money to the pomegranate trees.

Only for the time being, he said. Until we begin to market the pomegranates and get our money back.

Yes, sir, I said.

I didn't know for sure, but I figured we wouldn't be getting any pomegranates to speak of[33] off those little trees for two or three years at least, but I didn't say anything. My uncle got rid of the Mexican workers and he and I took over the farm. We had the tractor and a lot of land, so every now and then we drove out to the farm and drove the tractor around, plowing up cactus and turning over the soil between the        320
pomegranate trees. This went on for three years.

One of these days, my uncle said, you'll see the loveliest garden in the world in this desert.

The water situation didn't improve with time, either. Every once in a while there would be a sudden generous spurt[34] of water containing only a few pebbles and my uncle would be greatly pleased, but the next

---

[31]**trickle:** A very small stream.
[32]**absurdity:** Ridiculous thing.
[33]**any pomegranates to speak of:** Any

pomegranates worth mentioning or counting on (that is, very few—if any—pomegranates).
[34]**spurt:** Sudden large quantity.

day it would be muddy again and there would be only a little trickle. The pomegranate trees fought bravely for life, but they never did get enough water to come out with any fruit.

330     There were blossoms after the fourth year. This was a great triumph for my uncle. He went out of his head with joy when he saw them.

Nothing much ever came of the blossoms,[35] though. They were very beautiful, but that was about all. Purple and lonely.

That year my uncle harvested three small pomegranates.

I ate one, he ate one, and we kept the other one up in his office.

The following year I was fifteen. A lot of wonderful things had happened to me. I mean, I had read a number of good writers and I'd grown as tall as my uncle. The farm was still our secret. It had cost my

340 uncle a lot of money, but he was always under the impression that very soon he was going to start marketing his pomegranates and get his money back and go on with his plan to make a garden in the desert.

The trees didn't fare very well.[36] They grew a little, but it was hardly noticeable. Quite a few of them withered[37] and died.

That's average, my uncle said. Twenty trees to an acre is only average. We won't plant new trees just now. We'll do that later.

He was still paying for the land, too.

The following year he harvested about two hundred pomegranates. He and I did the harvesting. They were pretty sad-looking

350 pomegranates. We packed them in nice-looking boxes and my uncle shipped them to a wholesale produce house in Chicago. There were eleven boxes.

We didn't hear from the wholesale produce house[38] for a month, so one night my uncle made a long-distance phone call. The produce man, D'Agostino, told my uncle nobody wanted pomegranates.

How much are you asking per box? my uncle shouted over the phone.

One dollar, D'Agostino shouted back.

That's not enough, my uncle shouted. I won't take a nickel less

360 than five dollars a box.

They don't want them at one dollar a box, D'Agostino shouted.

Why not? my uncle shouted.

They don't know what they are, D'Agostino shouted.

What kind of a business man are you anyway? my uncle shouted. They're pomegranates. I want five dollars a box.

---

[35]**nothing ever came of the blossoms:** The blossoms didn't develop into fruit.
[36]**didn't fare very well:** Didn't do or grow very well.
[37]**withered:** Dried up.

[38]**wholesale produce house:** Place where produce (fruits and vegetables) purchased from the growers is sold and distributed to the retailers, who sell directly to the public.

I can't sell them, the produce man shouted. I ate one myself and I don't see anything so wonderful about them.

You're crazy, my uncle shouted. There is no other fruit in the world like a pomegranate. Five dollars a box isn't half enough.

What shall I do with them? D'Agostino shouted. I can't sell them. I don't want them.                                                                          370

I see, my uncle whispered. Ship them back. Ship them back express collect.[39]

The phone call cost my uncle about seventeen dollars.

So the eleven boxes came back.

My uncle and I ate most of the pomegranates.

The following year my uncle couldn't make any more payments on the land. He gave the papers back[40] to the man who had sold him the land. I was in the office at the time.

Mr. Griffith, my uncle said, I've got to give you back your property, but I would like to ask a little favor. I've planted twenty acres of pomegranate trees out there on that land and I'd appreciate it very much if you'd let me take care of those trees.                                         380

Take care of them? Mr. Griffith said. What in the world for?

My uncle tried to explain, but couldn't. It was too much to try to explain to a man who wasn't sympathetic.

So my uncle lost the land, and the trees, too.

About three years later he and I drove out to the land and walked out to the pomegranate orchard. The trees were all dead. The soil was heavy[41] again with cactus and desert brush. Except for the small dead pomegranate trees the place was exactly the way it had been all the years of the world.                                                                         390

We walked around in the orchard for a while and then went back to the car.

We got into the car and drove back to town.

We didn't say anything because there was such an awful lot[42] to say, and no language to say it in.

[39]**express collect:** By express (fast) shipment, the freight charge to be collected from the receiver rather than the sender.
[40]**gave the papers back:** Returned the ownership papers.

[41]**heavy:** Covered.
[42]**such an awful lot:** So very much.

---

## A LOOK AT THE IDEAS

---

1. Describe the situation when Uncle Melik first took his nephew with him to look at the land. Comment on (a) how much land Uncle Melik had bought and why he bought it;

(b) what kind of land it was; (c) whether or not Uncle Melik realized what the land was like; (d) how old his nephew was when Uncle Melik brought him to see the land; and (e) what Uncle Melik's reactions were to the plants and animals he saw on the land.

2. William Saroyan says that Uncle Melik "was just about the worst farmer that ever lived" because he was—

____ 1. an ignorant, stubborn man

____ 2. a poet and a dreamer

____ 3. a poor Armenian immigrant

Did Uncle Melik have the qualities that you think a successful farmer should have?

3. Which words do you think could be used to describe Uncle Melik and/or the nephew? Write *M* for Melik and *N* for the nephew next to the appropriate words. (This exercise can be done individually or in groups.)

| | | |
|---|---|---|
| 1. ____ poetic | 8. ____ sensitive | 15. ____ imaginative |
| 2. ____ practical | 9. ____ simple | 16. ____ ignorant |
| 3. ____ foolish | 10. ____ gentle | 17. ____ careful |
| 4. ____ happy | 11. ____ harmless | 18. ____ realistic |
| 5. ____ wise | 12. ____ proud | 19. ____ optimistic |
| 6. ____ sympathetic | 13. ____ curious | 20. ____ ridiculous |
| 7. ____ enthusiastic | 14. ____ stupid | 21. ____ efficient |

What other words or phrases would you use to describe Uncle Melik and his nephew?

4. Do you think Uncle Melik was correct in assuming that his nephew would understand why he bought the land? What do you think the eleven-year-old really thought of his uncle when he saw the land? How do you think the nephew felt about his uncle generally? Did he love and admire him? Was he sympathetic to his point of view? What would you have done in this situation?

5. Briefly summarize what happened after Uncle Melik's first visit to the land with his nephew. Comment on (a) why Uncle Melik wanted to keep the farm a secret and how successful he was in doing so; (b) what sorts of people he

hired to help him with the land and the kinds of problems these people faced and attempted to solve; (c) why Uncle Melik decided to plant only pomegranate trees; (d) how many pomegranates he had to sell and what he finally did with them.

6. Why do you think Uncle Melik told the wholesale dealer in Chicago to return the pomegranates?

_____ 1. He preferred to eat them himself and share them with his nephew.

_____ 2. He thought the dealer was cheating him when he offered him a low price.

_____ 3. He was hurt when he found out no one wanted or valued them.

_____ 4. None of the above reasons.

Give reasons for your choice. What would you have done with the pomegranates? Have you ever known anyone with attitudes and values that were or are similar to Uncle Melik's?

7. Explain why Uncle Melik finally gave up the land. Tell (a) what favor he asked and how the man reacted and (b) what happened to the land and how he felt about it.

8. Although Saroyan doesn't tell us how Uncle Melik feels, we can guess what his feelings are by the way he speaks, what he says, and what is said about him. What do you think Uncle Melik's feelings are in each of the following passages?

1. Here in this awful desolation a garden shall flower, fountains of cold water shall bubble out of the earth, and all things of beauty shall come into being. (lines 12-14)

2. This land, he said, is my land. He walked slowly, kicking the dry soil. A little horned toad scrambled over my uncle's feet. My uncle clutched my shoulder and came to a pious halt. (lines 29-32)

3. Wheat? my uncle shouted. What do I want with wheat? Bread is five cents a loaf. I'm going to plant pomegranate trees. (lines 169-170)

4. You're crazy, my uncle shouted. There is no other fruit in the world like the pomegranate. Five dollars a box isn't half enough. (lines 368-369)

5. I see, my uncle whispered. Ship them back. Ship them back express collect. (lines 372-373)

6. We didn't say anything because there was such an awful lot to say, and no language to say it in. (lines 396-397)

Find other similar passages and explain what Uncle Melik's feelings are.

9. Do you think Saroyan is sympathetic to Uncle Melik? Are you? Do you think Saroyan sees a place for dreamers like Uncle Melik in our society? How do you feel about it? What contribution, if any, does a dreamer make to society? Can you think of any historical figures who were considered impractical by their contemporaries but who ultimately made a significant contribution to society?

10. Write a composition in which you discuss the qualities you think make you primarily a dreamer or a realistic, practical person.

11. Imagine that Uncle Melik is your father's uncle and that your father was the nephew in the story. You receive the following letter from your Great Uncle Melik (your father's uncle would be your great uncle):

Date (to be filled in by you)

Dear (your name),

I greet you with my love and hope your health and spirits are in harmony. I am asking my dear nephew, your father, to write this letter for me because I am so busy. Your father is the one who was always closest to me, especially when he was young, and though I love him still, you have joined his place in my heart.

The most wonderful thing has happened, but only you, your father, and I shall know about it for now. With my savings, I have been able to buy 20 acres of land. Although the land is rocky and barren, I will transform it into a magical amusement park. It will be more magnificent than Disneyland, but not so large. You will remember that years ago I lost my beautiful pomegranate orchard because I did not have enough money to make payments on the land. But now I am more practical. This time there will be money coming in because people will be happy to pay to get into this splendid park. Everyone will pay except poor children, who will get in free.

Will you come home right away and help me? You are smart and can give me many suggestions. Also, like your father, you will understand what is in my heart and I can talk to you about it.

May your letter come with great speed and may your soul be always joyous.

Your loving Great Uncle,<br>Melik

Answer Uncle Melik's letter. *Suggestion:* In your answer, expose your own feelings and attitudes about the kind of man you think he is. You may also wish to compare or contrast the kinds of dreams you have with the dreams of Melik. In other words, your feelings about the character Melik should be made clear, as should any similarities or differences in your values and his. In addition, you might also give him advice and suggestions on what he should do about the amusement park. When you answer the letter, you might keep in mind that Uncle Melik seems to love and trust you.

## A LOOK AT THE LANGUAGE

1. Fill in the blanks in these sentences with the appropriate grammatical form of the *italicized* words.

   1. If you *fear* a situation, you are _____ .
   2. If something contains *poison*, it is _____ .
   3. You can say that a person who has more than his share of *misery* is _____ .
   4. Someone who speaks and acts *casually* is a _____ person.
   5. A person who acts with *consideration* for others is _____ .
   6. He said he didn't feel *brave*, but he was, nevertheless, praised for his _____ .
   7. Something that will *harm* you is _____ .

8. I don't think his whole plan was an *absurdity*, but certainly parts of it were _____ .

**2.** Supply the missing letters of the word in each sentence. The word you produce should be an antonym, or opposite, of the *italicized* word. (Most of the antonyms are explained in the footnotes.)

1. This land is very *valuable*, but that land is
   w o r _____ .

2. A rattlesnake is *dangerous*, but a horned toad is
   h a r _____ .

3. He usually is very *considerate* of other people, but in this case he was just plain t h o u _____ .

4. He gave us a *liberal* rather than a
   c o n _____ estimate.

5. This area is now *heavily populated*, but ten years ago it was lonely and d e s o _____ .

6. We expected to find *a lot of* water in the river, but there was only a t r i _____ .

**3.** Explain the *italicized* expression in the sentences by restating or paraphrasing them. Then use each idiom in a new sentence.

1. She talked about buying a house in the country, but *nothing ever came of it.*

2. He knew he couldn't be first in his class, but he decided *to give it all he had.*

3. Students can often produce very good compositions if you *turn them loose* on an assignment.

4. They are too kind and gentle *for their own good.*

**4.** In speaking, we omit many words and phrases because we know the person we are talking to can get the information from the context; and written dialogue reflects this practice. Read the following dialogue, adding the word or words that would precede or follow the *italicized* word or phrase if nothing were left out. As you read, notice the effect of the additions. Does the dialogue sound like conversation? You may want to revise some of the sentences as you add words.

The horned toad scrambled away.

These little things, I said, have been living on soil of this kind for centuries.

*Centuries?* my uncle said. Are you *sure?*

I'm not *sure,* I said, but I imagine they *have.* They're still here, anyway.

My uncle looked around at his land, at the cactus and brush growing out of it, at the sky overhead.

What have they been eating all this time? he shouted.

I don't *know,* I said.

What would you say they've been eating? he said.

*Insects,* I guess.

*Insects?* my uncle shouted. What sort of *insects?*

*Little bugs,* most likely, I said. I don't know their names. I can find *out* at school tomorrow.

5. In the story, Saroyan repeats the speaker identification tags, "I said," "he said," and "my uncle said" and does not use standard dialogue punctuation. In order to see how important the repetition of the speaker identification tags* and the omission of quotation marks are to Saroyan's style, examine the dialogue in lines 98-149.

   1. Read lines 98 through 149, substituting different verbs, such as *asked, answered, replied,* and *told,* for *said* and omitting some of the identification tags completely. What effect, if any, do these changes have?

   2. Rewrite lines 101 through 118 using standard dialogue punctuation—that is, using quotation marks. Then read both your version and Saroyan's version. What effect, if any, does the addition of quotation marks have?

6. When Uncle Melik and his nephew were together, they probably spoke Armenian at least some of the time. Do parts of their conversation sound like a direct translation from another language? Point out features of Uncle Melik's

---

*Speaker identification tags with pronouns usually appear in the order pronoun + verb (*she said*). The order verb + pronoun (*said she*) is much less common.

speech—phrases and sentences—that do not sound like a native speaker of English. Change these phrases and sentences to more ordinary or conventional English. What is the effect of these changes? In what way does Saroyan's style of writing seem more appropriate for this story?

7. Some of Saroyan's sentences contain paradoxes or phrases with an unusual combination of words. For example, he writes: "He knew I was a poet at heart, and he believed I would understand the magnificent impulse that was driving him to *glorious ruin*." One would not expect to find *ruin* in combination with *glorious*.

    1. Find other sentences that contain a paradox or an unusual combination of words.
    2. What is the effect of these combinations? How do these unlikely combinations of words influence the tone and mood of the story?

8. Saroyan uses many short, simple sentences in this story. But there are passages, such as the one below, where a series of short sentences is followed by a long sentence. Read the passage and describe the effect created by the change of sentence patterns.

    > Only they wouldn't grow. It was on account of the soil. The soil was desert soil. It was dry. My uncle waved at the six hundred and eighty acres of desert he had bought and he said in the most poetic Armenian anybody ever heard, Here in this awful desolation a garden shall flower, fountains of cold water shall bubble out of the earth, and all things of beauty shall come into being.

    Find other passages where Saroyan uses short, simple sentences followed by long, complex ones and describe the effect of the combination.

9. In a short composition, discuss Uncle Melik's dream and the steps he took to make his dream come true. In describing the steps he took, you might use such words as "*First*, Uncle Melik... *Second*, he... *Then*, he... *Finally*, he..." After you have discussed the steps, give your reaction to them. For example, do you think the steps he took were reasonable? What do you think he should have done or not done?

**10.** In what ways would the story be different if it were told by Uncle Melik rather than the nephew? How would it be different if it were told by an observer outside the story? Write a brief account of the story from the point of view of either Uncle Melik or a person who lived in their home town.

## Anne Tyler (b. 1941)

*Although Anne Tyler was born in Minneapolis, Minnesota, she considers herself a Southerner because she grew up in Raleigh, North Carolina, and attended Duke University. She was a member of Phi Beta Kappa and had twice won the Anne Flexner award for creative writing by the time she graduated from Duke at only nineteen. Later she did graduate work in Russian studies at Columbia University and worked at the Duke University Library for a year as the Russian bibliographer.*

*In 1977 Tyler's seventh novel,* Earthly Possessions, *was published. This novel, like the others and her many short stories, was highly praised by reviewers and literary critics, who use words like "wonderful, magic, and true" in describing her work. Tyler is especially noted for her true, wise, and loving treatment of the complex and sometimes troublesome aspects of family relationships. Her marriage to Taghi Mohammed Modarressi, a psychiatrist, and their life together in Baltimore, Maryland, with their young children no doubt gave her insight into the delicate relationships in a cross-cultural marriage, which she explores in "Your Place is Empty."*

# 9

# Your Place

# Is

# Empty

E arly in October, Hassan Ardavi invited his mother to come from
Iran for a visit. His mother accepted immediately. It wasn't clear how
long the visit was to last. Hassan's wife thought three months would be
a good length of time. Hassan himself had planned on six months, and
said so in his letter of invitation. But his mother felt that after such a long
trip six months would be too short, and she was counting on staying a
year. Hassan's little girl, who wasn't yet two, had no idea of time at all.
She was told that her grandmother was coming but she soon forgot
about it.

Hassan's wife was named Elizabeth, not an easy word for Iranians    10
to pronounce. She would have been recognized as American the world
over—a blond, pretty girl with long bones and an ungraceful way of
walking. One of her strong points was an ability to pick up foreign
languages, and before her mother-in-law's arrival she bought a textbook
and taught herself Persian. "*Salaam aleikum,*"[1] she told the mirror every
morning. Her daughter watched, startled, from her place on the potty-
chair.[2] Elizabeth ran through possible situations in her mind and looked
up the words for them. "Would you like more tea? Do you take sugar?"

[1]"**Salaam aleikum**": a Farsi (Persian) greeting.    [2]**potty-chair:** A toilet for a small child.

107

At suppertime she spoke Persian to her husband, who looked amused at
20 the new tone she gave his language, with her flat, factual American
voice.[3] He wrote his mother and told her Elizabeth had a surprise for her.

Their house was a three-story brick Colonial,[4] but only the first
two stories were in use. Now they cleared the third of its trunks and
china barrels[5] and *National Geographics*, and they moved in a few pieces
of furniture. Elizabeth sewed flowered curtains for the window. She was
unusually careful with them; to a foreign mother-in-law, fine seams[6]
might matter. Also, Hassan bought a pocket compass, which he placed
in the top dresser drawer. "For her prayers," he said. "She'll want to
face Mecca.[7] She prays three times a day."

30 "But which direction is Mecca from here?" Elizabeth asked.

Hassan only shrugged.[8] He had never said the prayers himself, not
even as a child. His earliest memory was of tickling the soles of his
mother's feet[9] while she prayed steadfastly[10] on; everyone knew it was
forbidden to pause once you'd started.

Mrs. Ardavi felt nervous about the descent from the plane. She
inched down the staircase sideways, one hand tight on the railing, the
other clutching her shawl.[11] It was night, and cold. The air seemed
curiously opaque.[12] She arrived on solid ground and stood collecting
herself—a small, stocky[13] woman in black, with a kerchief[14] over her
40 smooth gray hair. She held her back very straight, as if she had just had
her feelings hurt. In picturing this moment she had always thought
Hassan would be waiting beside the plane, but there was no sign of him.
Blue lights dotted the darkness behind her, an angular[15] terminal
loomed ahead, and an official was herding the passengers toward a
plate-glass door. She followed, entangled in a web of meaningless
sounds such as those you might hear in a fever dream.

Immigration. Baggage Claims. Customs. To all she spread her
hands and beamed[16] and shrugged, showing she spoke no English.
Meanwhile her fellow-passengers waved to a blur[17] of faces beyond a

---

[3]**flat, factual American voice:** A flat voice; a voice
that is not musical, as if it were made to tell facts.
[4]**Colonial:** Referring to a colonial style of
architecture—a style from the time before the
American independence of 1776.
[5]**china barrels:** Large, round wooden containers,
used in this case to pack dishes (china) for moving.
[6]**seams:** The sewn edges where clothing is put
together; in this case, the sewn edges of the
curtains.
[7]**She'll . . . Mecca:** Moslems face the city of Mecca
in Saudi Arabia when they pray; in this case, she
could determine the direction of Mecca with the
compass.
[8]**shrugged:** Moved his shoulders—a gesture used
in some cultures when one doesn't know or doesn't
care.
[9]**tickling . . . feet:** Touching the bottoms (soles) of
the feet to make her laugh.
[10]**steadfastly:** Firmly; faithfully.
[11]**shawl:** A large piece of cloth worn over the
shoulders for warmth.
[12]**opaque:** Not allowing light to pass through; in
this case, not clear.
[13]**stocky:** Solidly built.
[14]**kerchief:** Handkerchief.
[15]**angular:** Having many angles or corners;
rectangular.
[16]**beamed:** Smiled brightly.
[17]**blur:** Unclear mass.

glass wall. It seemed they all knew people here; she was the only one    50
who didn't. She had issued from the plane like a newborn baby,
speechless and friendless. And the customs official didn't seem pleased
with her. She had brought too many gifts. She had stuffed her bags with
them, discarding[18] all but the most necessary pieces of her clothing so
that she would have more room. There were silver tea sets and gold
jewelry for her daughter-in-law, and for her granddaughter a doll
dressed in the complicated costume of a nomad tribe,[19] an embroidered[20]
sheepskin vest, and two religious medals[21] on chains—one a disc
inscribed with the name of Allah,[22] the other a tiny gold Koran,[23] with a
very effective prayer for long life folded up within it. The customs    60
official sifted[24] gold through his fingers like sand and frowned at the
Koran. "Have I done something wrong?" she asked. But of course he
didn't understand her. Though you'd think, really, that if he would just
*listen* hard enough, just meet her eyes once . . . it was a very simple
language, there was no reason why it shouldn't come through to him.

For Hassan, she'd brought food. She had gathered all his favorite
foods and put them in a drawstring bag embroidered with peacocks.[25]
When the official opened the bag he said something under his breath
and called another man over. Together they unwrapped tiny newspaper
packets and sniffed at various herbs. "Sumac," she told them. "Powder    70
of lemons. Shambahleh." They gazed at her blankly. They untied a
small cloth sack and rummaged[26] through the kashk she had brought for
soup. It rolled beneath their fingers and across the counter—hard white
balls of yogurt curd,[27] stuck with bits of sheep hair and manure.[28] Some
peasant[29] had labored for hours to make that kashk. Mrs. Ardavi picked
up one piece and replaced it firmly in the sack. Maybe the official
understood her meaning: she was running out of patience. He threw up
his hands.[30] He slid her belongings down the counter. She was free to go.

Free to go where?

Dazed and stumbling,[31] a pyramid of knobby parcels and bags,[32]    80

---

[18]**discarding:** Throwing away; in this case, leaving behind.

[19]**nomad tribe:** A tribe that moves from place to place so that the animals will have food as the season changes.

[20]**embroidered:** Decorated with sewn threads of different colors.

[21]**medals:** Flat pieces of metal, usually in the shape of a coin.

[22]**disc . . . Allah:** Coin-shaped with the Arabic name for God written on it.

[23]**Koran:** The holy book of the Moslem religion.

[24]**sifted:** Let the gold fall through his hands like flour passing through a screened container used in baking.

[25]**peacocks:** Birds famous for their very large, beautiful tails in the shape of a fan.

[26]**rummaged:** Searched.

[27]**yogurt curd:** A thick, creamy food made from milk; the curd is the thick, nonliquid part of the yogurt.

[28]**manure:** Animal waste material.

[29]**peasant:** A countryman; a farmer.

[30]**threw up his hands:** Raised his hands, a gesture used in some cultures to show that a person gives up or surrenders.

[31]**dazed and stumbling:** Unable to think or walk normally.

[32]**a pyramid . . . bags:** A large, high pile of bulky parcels and bags.

scraps of velvet and brocade and tapestry,[33] she made her way to the
glass wall. A door opened out of nowhere and a stranger blocked her
path. "Khanom Jun," he said. It was a name that only her children
would use, but she passed him blindly and he had to touch her arm
before she would look up.

    He had put on weight. She didn't know him. The last time she'd
seen him he was a thin, stoop-shouldered medical student disappearing
into an Air France jet without a backward glance. "Khanom Jun, it's
me," this stranger said, but she went on searching his face with cloudy
90    eyes. No doubt he was a bearer of bad news. Was that it? A recurrent[34]
dream had warned her that she would never see her son again—that he
would die on his way to the airport, or had already been dead for
months but no one wanted to break the news; some second or third
cousin in America had continued signing Hassan's name to his cheerful,
anonymous[35] letters. Now here was this man with graying hair and a
thick mustache, his clothes American but his face Iranian, his eyes sadly
familiar, as if they belonged to someone else. "Don't you believe me?"
he said. He kissed her on both cheeks. It was his smell she recognized
first—a pleasantly bitter, herblike smell that brought her the image of
100   Hassan as a child, reaching thin arms around her neck. "It's you,
Hassan," she said, and then she starting crying against his gray tweed[36]
shoulder.

    They were quiet during the long drive home. Once she reached
over to touch his face, having wanted to do so for miles. None of the
out-of-focus snapshots he'd sent had prepared her for the way he had
aged. "How long has it been?" she asked."Twelve years?" But both of
them knew to the day how long it had been. All those letters of hers:
"My dear Hassan, ten years now and still your place is empty." "Eleven
years and still . . ."
110    Hassan squinted[37] through the windshield at the oncoming
headlights. His mother started fretting[38] over her kerchief, which she
knew she ought not to have worn. She'd been told so by her youngest
sister, who had been to America twice. "It marks you," her sister had
said. But that square of silk was the last, shrunken reminder[39] of the veil
she used to hide beneath, before the previous Shah had banished[40] such
things. At her age, how could she expose herself? And then her teeth;
her teeth were a problem too. Her youngest sister had said, "You ought

[33]**scraps . . . tapestry:** Pieces of cloth of different kinds.
[34]**recurrent:** Repeated; frequent.
[35]**anonymous:** Unknown; in this case, not personal or unfamiliar.
[36]**tweed:** A heavy, rough woolen cloth.
[37]**squinted:** Looked through half-closed eyes.
[38]**fretting:** Worrying.
[39]**shrunken reminder:** A last small reminder.
[40]**banished:** Forbidden.

to get dentures[41] made. I'm sure there aren't three whole teeth in your head." But Mrs. Ardavi was scared of dentists. Now she covered her mouth with one hand and looked sideways at Hassan, though so far he    120
hadn't seemed to notice. He was busy maneuvering[42] his car into the right-hand lane.

This silence was the last thing she had expected. For weeks she'd been saving up stray bits of gossip,[43] weaving together the family stories she would tell him. There were three hundred people in her family— most of them related to each other in three or four different ways, all leading intricate[44] and scandalous lives[45] she had planned to discuss in detail, but instead she stared sadly out the window. You'd think Hassan would ask. You'd think they could have a better conversation than this, after such a long time. Disappointment made her cross,[46] and now she    130
stubbornly[47] refused to speak even when she saw something she wanted to comment on, some imposing[48] building or unfamiliar brand of car sliding past her into the darkness.

By the time they arrived it was nearly midnight. None of the houses were lit but Hassan's—worn brick, older than she would have expected. "Here we are," said Hassan. The competence[49] with which he parked the car, fitting it neatly into a small space by the curb, put him firmly on the other side of the fence, the American side. She would have to face her daughter-in-law alone. As they climbed the front steps she whispered, "How do you say it again?"    140

"Say what?" Hassan asked.

"Her name. Lizabet?"

"Elizabeth. Like Elizabeth Taylor. *You* know."

"Yes, yes, of course," said his mother. Then she lifted her chin, holding tight to the straps of her purse.

Elizabeth was wearing bluejeans and a pair of fluffy[50] slippers. Her hair was blond as corn silk,[51] cut short and straight, and her face had the grave, sleepy look of a child's. As soon as she had opened the door she said, "*Salaam aleikum.*" Mrs. Ardavi, overcome with relief at the Persian greeting, threw her arms around her and kissed both cheeks. Then they    150
led her into the living room, which looked comfortable but a little too plain. The furniture was straight-edged, the rugs uninteresting, though the curtains had a nice figured pattern that caught her eye. In one corner

---

[41]**dentures:** False teeth.
[42]**maneuvering:** Moving.
[43]**stray bits of gossip:** Bits of information she had picked up here and there about the affairs of other people.
[44]**intricate:** Complicated; complex.
[45]**scandalous lives:** Shocking lives; behavior which is not approved of by other people.

[46]**cross:** Bad-humored.
[47]**stubbornly:** Unreasonably.
[48]**imposing:** Impressive.
[49]**competence:** Skill; ability.
[50]**fluffy:** Soft and light, probably furry.
[51]**corn silk:** The soft, bright yellow threads or strands on an ear of corn.

sat a shiny red kiddie car complete with license plates. "Is that the child's?" she asked. "Hilary's?" She hesitated over the name. "Could I see her?"

"*Now?*" said Hassan.

But Elizabeth told him, "That's all right." (Women understood these things.) She beckoned[52] to her mother-in-law. They climbed the stairs together, up to the second floor, into a little room that smelled of milk and rubber and talcum powder, smells she would know anywhere. Even in the half-light from the hallway, she could tell that Hilary was beautiful. She had black, tumbling hair, long black lashes, and skin of a tone they called wheat-colored, lighter than Hassan's. "There," said Elizabeth. "Thank you," said Mrs. Ardavi. Her voice was formal, but this was her first grandchild and it took her a moment to recover herself. Then they stepped back into the hallway. "I brought her some medals," she whispered. "I hope you don't mind."

"Medals?" said Elizabeth. She repeated the word anxiously, mispronouncing it.

"Only an Allah and a Koran, both very tiny. You'll hardly know they're there. I'm not used to seeing a child without a medal. It worries me."

Automatically her fingers traced a chain around her neck, ending in the hollow of her collarbone. Elizabeth nodded, looking relieved. "*Oh* yes. Medals," she said.

"Is that all right?"

"Yes, of course."

Mrs. Ardavi took heart.[53] "Hassan laughs," she said. "He doesn't believe in these things. But when he left I put a prayer in his suitcase pocket, and you see he's been protected. Now if Hilary wore a medal, I could sleep nights."

"Of course," Elizabeth said again.

When they re-entered the living room, Mrs Ardavi was smiling, and she kissed Hassan on the top of his head before she sat down.

American days were tightly scheduled, divided not into morning and afternoon but into 9:00, 9:30, and so forth, each half hour possessing its own set activity. It was marvelous. Mrs. Ardavi wrote her sisters: "They're more organized here. My daughter-in-law never wastes a minute." How terrible, her sisters wrote back. They were all in Teheran, drinking cup after cup of tea and idly guessing who might come and visit. "No, you misunderstand," Mrs. Ardavi protested. "I like it this

[52]**beckoned:** Motioned to her to follow by moving her arm.
[53]**took heart:** Felt encouraged; became braver.

way. I'm fitting in wonderfully." And to her youngest sister she wrote, "You'd think I was American. No one guesses otherwise." This wasn't true, of course, but she hoped it would be true in the future.

Hassan was a doctor. He worked long hours, from six in the morning until six at night. While she was still washing for her morning prayers she could hear him tiptoe[54] down the stairs and out the front door. His car would start up, a distant rumble[55] far below her, and from her bathroom window she could watch it swing out from beneath a 200 tatter[56] of red leaves and round the corner and disappear. Then she would sigh and return to her sink. Before prayers she had to wash her face, her hands, and the soles of her feet. She had to draw her wet fingers down the part in her hair. After that she returned to her room, where she swathed[57] herself tightly in her long black veil and knelt on a beaded velvet prayer mat.[58] East was where the window was, curtained by chintz[59] and misted over.[60] On the east wall she hung a lithograph of the Caliph Ali[61] and a color snapshot of her third son, Babak, whose marriage she had arranged just a few months before this visit. If Babak hadn't married, she never could have come. He was the youngest, 210 spoiled by being the only son at home. It had taken her three years to find a wife for him. (One was too modern, one too lazy, one so perfect she had been suspicious.) But finally the proper girl had turned up, modest and well-mannered and sufficiently wide of hip, and Mrs. Ardavi and the bridal couple had settled in a fine new house on the outskirts[62] of Teheran. Now every time she prayed, she added a word of thanks that at last she had a home for her old age. After that, she unwound her veil and laid it carefully in a drawer. From another drawer she took thick cotton stockings and elastic garters;[63] she stuffed her swollen feet[64] into open-toed vinyl sandals.[65] Unless she was going out, 220 she wore a housecoat. It amazed her how wasteful Americans were with their clothing.

Downstairs, Elizabeth would have started her tea and buttered a piece of toast for her. Elizabeth and Hilary ate bacon and eggs, but bacon of course was unclean and Mrs. Ardavi never accepted any. Nor had it even been offered to her, except once, jokingly, by Hassan. The distinctive, smoky smell rose to meet her as she descended the stairs. "What does it taste like?" she always asked. She was dying to know. But

---

[54]**tiptoe:** Walk quietly on the toes.
[55]**rumble:** A deep, rolling sound.
[56]**tatter:** A small disorderly pile.
[57]**swathed:** Wrapped.
[58]**beaded . . . mat:** A rug or carpet used for prayer that is decorated with beads.
[59]**chintz:** A shiny cotton cloth.
[60]**misted over:** Covered with mist—a light, watery film.

[61]**a lithograph of the Caliph Ali:** A printed picture of one of the holy men of the Shiite Moslems.
[62]**outskirts:** Edge of the city.
[63]**elastic garters:** Rubberized bands or strips used to hold up stockings.
[64]**swollen feet:** Feet that have become enlarged because of inside pressure (verb: *swell*).
[65]**open-toed vinyl sandals:** Open shoes made of plastic.

Elizabeth's vocaculary didn't cover the taste of bacon; she only said it
230  was salty and then laughed and gave up. They had learned very early to
travel a well-worn conversational path, avoiding the dead ends[66] caused
by unfamiliar words. "Did you sleep well?" Elizabeth always asked in
her funny, childish accent, and Mrs. Ardavi answered, "So-so." Then
they would turn and watch Hilary, who sat on a booster seat[67] eating
scrambled eggs, a thin chain of Persian gold crossing the back of her
neck. Conversation was easier, or even unnecessary, as long as Hilary
was there.

In the mornings Elizabeth cleaned house. Mrs. Ardavi used that
time for letter writing. She had dozens of letters to write, to all her aunts
240  and uncles and her thirteen sisters. (Her father had had three wives, and
a surprising number of children even for that day and age.) Then there
was Babak. His wife was in her second month of pregnancy, so Mrs.
Ardavi wrote long accounts of the American child-rearing methods.[68]
"There are some things I don't agree with," she wrote. "They let Hilary
play outdoors by herself, with not even a servant to keep an eye on her."
Then she would trail off[69] and gaze thoughtfully at Hilary, who sat on
the floor watching a television program called "Captain Kangaroo."

Mrs. Ardavi's own childhood had been murky and grim.[70] From
the age of nine she was wrapped in a veil, one corner of it clenched[71] in
250  her teeth to hide her face whenever she appeared on the streets. Her
father, a respected man high up in public life, used to chase servant girls
through the halls and trap them, giggling,[72] in vacant bedrooms. At the
age of ten she was forced to watch her mother bleed to death in
childbirth, and when she screamed the midwife[73] had struck her across
the face and held her down till she had properly kissed her mother
goodbye. There seemed no connection at all between her and this little
overalled[74] American. At times, when Hilary had one of her temper
tantrums,[75] Mrs. Ardavi waited in horror for Elizabeth to slap her and
then, when no slap came, felt a mixture of relief and anger. "In Iran—"
260  she would begin, and if Hassan was there he always said, "But this is
not Iran, remember?"

After lunch Hilary took a nap, and Mrs. Ardavi went upstairs to
say her noontime prayers and take a nap as well. Then she might do a
little laundry in her bathtub. Laundry was a problem here. Although she
liked Elizabeth, the fact was that the girl was a Christian, and therefore

---

[66]**dead ends:** Stops with no chance to continue.
[67]**booster seat:** A small seat for a child placed on a regular chair.
[68]**child-rearing methods:** Methods of bringing up or raising children.
[69]**trail off:** Gradually stop writing.
[70]**murky and grim:** Extremely unpleasant.

[71]**clenched:** Held tightly.
[72]**giggling:** Laughing.
[73]**midwife:** A woman who helps at the birth of a baby.
[74]**overalled:** Wearing overalls or blue jeans.
[75]**temper tantrums:** Fits or periods of uncontrolled anger.

unclean; it would never do to have a Christian wash a Moslem's clothes. The automatic dryer was also unclean, having contained, at some point, a Christian's underwear. So she had to ask Hassan to buy her a drying rack. It came unassembled. Elizabeth put it together for her, stick by stick, and then Mrs. Ardavi held it under her shower and rinsed it off,          270 hoping that would be enough to remove any taint.[76] The Koran didn't cover this sort of situation.[77]

When Hilary was up from her nap they walked her to the park— Elizabeth in her eternal bluejeans and Mrs. Ardavi in her kerchief and shawl, taking short painful steps in small shoes that bulged over her bunions.[78] They still hadn't seen to her teeth, although by now Hassan had noticed them. She was hoping he might forget about the dentist, but then she saw him remembering every time she laughed and revealed her five brown teeth set wide apart.

At the park she laughed a great deal. It was her only way of          280 communicating with the other women. They sat on the benches ringing the playground, and while Elizabeth translated their questions Mrs. Ardavi laughed and nodded at them over and over. "They want to know if you like it here," Elizabeth said. Mrs. Ardavi answered at length, but Elizabeth's translation was very short. Then gradually the other women forgot her, and conversation rattled on while she sat silent and watched each speaker's lips. The few recognizable words—"telephone," "television," "radio"—gave her the impression that American conversations were largely technical, even among women. Their gestures were wide and slow, disproving her youngest sister's statement that in America          290 everyone was in a hurry. On the contrary, these women were dreamlike, moving singly or in twos across wide flat spaces beneath white November skies when they departed.

Later, at home, Mrs. Ardavi would say, "The red-haired girl, is she pregnant? She looked it, I thought. Is that fat girl happy in her marriage?" She asked with some urgency,[79] plucking[80] Elizabeth's sleeve when she was slow to answer. People's private lives fascinated her. On Saturday trips to the supermarket she liked to single out some interesting stranger. "What's the matter with that *jerky*-moving[81] man? That girl, is she one of your dark-skinned people?" Elizabeth answered          300 too softly, and never seemed to follow Mrs. Ardavi's pointing finger.

Supper was difficult; Mrs. Ardavi didn't like American food. Even when Elizabeth made something Iranian, it had an American taste to

---

[76]**taint:** A remaining bit or trace of a bad quality.
[77]**The Koran ... situation:** The Koran didn't tell what to do in this kind of situation.
[78]**bulged over her bunions:** Stuck out over the swellings or growths on her toes.

[79]**urgency:** With a need for prompt action; in this case, Mrs. Ardavi felt she needed a quick answer.
[80]**plucking:** Pulling on.
[81]**jerky-moving:** Moving in an unsmooth manner.

it—the vegetables still faintly crisp,[82] the onions transparent[83] rather than nicely blackened. "Vegetables not thoroughly cooked retain a certain acidity," Mrs. Ardavi said, laying down her fork. "This is a cause of constipation[84] and stomach aches. At night I often have heartburn. It's been three full days since I moved my bowels." Elizabeth merely bent over her plate, offering no symptoms of her own in return. Hassan
310    said, "At the table, Khanom? At the table?"

Eventually she decided to cook supper herself. Over Elizabeth's protests she began at three every afternoon, filling the house with the smell of dillweed and arranging pots on counters and cabinets and finally, when there was no more space, on the floor. She squatted[85] on the floor with her skirt tucked between her knees and stirred great bowls of minced greens[86] while behind her, on the gas range, four different pots of food bubbled and steamed. The kitchen was becoming more homelike, she thought. A bowl of yogurt brewed[87] beside the stove, a kettle of rice soaked in the sink, and the top of the dishwasher was
320    curlicued with the yellow dye from saffron.[88] In one corner sat the pudding pan, black on the bottom from the times she had cooked down sugar to make a sweet for her intestines.[89] "Now, this is your rest period," she always told Elizabeth. "Come to the table in three hours and be surprised." But Elizabeth only hovered[90] around the kitchen, disturbing the serene,[91] steamed-filled air with clatters and slams[92] as she put away pots, or pacing between stove and sink, her arms folded across her chest. At supper she ate little; Mrs. Ardavi wondered how Americans got so tall on such small suppers. Hassan, on the other hand, had second and third helpings. "I must be gaining five pounds a week,"
330    he said. "None of my clothes fit."

"That's good to hear," said his mother. And Elizabeth added something but in English, which Hassan answered in English also. Often now they broke into English for paragraphs at a time—Elizabeth speaking softly, looking at her plate, and Hassan answering at length and sometimes reaching across the table to cover her hand.

At night, after her evening prayers, Mrs. Ardavi watched television on the living-room couch. She brought her veil downstairs

---

[82]**faintly crisp:** A bit hard; in this case, slightly undercooked.
[83]**onions transparent:** Onions only lightly cooked; something that is transparent permits light to pass through (the opposite of opaque).
[84]**constipation:** Lack of regularity in bowel movements.
[85]**squatted:** Sat on the heels of her feet.
[86]**minced greens:** Very finely cut green leafy vegetables.

[87]**brewed:** Cooked.
[88]**curlicued . . . saffron:** Circles of yellow color from the spice saffron.
[89]**Intestines:** Part of the digestive tract.
[90]**hovered:** Stood close by.
[91]**serene:** Calm.
[92]**clatters and slams:** Loud noises.

and wrapped it around her to keep the drafts away. Her shoes lay on the rug beneath her, and scattered down the length of the couch were her knitting bag, her sack of burned sugar, her magnifying glass, and *My* 340 *First Golden Dictionary*. Elizabeth read novels in an easy chair, and Hassan watched TV so that he could translate the difficult parts of the plot. Not that Mrs. Ardavi had much trouble. American plots were easy to guess at, particularly the Westerns. And when the program was boring—a documentary or a special news feature—she could pass the time by talking to Hassan. "Your cousin Farah wrote," she said. "Do you remember her? A homely[93] girl, too dark. She's getting a divorce and in my opinion it's fortunate; he's from a lower class. Do you remember Farah?"

Hassan only grunted,[94] his eyes on the screen. He was interested 350 in American politics. So was she, for that matter. She had wept for President Kennedy, and carried Jackie's picture in her purse. But these news programs were long and dry, and if Hassan wouldn't talk she was forced to turn at last to her *Golden Dictionary*.

In her childhood, she had been taught by expensive foreign tutors. Her mind was her great gift, the compensation[95] for a large, plain face and a stocky figure. But now what she had learned seemed lost, forgotten utterly or fogged[96] by years, so that Hassan gave a snort[97] whenever she told him some fact that she had dredged up[98] from her memory. It seemed that everything she studied now had to penetrate[99] 360 through a great thick layer before it reached her mind. "Tonk you," she practiced. "Tonk you. Tonk you." "Thank you," Hassan corrected her. He pointed out useful words in her dictionary—grocery-store words, household words—but she grew impatient with their woodenness. What she wanted was the language to display her personality, her famous courtesy, and her magical intuition[100] about the inside lives of other people. Nightly she learned "salt," "bread," "spoon," but with an inner sense of dullness, and every morning when she woke her English was once again confined to "thank you" and "NBC."

Elizabeth, meanwhile, read on, finishing one book and reaching 370 for the next without even glancing up. Hassan chewed a thumbnail and watched a senator. He shouldn't be disturbed, of course, but time after time his mother felt the silence and the whispery turning of pages stretching her nerves until she had to speak. "Hassan?"

[93]**homely:** In American English, ugly or unattractive.
[94]**grunted:** Make a low noise to show that he heard but wasn't interested.
[95]**compensation:** Payment making up for some loss or deficiency.
[96]**fogged:** Made unclear.

[97]**snort:** A sound through the nose showing impatience.
[98]**dredged up:** Pulled to the surface.
[99]**penetrate:** Enter.
[100]**intuition:** Understanding without reason or study.

"Hmm."

"My chest seems tight. I'm sure a cold is coming on. Don't you have a tonic?"[101]

"No," said Hassan.

380 He dispensed[102] medicines all day; he listened to complaints. Common sense told her to stop, but she persisted,[103] encouraged by some demon[104] that wouldn't let her tongue lie still. "Don't you have some syrup? What about that liquid you gave me for constipation? Would that help?"

"No, it wouldn't," said Hassan.

He drove her on,[105] somehow. The less he gave, the more she had to ask. "Well, aspirin? Vitamins?" Until Hassan said, "Will you just let me *watch?*" Then she could lapse into silence[106] again, or even gather up the clutter[107] of her belongings and bid the two of them good night.

390 She slept badly. Often she lay awake for hours, fingering the edge of the sheet and staring at the ceiling. Memories crowded in on her, old grievances[108] and fears, injustices that had never been righted. For the first time in years she thought of her husband, a gentle, weak man given to surprising outbursts of temper.[109] She hadn't loved him when she married him, and at his death from a liver ailment[110] six years later her main feeling had been resentment.[111] Was it fair to be widowed so young, while other women were supported and protected? She had moved from her husband's home back to the old family estate, where five of her sisters still lived. There she had stayed till Babak's wedding, drinking tea all day with her sisters and pulling the strings by which the

400 rest of the family was attached. Marriages were arranged, funerals attended, childbirth discussed in fine detail; servants' disputes were settled, and feuds patched up[112] and then restarted. Her husband's face had quickly faded, leaving only a vacant spot in her mind. But now she could see him so clearly—a wasted[113] figure on his deathbed, beard untrimmed, turban[114] coming loose, eyes imploring[115] her for something more than an absentminded[116] pat on the cheek as she passed through his room on her way to check the children.

She saw the thin faces of her three small boys as they sat on the rug

[101]**tonic:** A drink or medicine to give strength.
[102]**dispensed:** Distributed; gave people prescriptions.
[103]**persisted:** Continued in spite of opposition.
[104]**demon:** Evil spirit; devil.
[105]**He drove her on:** Made her continue.
[106]**lapse into silence:** Become quiet.
[107]**clutter:** Disorderly collection.
[108]**grievances:** Complaints based on some real or imagined cause.
[109]**outbursts of temper:** Sudden fits or bursts of anger.
[110]**ailment:** Sickness.
[111]**resentment:** Feeling that one has been hurt or badly treated by another person.
[112]**feuds patched up:** Quarrels or fights repaired or finished.
[113]**wasted:** Very thin, as if from sickness.
[114]**turban:** A head covering made of long strips of cloth wrapped around the head.
[115]**imploring:** Begging; requesting earnestly.
[116]**absentminded:** Unthinking.

eating rice. Hassan was the stubborn, mischievous[117] one, with perpetual scabs[118] on his knees. Babak was the cuddly[119] one. Ali was    410
the oldest, who had caused so much worry—weak, like his father, demanding, but capable of turning suddenly charming. Four years ago he had died of a brain hemorrhage,[120] slumping[121] over a dinner table in faraway Shîrāz where he'd gone to be free of his wife, who was also his double first cousin. Ever since he was born he had disturbed his mother's sleep, first because she worried over what he would amount to and now, after his death, because she lay awake listing all she had done wrong with him. She had been too lenient.[122] No, too harsh.[123] There was no telling. Mistakes she had made floated on the ceiling like ghosts—allowances she'd made when she knew she shouldn't have,    420
protections he had not deserved, blows which perhaps he had not deserved either.

She would have liked to talk to Hassan about it, but any time she tried he changed the subject. Maybe he was angry about the way he had heard of Ali's death. It was customary to break such news gradually. She had started a series of tactful[124] letters, beginning by saying that Ali was seriously ill when in truth he was already buried. Something in the letter had given her away—perhaps her plans for a rest cure by the seaside, which she never would have considered if she'd had an ailing son at home. Hassan had telephoned overseas, taking three nights to    430
reach her. "Tell me what's wrong," he said. "I know there's something." When her tears kept her from answering, he asked, "Is he dead?" His voice sounded angry, but that might have been due to a poor connection. And when he hung up, cutting her off before she could say all she wanted, she thought, I should have told him straight out.[125] I had forgotten that about him. Now when she spoke of Ali he listened politely, with his face frozen. She would have told him anything, all about the death and burial and that witch of a wife throwing herself, too late, into the grave; but Hassan never asked.

Death was moving in on her. Oh, not on her personally (the    440
women in her family lived a century or longer, burying the men one by one) but on everybody around her, all the cousins and uncles and brothers-in-law. No sooner had she laid away her mourning clothes than it was time to bring them out again. Recently she had begun to feel

---

[117]**mischievous:** Likely to cause harm to, or make trouble for, or annoy other people.
[118]**perpetual scabs:** Never-ending dry patches of blood over wounds or sores.
[119]**cuddly:** Making one want to hold the person close and hug affectionately.
[120]**brain hemorrhage:** Very hard bleeding in the brain due to broken blood vessels.

[121]**slumping:** Falling lifelessly.
[122]**lenient:** Mild or gentle in treatment of him.
[123]**harsh:** The opposite of lenient.
[124]**tactful:** Diplomatic; skillful in handling people without making them angry or upset.
[125]**straight out:** Frankly; without trying to be polite or tactful.

she would outlive her two other sons as well, and she fought off sleep because of the dreams it brought—Babak lying stiff and cold in his grave, Hassan crumpled[126] over in some dark American alley.[127] Terrifying images would zoom at her out of the night. In the end she had to wrap herself in her veil and sleep instead on the Persian rug, which
450 had the dusty smell of home and was, anyway, more comfortable than her unsteady foreign mattress.

At Christmas time, Hassan and Elizabeth gave Mrs. Ardavi a brightly colored American dress with sleeves. She wore it to an Iranian party, even leaving off her kerchief in a sudden fit of daring.[128] Everyone commented on how nice she looked. "Really you fit right in," a girl told her. "May I write to my mother about you? She was over here for a year and a half and never once stepped out of the house without her kerchief." Mrs. Ardavi beamed. It was true she would never have associated with these people at home—children of civil servants and
460 bank clerks, newly rich now they'd finished medical school. The wives called their husbands "Doctor" even in direct address. But still it felt good to be speaking so much Persian; her tongue nearly ran away with her. "I see you're expecting a baby," she said to one of the wives. "Is it your first? I could tell by your eyes. Now don't be nervous. I had three myself; my mother had seven and never felt a pain in her life. She would squat down to serve my father's breakfast and 'Eh?' she would say. 'Aga Jun, it's the baby!' and there it would be on the floor between her feet, waiting for her to cut the cord and finish pouring the tea." She neglected to mention how her mother had died. All her natural tact
470 came back to her, her gift with words and her knowledge of how to hold an audience. She bubbled and sparkled like a girl, and her face fell when it was time to go home.

After the party, she spent two or three days noticing more keenly than ever the loss of her language, and talking more feverishly when Hassan came home in the evening. This business of being a foreigner was something changeable. Boundaries kept shifting, and sometimes it was she who was the foreigner but other times Elizabeth, or even Hassan. (Wasn't it true, she often wondered, that there was a greater distance between men and women than between Americans and
480 Iranians, or even *Eskimos* and Iranians?) Hassan was the foreigner when she and Elizabeth conspired[129] to hide a miniature Koran in his glove

---

[126]**crumpled:** Fallen like a piece of old, wrinkled newspaper.
[127]**alley:** A narrow street or passage between buildings.

[128]**fit of daring:** Sudden feeling to be bold and adventurous.
[129]**conspired:** Made a secret plan or agreement.

compartment;[130] he would have laughed at them. "You see," she told Elizabeth, "I know there's nothing to it, but it makes me feel better. When my sons were born I took them all to the bath attendant to have their blood let.[131] People say it brings long life. I know that's superstition, but whenever afterward I saw those ridges down their backs I felt safe. Don't you understand?" And Elizabeth said, "Of course." She smuggled[132] the Koran into the car herself, and hid it beneath the Texaco maps. Hassan saw nothing.

Hilary was a foreigner forever. She dodged[133] her grandmother's        490
yearning[134] hands, and when the grownups spoke Persian she fretted[135] and misbehaved and pulled on Elizabeth's sleeve. Mrs. Ardavi had to remind herself constantly not to kiss the child too much, not to reach out for a hug,[136] not to offer her lap. In this country people kept more separate. They kept so separate that at times she felt hurt. They tried to be subtle,[137] so undemonstrative. She would never understand this place.

In January they took her to a dentist, who made clucking noises[138] when he looked in her mouth. "What does he say?" she asked. "Tell me the worst." But Hassan was talking in a low voice to Elizabeth, and he        500
waved her aside. They seemed to be having a misunderstanding of some sort. "What does he *say*, Hassan?"

"Just a minute."

She craned[139] around in the high-backed chair, fighting off the dentist's little mirror. "I have to know," she told Hassan.

"He says your teeth are terrible. They have to be extracted[140] and the gums surgically smoothed.[141] He wants to know if you'll be here for another few months; he can't schedule you till later."

A cold lump of fear swelled in her stomach. Unfortunately she *would* be here; it had only been three months so far and she was        510
planning to stay a year. So she had to watch numbly[142] while her life was signed away, whole strings of appointments made, and little white cards filled out. And Hassan didn't even look sympathetic. He was still

---

[130]**glove compartment:** A small space in a car used to keep gloves, maps, flashlights, etc.
[131]**blood let:** To have some of their blood taken out; blood letting was thought to improve health.
[132]**smuggled:** To import or export illegally; in this case, put in the car secretly.
[133]**dodged:** Moved quickly to avoid.
[134]**yearning:** Strongly desiring.
[135]**fretted:** Became nervous and unhappy; bad-tempered.
[136]**hug:** An embrace; putting one's arms around someone.

[137]**subtle:** Not obvious in their actions.
[138]**clucking noises:** The noises of a hen; noises that people make to show that something is bad.
[139]**craned:** Turned her head around like a crane— a kind of bird with a very long neck.
[140]**extracted:** Taken out.
[141]**surgically smoothed:** Made smooth by a medical operation.
[142]**numbly:** Without being able to feel or move.

involved in whatever this argument was with Elizabeth. The two of them failed to notice how her hands were shaking.

It snowed all of January, the worst snow they had had in years. When she came downstairs in the mornings she found the kitchen icy cold, crisscrossed[143] by drafts. "The sort of cold enters your bones," she told Elizabeth. "I'm sure to fall sick."Elizabeth only nodded. Some
520   mornings now her face was pale and puffy,[144] as if she had a secret worry, but Mrs. Ardavi had learned that it was better not to ask about it.

Early in February there was a sudden warm spell.[145] Snow melted and all the trees dripped[146] in the sunshine. "We're going for a walk," Elizabeth said, and Mrs. Ardavi said, "I'll come too." In spite of the warmth, she toiled[147] upstairs for her woolen shawl. She didn't like to take chances. And she worried over Hilary's bare ears. "Won't she catch cold?" she asked. "I think we should cover her head."

"She'll be all right," said Elizabeth, and then shut her face in a certain stubborn way she had.
530   In the park, Elizabeth and Hilary made snowballs from the last of the snow and threw them at each other, narrowly missing Mrs. Ardavi, who stood watching with her arms folded and her hands tucked in her sleeves.

The next morning, something was wrong with Hilary. She sat at the breakfast table and cried steadily, refusing all food. "Now, now," her grandmother said, "won't you tell old Ka Jun what's wrong?" But when she came close Hilary screamed louder. By noon she was worse, Elizabeth called Hassan, and he came home immediately and laid a hand on Hilary's forehead and said she should go to the pediatrician.[148] He
540   drove them there himself. "It's her ears, I'm sure of it," Mrs. Ardavi said in the waiting room. For some reason Hassan grew angry. "Do you always know better than the experts?" he asked her. "What are we coming to the doctor for? We could have talked to you and saved the trip." His mother lowered her eyes and examined her purse straps. She understood that he was anxious, but all the same her feelings were hurt and when they rose to go into the office she stayed behind.

Later Hassan came back and sat down again. "There's an infection in her middle ear," he told her. "The doctor's going to give her a shot of penicillin." His mother nodded, careful not to annoy him by reminding
550   him she had thought as much. Then Hilary started crying. She must be getting her shot now. Mrs. Ardavi herself was terrified of needles, and

---

[143]**crisscrossed:** Crossed in many directions.
[144]**pale and puffy:** Without much color (pale) and somewhat swollen (puffy).
[145]**warm spell:** A period of warm weather.

[146]**dripped:** Had water falling in small drops.
[147]**toiled:** Moved with difficulty.
[148]**pediatrician:** A doctor specializing in taking care of children.

she sat gripping her purse until her fingers turned white, staring around the waiting room, which seemed pathetically[149] cheerful, with its worn wooden toys and nursery-school paintings. Her own ear ached in sympathy. She thought of a time when she had boxed Ali's ears[150] too hard and he had wept all that day and gone to sleep sucking his thumb.

While Hassan was there she was careful not to say anything, but the following morning at breakfast she said, "Elizabeth dear, do you remember that walk we took day before yesterday?"

"Yes," said Elizabeth. She was squeezing oranges for Hilary,   560
who'd grown cheerful again and was eating a huge breakfast.

"Remember I said Hilary should wear a hat? Now you see you should have been more careful. Because of you she fell sick; she could have died. Do you see that now?"

"No," said Elizabeth.

Was her Persian that scanty?[151] Lately it seemed to have shrunk and hardened, like a stale[152] piece of bread. Mrs. Ardavi sighed and tried again. "Without a hat, you see—" she began. But Elizabeth had set down her orange, picked up Hilary, and walked out of the room. Mrs. Ardavi stared after her, wondering if she's said something wrong.   570

For the rest of the day, Elizabeth was busy in her room. She was cleaning out bureaus and closets. A couple of times Mrs. Ardavi advanced as far as the doorway, where she stood awkwardly[153] watching. Hilary sat on the floor playing with a discarded[154] perfume bottle. Everything, it seemed, was about to be thrown away—buttonless blouses and stretched-out sweaters, stockings and combs and empty lipstick tubes. "Could I be of any help?" Mrs. Ardavi asked, but Elizabeth said, "Oh, no. Thank you very much." Her voice was cheerful. Yet when Hassan came home he went upstairs and stayed a long time, and the door remained shut behind him.   580

Supper that night was an especially fine stew, Hassan's favorite ever since childhood, but he didn't say a word about it. He hardly spoke at all, in fact. Then later, when Elizabeth was upstairs putting Hilary to bed, he said, "Khanoum Jun, I want to talk to you."

"Yes, Hassan," she said, laying aside her knitting. She was frightened by his seriousness, the black weight of his mustache, and her own father's deep black eyes. But what had she done? She knotted her hands and looked up at him, swallowing.

"I understand you've been interfering," he said.

"I, Hassan?"   590

[149]**pathetically:** Sadly; pitifully.
[150]**boxed Ali's ears:** Punished him by hitting his ears.
[151]**scanty:** Little or limited.
[152]**stale:** Old, hard.
[153]**awkwardly:** Uncomfortably and ungracefully.
[154]**discarded:** Thrown away.

"Elizabeth isn't the kind you can do that with. And she's raising the child just fine on her own."

"Well, of course, she is," said his mother. "Did I ever say otherwise?"

"Show it, then. Don't offer criticisms."

"Very well," she said. She picked up her knitting and began counting stitches,[155] as if she'd forgotten the conversation entirely. But that evening she was unusually quiet, and at nine o' clock she excused herself to go to bed. "So early?" Hassan asked.

600     "I'm tired," she told him, and left with her back very straight.

Her room surrounded her like a nest. She had built up layers of herself on every surface—tapestries and bits of lace and lengths of Paisley.[156] The bureau was covered with gilt[157]-framed pictures of the saints,[158] and snapshots of her sisters at family gatherings. On the windowsill were little plants in orange and aqua[159] plastic pots—her favorite American colors. Her bedside table held bottles of medicine, ivory prayer beads,[160] and a tiny brick of holy earth. The rest of the house was bare and shiny, impersonal; this room was as comforting as her shawl.

610     Still, she didn't sleep well. Ghosts rose up again, tugging[161] at her thoughts. Why did things turn out so badly for her? Her father had preferred her brothers, a fact that crushed her even after all these years. Her husband had had three children by her and then complained that she was cold. And what comfort were children? If she had stayed in Iran any longer Babak would have asked her to move; she'd seen it coming. There'd been some disrespect creeping into his bride's behavior, some unwillingness to take advice, which Babak had overlooked even when his mother pointed it out to him. And Hassan was worse—always so stubborn, much too independent. She had offered him anything if he

620     would just stay in Iran but he had said no; he was set on leaving her. And he had flatly[162] refused to take along his cousin Shora as his wife, though everyone pointed out how lonely he would be. He was so anxious to break away, to get *going*, to come to this hardhearted country and take up with a Christian girl. Oh, she should have laughed when he left, and saved her tears for someone more deserving. She never should have come here, she never should have asked anything of him again.

---

[155]**counting stitches:** Counting the complete turns of the wool.
[156]**tapestries . . . Paisley:** Kinds of cloth.
[157]**gilt:** Gold covered or gold colored.
[158]**saints:** Holy people.
[159]**aqua:** Blue-green color.

[160]**ivory prayer beads:** Round ivory balls on a string which are used for prayer. Ivory comes from the long teeth (tusks) of an elephant.
[161]**tugging:** Pulling.
[162]**flatly:** Absolutely; completely.

When finally she went to sleep it seemed that her eyes remained open, burning large and dry beneath her lids.

In the morning she had a toothache. She could hardly walk for the pain. It was only Friday (the first of her dental appointments was for Monday), but the dentist made time for her during the afternoon and pulled the tooth. Elizabeth said it wouldn't hurt, but it did. Elizabeth treated it as something insignificant, merely a small break in her schedule, which required the hiring of a babysitter. She wouldn't even call Hassan home from work. "What could he do?" she asked.

So when Hassan returned that evening it was all a surprise to him—the sight of his mother with a bloody cotton cylinder[163] hanging out over her lower lip like a long tooth. "What *happened* to you?" he asked. To make it worse, Hilary was screaming and had been all afternoon. Mrs. Ardavi put her hands over her ears, wincing.[164] "Will you make that child hush?"[165] Hassan told Elizabeth. "I think we should get my mother to bed." He guided her toward the stairs, and she allowed herself to lean on him. "It's mainly my heart," she said. "You know how scared I am of dentists." When he had folded back her bedspread and helped her to lie down she closed her eyes gratefully, resting one arm across her forehead. Even the comfort of hot tea was denied her; she had to stay on cold foods for twelve hours. Hassan fixed her a glass of ice water. He was very considerate, she thought. He seemed as shaken at the sight of her as Hilary had been. All during the evening he kept coming to check on her, and twice in the night she heard him climbing the stairs to listen at her door. When she moaned he called, "Are you awake?"

"Of course," she said.

"Can I get you anything?"

"No, no."

In the morning she descended the stairs with slow, groping feet,[166] keeping a tight hold on the railing. "It was a very hard night," she said. "At four my gum started throbbing.[167] Is that normal? I think these American pain pills are constipating. Maybe a little prune juice would restore my regularity."

"I'll get it," Hassan said. "You sit down. Did you take the milk of magnesia?"[168]

---

[163]**cylinder:** Roll.
[164]**wincing:** Moving in pain.
[165]**hush:** Be quiet.
[166]**groping feet:** Feet that reached or searched for each step uncertainly.

[167]**throbbing:** Beating rapidly with pain.
[168]**milk of magnesia:** A medicine for constipation.

"Oh, yes, but I'm afraid it wasn't enough," she said.

Elizabeth handed Hassan a platter[169] of bacon, not looking at him.

After breakfast, while Hassan and his mother were still sitting over their tea, Elizabeth started cleaning the kitchen. She made quite a bit of noise. She sorted the silverware and then went through a tangle of utensils,[170] discarding bent spatulas and rusty tongs.[171] "May I help?" asked Mrs. Ardavi. Elizabeth shook her head. She seemed to have these

670  fits[172] of throwing things away. Now she was standing on the counter to take everything from the upper cabinets—crackers, cereals, half-empty bottles of spices. On the very top shelf was a flowered tin confectioner's[173] box with Persian lettering on it, forgotten since the day Mrs. Ardavi had brought it. "My!" said Mrs. Ardavi. "Won't Hilary be surprised!" Elizabeth pried the lid off.[174] Out flew a cloud of insects, grayish-brown with V-shaped wings. They brushed past Elizabeth's face and fluttered through her hair and swarmed toward the ceiling, where they dimmed the light fixture. Elizabeth flung the box as far from her as possible and climbed down from the counter. "Goodness!" said

680  Mrs. Ardavi. "Why, *we* have those at home!" Hassan lowered his teacup. Mixed nuts and dried currants[175] rolled every which way on the floor; more insects swung toward the ceiling. Elizabeth sat on the nearest chair and buried her head in her hands. "Elizabeth?" said Hassan.

But she wouldn't look at him. In the end she simply rose and went upstairs, shutting the bedroom door with a gentle, definite click, which they heard all the way down in the kitchen because they were listening so hard.

"Excuse me," Hassan said to his mother.

690  She nodded and stared into her tea.

After he was gone she went to find Hilary, and she set her on her knee, babbling[176] various folk rhymes[177] to her while straining her ears toward the silence overhead. But Hilary squirmed[178] off her lap and went to play with a truck. Then Hassan came downstairs again. He didn't say a word about Elizabeth.

On the following day, when Mrs. Ardavi's tooth was better, she and Hassan had a little talk upstairs in her room. They were very polite with each other. Hassan asked his mother how long they could hope for

---

[169]**platter:** Large plate for serving food.
[170]**tangle of utensils:** Disorderly or mixed up pile of kitchen equipment.
[171]**discarding . . . tongs:** Throwing away some types of kitchen equipment not in working order.
[172]**(to have) fits:** Sudden period of great activity.
[173]**confectioner's:** Candy maker's.

[174]**pried the lid off:** Removed the cover.
[175]**currants:** Small fruit similar to grapes.
[176]**babbling:** Saying meaningless or foolish things; in this case, saying from memory without paying attention to meaning.
[177]**folk rhymes:** Old, traditional poems.
[178]**squirmed:** Twisted.

her to stay. His mother said she hadn't really thought about it. Hassan
said that in America it was the custom to have house guests for three    700
months only. After that they moved to a separate apartment nearby,
which he'd be glad to provide for her as soon as he could find one,
maybe next week. "Ah, an apartment," said his mother, looking
impressed. But she had never lived alone a day in her life, and so after a
suitable pause she said that she would hate to put him to so much
expense. "Especially," she said, "when I'm going in such a short time
anyway, since I'm homesick for my sisters."

"Well, then, " said Hassan.

At supper that night, Hassan announced that his mother was
missing her sisters and would like to leave. Elizabeth lowered her glass.    710
"Leave?" she said.

Mrs. Ardavi said, "And Babak's wife, of course, will be asking for
me when the baby arrives."

"Well . . . but what about the dentist? You were supposed to start
your appointments on Monday."

"It's not important," Mrs. Ardavi said.

"But we set up all those—"

"There are plenty of dentists she can see at home," Hassan told
Elizabeth. "We have dentists in Iran, for God's sake. Do you imagine
we're barbarians?"[179]                                                                              720

"No," Elizabeth said.

On the evening of the third of March, Hassan drove his mother to
the airport. He was worrying about the road, which was slippery after a
snowfall. He couldn't find much to say to his mother. And once they
had arrived, he deliberately kept the conversation to trivia[180]—the
verifying of tickets, checking of departure times, weighing of baggage.
Her baggage was fourteen pounds overweight. It didn't make sense; all
she had were her clothes and a few small gifts for her sisters. "Why is it
so heavy?" Hassan asked. "What have you got in there?" But his mother
only said, "I don't know," and straightened her shawl, looking    730
elsewhere. Hassan bent to open a tooled-leather[181] suitcase. Inside he
found three empty urn-shaped[182] wine bottles, the permanent-press
sheets from her bed, and a sample box of detergent that had come in
yesterday's mail. "Listen," said Hassan, "do you know how much I'd
have to pay to fly these things over? What's the matter with you?"

"I wanted to show my sisters," his mother said.

"Well, forget it. Now, what else have you got?"

---

[179]**barbarians:** People without civilization or
culture.
[180]**trivia:** Small, unimportant things.

[181]**tooled-leather:** Decorated leather.
[182]**urn-shaped:** Shaped like a vase—a container
to hold flowers.

740 But something about her—the vague, childlike eyes set upon some faraway object—made him give in. He opened no more bags. He even regretted his sharpness, and when her flight was announced he hugged her closely and kissed the top of her head. "Go with God," he said. "Goodbye, Hassan."

She set off down the corridor by herself, straggling behind[183] a line of businessmen. They all wore hats. His mother wore her scarf, and of all the travelers she alone, securely kerchiefed and shawled, setting her small shoes resolutely[184] on the gleaming tiles,[185] seemed undeniably a foreigner.

[183]**straggling behind:** Walking behind.
[184]**resolutely:** Firmly.

[185]**gleaming tiles:** A floor made of squares of shiny baked clay.

--- **A LOOK AT THE IDEAS** ---

1. Summarize the situation before Mrs. Ardavi arrived to visit her son Hassan, his wife Elizabeth, and their daughter Hilary. Comment on (a) where Mrs. Ardavi was coming from and how long it had been since she had seen her son; (b) how long each of the characters expected she would stay; (c) what preparations Hassan and Elizabeth had made for her visit and how they felt about her coming.

2. When Hassan greeted his mother at the airport, why did she think he was a stranger?

   ____ 1. He was thin, stoop-shouldered, and gray-haired.

   ____ 2. She didn't expect him to meet her at the airport.

   ____ 3. He had changed so very much in appearance.

   What did she do when she finally recognized Hassan?

3. During the ride home, Hassan said very little. Why? What had Mrs. Ardavi expected? How did she react to Hassan's silence?

4. Describe the meeting between Mrs. Ardavi and Elizabeth. Comment on (a) how Elizabeth looked and acted; (b) what Mrs. Ardavi thought about the house; (c) Elizabeth's response to Mrs. Ardavi's request to see the child; (d) what Mrs. Ardavi did when she saw Hilary and how Elizabeth felt about it.

**5.** Which words would you use to describe Mrs. Ardavi, Hassan, and/or Elizabeth? Write *A* for Mrs. Ardavi; *H* for Hassan, and *E* for Elizabeth next to the appropriate words. (This exercise can be done individually or in groups.)

| | | | | | |
|---|---|---|---|---|---|
| 1. ___ attractive | 8. ___ nervous | 15. ___ loving |
| 2. ___ frightened | 9. ___ confused | 16. ___ excited |
| 3. ___ inconsiderate | 10. ___ distant | 17. ___ busy |
| 4. ___ worried | 11. ___ generous | 18. ___ insensitive |
| 5. ___ hurt | 12. ___ religious | 19. ___ efficient |
| 6. ___ thoughtful | 13. ___ dazed | 20. ___ understanding |
| 7. ___ cooperative | 14. ___ disappointed | 21. ___ thoughtful |

What other words or phrases would you use to describe each character?

**6.** What are some of the problems Mrs. Ardavi found in adjusting to her new environment, and how did she attempt to handle them?

How did Mrs. Ardavi's schedule in the United States differ from her schedule and the schedule of her sisters in Iran?

**7.** Indicate how Hassan, Elizabeth, and/or Mrs. Ardavi felt about each situation below. If the character felt pleased or *positive*, mark *P* in the appropriate column. If the character felt displeased or *negative*, mark *N* in the appropriate column.

| | Hassan | Elizabeth | Mrs. Ardavi |
|---|---|---|---|
| 1. When Mrs. Ardavi spoke of her physical ailments | ___ | ___ | ___ |
| 2. When Mrs. Ardavi began to cook the dinners | ___ | ___ | ___ |
| 3. When Hassan ate second and third helpings | ___ | ___ | ___ |
| 4. When Mrs. Ardavi brought her things into the living room | ___ | ___ | ___ |

5. When Hassan
   watched TV in the
   evenings and
   wouldn't talk           _____   _____   _____

6. When Mrs. Ardavi
   tried to speak English  _____   _____   _____

7. When Mrs. Ardavi
   asked Hassan for
   medicine                _____   _____   _____

8. When the dentist said
   he couldn't give Mrs.
   Ardavi an appoint-
   ment right away         _____   _____   _____

9. When Mrs. Ardavi
   offered suggestions
   about taking care of
   Hilary                  _____   _____   _____

10. When Mrs. Ardavi
    became silent and
    went to her room
    early                  _____   _____   _____

11. When Elizabeth
    started cleaning out
    the kitchen cupboards  _____   _____   _____

12. After the dentist
    pulled out Mrs.
    Ardavi's tooth         _____   _____   _____

13. When Hassan
    suggested that his
    mother move to her
    own apartment          _____   _____   _____

14. When Mrs. Ardavi
    announced that she
    was going back home    _____   _____   _____

If your mother or mother-in-law were visiting you at your
home, how would you feel in these situations?

8. Mrs. Ardavi became increasingly aware of the loss of her
   own language during her stay in the United States, and
   she couldn't seem to make any progress in learning
   English. Why?

Compare Mrs. Ardavi's elation at the Iranian party with her attempts to communicate with Hassan, Elizabeth, and the women in the park. Why were Elizabeth's brief translations unsatisfactory to her?

9. As the visit wore on, communication in either English or Persian began to break down and Hassan, Elizabeth, and Mrs. Ardavi withdrew more and more into themselves. What did Hassan and Elizabeth do? What did Mrs. Ardavi do?

   What did Mrs. Ardavi think about when she went to her room early or when she couldn't sleep at night? What were Hassan's and Elizabeth's thoughts?

10. Although cultural differences were no doubt responsible for a large part of the tension and misunderstanding that developed, more or less the same situation might have occurred had Mrs. Ardavi been American rather than Iranian. Also, at one point Mrs. Ardavi wonders if there aren't greater differences between men and women than between Americans and Iranians. Why does Mrs. Ardavi feel this is true? What examples in the story support her views? Do you believe this is true? Describe a situation from your own experience or observations that supports your view.

11. Mrs. Ardavi feels that Hilary will be a foreigner forever and possibly Mrs. Ardavi will be a foreigner to Hilary. Have you ever felt like a foreigner to a close relative or family friend? How do you account for this feeling?

12. When Elizabeth opened the box with the Persian lettering on it and insects flew out, how did everyone react? Do you think they would have reacted the same way if Elizabeth had opened the box the day after Mrs. Ardavi arrived?

   What other types of gifts did Mrs. Ardavi bring? How did these compare with the gifts she wanted to take home with her?

13. Mrs. Ardavi finally decided to return to Iran. Why?

   _____ 1. She was too proud to continue going to the expensive dentist.

_____ 2. She was homesick for her sisters and her son Babak and his family.

_____ 3. She couldn't bear the tension and isolation she felt.

_____ 4. She realized she would have to move and had never lived alone.

When Mrs. Ardavi returned to Iran, do you think she lived with Babak and his wife or with her sisters? Explain your reasons.

14. Read the statements below and decide whether you agree or disagree with them. Explain your reasons.

1. Hassan should never have left home.
2. Hassan had an obligation to take care of his mother even if he had left home.
3. Hassan should have let his mother stay as long as she wanted.
4. Hassan had an understandable concern about his mother's health.
5. Hassan tried hard to make the visit a success.
6. Elizabeth tried hard to make the visit a success.
7. Elizabeth had good reasons to become annoyed with Mrs. Ardavi.
8. Elizabeth should have been more considerate.
9. Elizabeth was right in wanting her mother-in-law to move into a separate apartment.
10. Mrs Ardavi tried hard to make the visit a success.
11. Mrs. Ardavi wasn't sure what she was doing wrong.
12. Mrs. Ardavi wouldn't be happy no matter where she was.
13. Mrs. Ardavi should have tried harder to adapt to the customs of the United States.
14. Mrs. Ardavi should never have come to visit her son and his family.
15. Mrs. Ardavi had no business telling Elizabeth how to raise Hilary and run the household.

15. Do you think the author is sympathetic to all of the

characters in the story? What strengths and weaknesses does each person have? Do any of the characters change as a result of the experience they undergo, or are they more or less the same at the beginning and end of the story?

Given the personalities of Hassan, his mother, and Elizabeth, with all their strengths and weaknesses, and the situation in which they found themselves, do you think the outcome of the visit could have been otherwise? If not, why not? If so, what could each person have done to make the visit more successful?

16. Write an essay in which you discuss the expectations you think a mother, father, mother-in-law, or father-in-law would have if one of them came to visit you when you were living in another country. What mutual obligations do you think you and the person visiting would have? Would you expect "this business of being a foreigner" to be changeable, as Mrs. Ardavi did? How would you deal with such a visit in order to make it a successful one? In your essay, be sure to identify your relationship with the person visiting and the location of "home" for both you and your visitor.

17. In "My Turkish Grandmother," Anaïs Nin refers to the old woman as a universal grandmother. Do you think Mrs. Ardavi is a universal mother-in-law or is she a unique personality? Write an essay in which you discuss the universal or individual qualities of these two women. Here are some suggestions:

   1. You could begin your essay by indicating whether or not you agree that the Turkish woman was a universal type and briefly identify the qualities in her personality that support your view.

   2. Then consider Mrs. Ardavi. What qualities in her personality make her a universal or an individual mother-in-law?

   3. In your conclusion, you can summarize the ways in which the two women were alike or different and explain whether you like or sympathize with one character more than the other.

**1.** Supply the missing word in each sentence. The word you produce should be an antonym, or opposite, of the *italicized* word.

1. The air inside the waiting room seemed curiously *opaque*, but outside the air was _____.

2. Mrs. Ardavi was short and *stocky*, but her daughter-in-law was _____.

3. Hilary was sometimes *cross* when she got tired, but she was usually _____.

4. Hassan was *sharp* with his mother that morning; he was usually _____, however.

5. On that subject, he was surprisingly *stubborn*, particularly since he was usually so accomodating and

_____.

6. What some people consider *trivial*, other people may consider _____.

7. Elizabeth liked her vegetables *crisp*. Mrs. Ardavi preferred hers _____.

8. She thought Americans tried to be too *subtle*. She would have preferred them to be more _____ in their actions.

9. People who lead *intricate* lives usually give others more to talk about than those who lead _____ lives.

10. Sometimes she thought she was too *lenient* with her children. Other times she thought she was too

_____.

**2.** Supply the missing letters of the word in each sentence. The word you produce should have the same meaning as the *italicized* word.

1. Some people have no problem *fitting in* to a new environment, but others have serious problems
a d j _____ to a new routine.

2. That building is very *imposing*, but this one is not very
i m p _____.

3. She *flatly* refused; in other words, she
a b s _____ turned down his offer.

4. Her Persian became *scanty*—that is, it became more
   *l i m ____ .*

5. It was only an *insignificant* matter, but sometimes
   *s m ____* things can assume large proportions.

3. The *italicized* words and phrases indicate devices that relate parts of the passage below. Explain what is omitted, referred to, linked, or replaced, and tell how these devices function in relating ideas in the passage. (For further information on this type of exercise, see Steinbeck, "A Look at the Language," question 4, page 12.)

> "I brought her some medals," she whispered. "I hope you don't mind."
>
> "*Medals?*" said Elizabeth. She repeated *the word* anxiously, mispronouncing *it*.
>
> "*Only* an Allah and a Koran, *both* very tiny. You'll hardly know *they*'re there. I'm not used to seeing a child without a medal. *It* worries me."

In the sentence "You'll hardly know they're *there,*" *there* does not relate to anything in this passage. Mrs. Ardavi knows that Elizabeth will understand. In place of *there,* what could Mrs. Ardavi have said?

4. The meaning a speaker intends to communicate may be quite different from the meaning conveyed by the actual words, phrases, and sentences. For example, when Mrs. Ardavi lays down her fork and says, "Vegetables not thoroughly cooked retain a certain acidity," she is not making a general statement about vegetable cookery but voicing a criticism of American food and possibly Elizabeth's cooking. We can never, of course, be certain about the intention of a speaker, but we must always be prepared for the fact that what a person is saying is not always exactly what he or she means. We must, so to speak, learn to interpret the *tone* of the statement.

With this in mind, decide the meaning you think each speaker intends to convey.

1. *Hassan:* "At the table, Khanom? At the table?" (line 310)

2. *Mrs. Ardavi:* "Now, this is your rest period. Come to the table in three hours and be surprised." (lines 322-324)

3. *Hassan:* "I must be gaining five pounds a week. None of my clothes fit." (lines 329-330)

4. *Mrs. Ardavi:* "That's good to hear." (line 331)

5. *Mrs. Ardavi:* "It's her ears, I'm sure of it." (line 540)

6. *Hassan:* "Do you always know better than the experts? What are we coming to the doctor for? We could have talked to you and saved the trip." (lines 541-544)

5. In accordance with Iranian custom, Mrs. Ardavi decided to break the news of Ali's death to Hassan gradually by telling him that Ali was very ill when he was, in fact, already dead. Later she realized her mistake. She remembered that Hassan liked to be told things directly.

This incident suggests that handling news of death or other misfortunes can be quite individualistic. Nevertheless, cultural patterns are important and a person needs to be aware of them. Decide on when and how you would break the news and what you might say in the following situations in the United States. How might you handle the situation in another culture?

1. Your roommate has been in an automobile accident and is in the hospital. The injuries are serious but fortunately not fatal. You are the logical one to call your roommate's parents, whom you have met on one or two occasions.

2. A close friend of yours is on his way to your house for dinner. Your friend's mother has just called to tell you that his father has had a heart attack and is in the intensive care unit of the local hospital. You are faced with the job of telling your friend about it when he arrives.

3. Your neighbors have been away on a three-week vacation. By previous arrangement, you are meeting them at the airport. You have the unpleasant task of telling them that their house was robbed the night before.

6. Mrs. Ardavi was not very tactful or diplomatic when she made her comment about vegetables retaining acidity. What could she have said and how might she have handled the situation?

Tell what you think the people in the following situations might say if they wish to be tactful and diplomatic.

1. Tom is a dinner guest of a family he has met through a school organization. His hostess is about to serve him a very generous slice of blood-rare roast beef, the sight of which makes him ill. He says to the hostess:

2. Somebody spills milk on you, and you don't want the person to feel embarrassed. You say:

3. A neighbor has enthusiastically offered to drive you to the shopping center or market. You want to go alone, even if it means taking the bus, because you are planning to meet a friend there for a cup of coffee and want to have a private conversation. You say:

7. The organization of short stories varies greatly. Some stories are told in chronological order; some may begin at the end and work backward; some rely heavily on "flashbacks"—parts of the story that have happened some time before the main action begins. Some, of course, contain a combination of these patterns. Analyze the organizational pattern of "Your Place is Empty":

1. Prepare two lists of events: (a) a list of the main events in the story in chronological order and (b) a list of the flashbacks.

2. When you have completed your lists, answer these questions: (a) Is the story told mainly in chronological order? (b) How many flashbacks are there? Explain the purpose of the flashbacks and how they relate to the main action.

3. Look over the two lists and decide how you will organize a short summary of the plot or main events in the story. Will you report only the main events in chronological order or will you include some flashbacks?

4. After you have written your summary, compare it with those written by other students to see if you have, in general, included the same material. Would people who had not read the story know what it was about after reading your summary? What would they miss, if anything?

## Margaret Mead (1901-1978)

*Margaret Mead began her distinguished career with an anthropological field trip to Samoa in the 1920s. Her studies of adolescents in Samoa and in the Admiralty Islands are reported in her books* Coming of Age in Samoa *(1928) and* Growing Up in New Guinea *(1930). In 1929, she returned to New York and in that same year received a Ph.D. degree in anthropology from Columbia University.*

*Dr. Mead was a giant in her field and had many interests. For many years, she served as Curator of Ethnology at the American Museum of Natural History in New York, carried a heavy teaching load at Columbia University, published extensively in her field, gave lectures around the world, held professional offices and served on many important committees, and wrote numerous articles expressing her views on various social and political issues. Her wise and common-sense opinions, based on her observations as a social scientist and her insights as a mother and grandmother, were of interest to millions of newspaper and magazine readers. In the selection from* Redbook *magazine that follows, she answers a reader's question about her earlier conclusions on sex and temperament.*

# 10

## Margaret Mead

## Answers

Do you still adhere to the notion[1] that it is temperament[2] rather than sex that determines social roles and that social conditioning determines an individual's temperament?

First let's clarify the terms. By temperament I mean the constellation[3] of traits[4] determined by the individual's biological heritage.[5] You are born with your own particular temperament—your way of approaching life.

Character is distinct from temperament. By character I mean the constellation of traits that are emphasized in the upbringing of individuals as members of a given culture—as Americans or Eskimos or Chinese. It is our shared cultural character that helps us to understand and communicate with one another as Americans.

Personality combines the two, temperament and character. It is the outcome of the combination. The personality of an individual with a

10

---

[1]**adhere to the notion:** Keep the idea or opinion.
[2]**temperament:** The manner in which one thinks or acts in general.
[3]**constellation:** A group of stars with fixed positions in relationship to each other; in this case, a collection.

[4]**traits:** Characteristics.
[5]**heritage:** Characteristics that are inherited or handed down from past generations.

certain inborn[6] temperament is shaped by the experience of growing up and living as a woman or a man in a particular cultural setting.

On the basis of research I have carried out, I believe that there are male and female versions[7] of the same temperament. Temperamentally there are male as well as female introverts and extroverts,[8] fiercely brave
20 women as well as fiercely brave men, shy and gentle men as well as shy and gentle women.

Every society emphasizes an expected personality for each sex. Sometimes both men and women are expected to have the same kind of personality. That is, both men and women are expected to be outgoing, active people or, on the contrary, introspective,[9] meditative[10] people. In cultures where this is so, sex differences are reflected in the particular ways in which a woman and a man are expected to behave and the activities each is expected to engage in. In a culture in which both men and women are expected to be outgoing and active, women may be
30 expected to take a lot of initiative[11] in personal relations between men and women, while men may be expected to take the initiative in public, community activities.

In other cultures it is expected that the personalities of women and men will be complementary.[12] The personality of women is based on one set of temperamental traits and that of men on another. In such a culture women may be expected to be passive, gentle and modest, while men may be expected to be active and self-assertive[13] in whatever activities persons of either sex engage in.

Neither sex nor temperament as such "determines" social roles.
40 But in different cultures social roles may be assigned on the basis of either sex or temperament. Sex is the easiest way of making a division in assigning social roles: Women do the fishing, men do the hunting; women care for the home, men run public life.

But since all temperaments are represented in both sexes, the assignment of social roles entirely on the basis of sex, rather than temperament, is likely to be very unsatisfactory to a great many individuals. What we should be aiming for, I think, is a kind of social world in which the great variety of personalities, masculine and feminine, is recognized, and in which individuals are free to choose social roles that are in keep-
50 ing with their temperament as well as with their trained skills.

[6]**inborn:** Natural; already possessed at the time of birth.
[7]**versions:** Varieties.
[8]**introverts and extroverts:** People whose interests center on their own inner thoughts and people who are more interested in the things around them.
[9]**Introspective:** Thoughtful; examining one's own thoughts.

[10]**meditative:** Thinking deeply and quietly.
[11]**(to take the) initiative:** To take the first step or to make the opening move.
[12]**complementary:** Completing; in this case, the personalities are different but together make a whole.
[13]**self-assertive:** Actively express oneself.

1. Compare the question Margaret Mead was asked with the restatement of the question below it. Is the restatement of the question accurate? Do the two questions in the restatement correspond to the two parts of the original question?

> Do you still adhere to the notion that it is temperament rather than sex that determines social roles and that social conditioning determines an individual's temperament?
>
> Restatement: *Do you still think that social roles are determined by sex rather than temperament? Do you also still believe that a person's temperament is shaped by his experiences in growing up in a particular culture?*

   Restate the original question in your own words. You can write one question with two parts like the original question or make the two parts into two questions. Compare your question with the original question. Does your question ask for essentially the same information?

2. Before answering the question, Mead explains what the terms *temperament*, *character*, and *personality* mean to her. Match the terms in column *A* with her idea of these terms in column *B*.

   | *A* | *B* |
   |---|---|
   | 1. character | _____ the traits one is born with |
   | 2. temperament | _____ the traits one acquires in growing up |
   | 3. personality | _____ a combination of one's inborn and culturally acquired traits |

   How do you use these terms? Do you use them in the same way that Mead uses them?

3. Which of the following reflects Mead's view of temperament?

   _____ 1. Women have different versions of one basic temperament.

   _____ 2. Men and women may have essentially the same temperaments.

141

_____ 3. Men in general have a more aggressive temperament than women.

Give reasons for your choice. Why would Mead not agree with the other two choices? What do you believe about statements 1, 2, and 3?

4. Mead points out that there are both male and female extroverts and introverts. Which of the following adjectives does she associate with extroverts? Which does she associate with introverts? Mark *E* for *extroverts* and *I* for *introverts*.

| | | | |
|---|---|---|---|
| 1. _____ active | 4. _____ aggressive | 7. _____ shy |
| 2. _____ outgoing | 5. _____ modest | 8. _____ self-assertive |
| 3. _____ gentle | 6. _____ introspective | 9. _____ passive |

How would you describe an extrovert and an introvert? Do you consider yourself fundamentally an introvert or an extrovert?

5. In Society A, men and women are expected to have the same personality. In Society B, men and women are expected to have different personalities. Would Mead probably say the statements below are true of Society A or Society B?

_____ 1. The personalities of men and women are based on two different sets of temperamental traits.

_____ 2. Men are expected to be aggressive and outgoing, while women are expected to be modest and passive in all activities.

_____ 3. Sex differences are reflected in patterns of behavior rather than personality type.

_____ 4. Both men and women are expected to be humble and modest even though they do different kinds of work.

Does either Society A or Society B appeal to you? Is your immediate cultural group more like Society A or Society B?

6. Write *A* before the statement if you think Mead would agree with it; write *D* if you think she would disagree with it. Then tell how you feel about the statement.

_____ 1. The best way to assign social roles (the parts men and women play in a particular society) is on the basis of sex.

_____ 2. People should have the freedom to choose the social roles they would like to play.

_____ 3. Temperament should be taken into consideration in assigning social roles.

_____ 4. Sex differences should not be reflected in patterns of behavior.

_____ 5. Social roles today should reflect an awareness of the great variety of personalities of men and women.

**7.** Do you think the following social roles should be primarily assigned to men or to women? Check the appropriate column to indicate your point of view. Check both columns if you think the activities should be more or less equally shared.

|  | Men | Women |
|---|---|---|
| 1. Being head of the family | _____ | _____ |
| 2. Taking responsibility for shopping, cooking, cleaning, and the running of the household | _____ | _____ |
| 3. Handling the major financial affairs of the family | _____ | _____ |
| 4. Taking care of the children | _____ | _____ |
| 5. Disciplining the children | _____ | _____ |
| 6. Making decisions about family outings and vacations | _____ | _____ |
| 7. Making major decisions concerning the education of the children | _____ | _____ |
| 8. Supervising or taking care of the garden and yard | _____ | _____ |
| 9. Deciding whether or not invitations should be accepted | _____ | _____ |
| 10. Writing social letters or making telephone calls to accept invitations | _____ | _____ |
| 11. Writing thank-you notes for gifts and hospitality | _____ | _____ |

12. Assuming chief responsibility for
    support of the family                          _____   _____

13. Assuming responsibility, if
    necessary, for the welfare of the
    extended family—that is, parents
    and other relatives                            _____   _____

14. Giving advice and moral support
    when needed to younger members of
    the extended family                            _____   _____

15. Providing love and emotional
    support for the entire family                  _____   _____

**8.** Write a composition in which you describe the social roles
of husband and wife in a family you know. Include information about such things as where the people live, how old
they are, how long they have been married, and how many
children they have. Also indicate whether one person tends
to take major responsibilities for certain matters or whether
they seem to share responsibilities and decision making.
Conclude by telling why you *do* or *do not* think the situation
is an ideal one.

## ——————— A LOOK AT THE LANGUAGE ———————

**1.** Circle the *italicized* word in each sentence that does not
seem to fit the context because it is noticeably different from
the other three italicized words.

1. He had an *outgoing, dynamic, aggressive, modest*
   personality.
2. She was *self-assertive, shy, gentle,* and *passive.*
3. They were *cooperative, temperamental, dependable,* and
   *supportive.*
4. He was a *shy, introspective, meditative, outgoing* introvert.
5. They were noted for their *adherence, opposition, loyalty,*
   and *allegiance* to company policy.
6. She was an *aggressive, self-assertive, dynamic, modest*
   extrovert.

**2.** The *italicized* words and phrases indicate devices that relate parts the passages below. Explain what is omitted, referred to, linked, or replaced, and tell how these devices function in relating ideas in the passage. (For further information on this type of exercise, see Steinbeck's, "A Look at the Language," question 4, page 12.)

1. Every society emphasizes an expected personality for each sex. Sometimes both men and women are expected to have the same kind of personality. *That is,* both men and women are expected to be outgoing, active people or, on the contrary, introspective, meditative people. In cultures where *this* is *so,* sex differences are reflected in the particular ways in which a woman and a man are expected to behave and the activities *each* is expected to engage in.

2. In *other cultures* it is expected that the personalities of women and men will be complementary. The personality of women is based on one set of temperamental traits and *that* of men on *another.*

**3.** The first sentence in each group is from the Mead selection. Clarify the meaning of Mead's sentence by completing the second sentence in each group.

1. Neither sex nor temperament as such "determines" social roles.

*Social roles are . . .*

2. What we should be aiming for, I think, is a kind of social world in which the great variety of personalities, masculine and feminine, is recognized, and in which individuals are free to choose social roles that are in keeping with their temperament as well as with their trained skills.

*A kind of social world . . .*

3. But since all temperaments are represented in both sexes, the assignment of social roles entirely on the basis of sex, rather than temperament, is likely to be very unsatisfactory to a great many individuals.

*A great many individuals are likely to find . . .*

Now compare the original and the rewritten sentences.

Does the rewritten sentence change the meaning or focus? Which version do you prefer? Why?

4. Indicate the order in which Mead answers the questions by writing *1* before the first thing she does, *2* before the second thing she does, and so on.

_____ Indicates dissatisfaction with means of assigning special roles in society in general

_____ Discusses personality in terms of the expectations of two contrasting societies

_____ Defines terms and focuses on the first part of the question; gives her own views about temperament in relation to the sexes

_____ Gives her views on the ideal basis for assigning social roles

_____ Turns to the second part of the question and indicates the basis for assigning social roles

5. Would you say that Mead answers the question she was asked directly? What are the assumptions on which the question is based? Does she accept or reject these assumptions before going on to answer the question?

6. Consider this question? Do you think intelligence, diligence, or personality is most important in getting ahead in the world?

1. First, analyze the question. What assumptions are built into the question? Do you accept or reject these assumptions?

2. Now, write an essay answer to the question. Here are some suggestions. First, define the terms in the question. Then, give your answer, using illustrations and/or giving reasons for your position. Conclude with a summary statement of your point of view.

## Joan Rubin (b. 1932)

*Joan Rubin, author of* National Bilingualism in Paraguay *(1965) and numerous other books and articles on language planning and bilingual education, received her Ph.D. degree in anthropology from Yale University in 1963. Her recent academic experience includes a Visiting Professorship at Georgetown University and a three-year appointment as Visiting Researcher at the East-West Culture Learning Institute in Hawaii. She has also served as a consultant on language planning and bilingual education in school systems here and abroad, including the Ministry of Education in Paraguay, and has lectured at many universities around the world.*

*Besides her scholarly pursuits, Dr. Rubin has maintained an active interest in language teaching. Her interest and concern are apparent in the article "How to Tell When Someone Is Saying 'No'" in which she draws on her experience as a language teacher as well as her vast knowledge of languages and cultures.*

# 11

# How to Tell When Someone Is Saying "No"

One of the more important communicative tasks that confronts[1] a traveler is the recognition of when a speaker has said "no." That is, one needs to be able to recognize that a respondent has refused or denied that which the speaker has demanded, solicited,[2] or offered. Equally, one needs to acquire the appropriate manner in which to respond in the negative when offered, solicited, or demanded something. Granted that it is sometimes difficult to recognize a refusal in one's mother tongue where the answer might be ambiguous[3] or deliberately obscure.[4] Nonetheless, in many encounters the meaning is clear if one knows how to read the appropriate signals.

A first task for the visitor abroad is to discover which forms are used to fulfill this function. If we compare form and function across cultures, it soon becomes clear that one form may be used to mean different things in another culture than in one's own. For example, in Turkish "no" is signaled by moving one's head backwards while rolling one's eyes upwards. However, to an American this movement is close to

10

[1]**confronts:** Faces.
[2]**solicited:** Asked for; requested.
[3]**ambiguous:** Unclear; having two or more possible meanings.

[4]**deliberately obscure:** Intentionally hidden.

the signal used for saying "yes." Further, in still other cultures, head shaking may have nothing to do with affirmation or negation. In parts of India, rolling the head slowly from side to side means something like
20 "Yes, go on. I'm listening." Thus, as one goes from culture to culture, form and function may not match.[5] If a foreigner wants to communicate appropriately, he must develop the competence[6] of sending and receiving "no" messages.

In order to understand the meaning of a new set of forms, it takes more than learning the forms that are used for denial or negation. A foreigner must also learn when and to whom he must use the proper form. That is to say, one must learn when and to whom it is appropriate to use a particular form which means "no." For example, how do employees refuse a request from their employer? This may well be
30 different from saying "no" to a peer.[7] It will be important as well to understand what the appropriate conditions for saying "no" are. A speaker may be insulting the foreigner deliberately by the form of "no" he uses. These conditions must be learned along with the form for "no" or important messages or conditions may be missed.

However, not only the appropriate form and setting must be learned but also the underlying values of a culture will alter what is meant by a particular form even if used in the right setting. We will find that deep-seated[8] cultural values will affect the proper interpretation of a particular form. Without knowledge of the central values, the traveler
40 may never understand properly what message the speaker is trying to convey. Each of us carries around certain central values which underlie our behavior. These might be values such as being hospitable, being respectful, "time is money," man as a mechanistic being[9] and the like.

Finally, individuals tend to have idiosyncratic[10] ways of sending and receiving "no." One of my students wrote a paper once on how she knew what was the most auspicious[11] time to ask her father for something so as to avoid his saying no and thus more easily gain the favor she was asking for.

We can all recount tales of misunderstanding while residing[12] in a
50 foreign culture. Here are a couple of my own: (1) While living abroad I invited people to parties or dinner at my house. Although I requested an RSVP[13] I never got any. As a result, it was necessary to prepare a large amount of food in case they all came. I was annoyed[14] that I hadn't

---

[5]**match:** Agree.
[6]**competence:** Ability.
[7]**peer:** An equal person; a person with the same social or professional position.
[8]**deep-seated:** Firmly established; deeply rooted.
[9]**man as a mechanistic being:** The theory that man is controlled by physical and chemical forces or laws over which he has no control.

[10]**idiosyncratic:** Their own, individualistic, or peculiar.
[11]**auspicious:** Favorable.
[12]**residing:** Living, being a resident.
[13]**RSVP:** Please reply—an abbreviation for the French *répondez s'il vous plaît* (respond, if you please), used on an invitation when an answer is expected.

understood the cues[15] for negation. (2) On several occasions, I found that I couldn't interpret the servants' ways of saying no. (3) In the United States negotiations with North Vietnam were often misinterpreted. The President often said: "I'll talk peace anywhere, anytime." I think that one meaning which can be attributed to this sentence is "No, I won't." The reason for this interpretation is that in most U.S. areas, when a person says "drop in any time" this is not an     60 invitation. Rather, if one really wanted to extend an invitation one would need to specify when and where to meet. By saying "anywhere, anytime" without being more specific, the President's willingness to negotiate seemed dubious.[16]

This paper will provide evidence for one of the claims of the new field of sociolinguistics which is concerned with understanding the speech act by looking at speech variation and social structure and rules. The claim is made that the interpretation of the speech act requires understanding it as a totality. Further, it is claimed that it won't do to merely look at the form-function relation inherent[17] in any speech act in     70 order to be able to interpret the message nor is it sufficient to look at the social parameters.[18] One must also look for the underlying values inherent in the speech act. All of this kind of knowledge comprises[19] what is meant by the term "communicative competence," i.e., the ability to interpret the full meaning of a message and the ability to properly formulate such messages.

Looked at in this deeper way, the teaching of language would greatly benefit from using this kind of information in teaching about the culture and the proper use of the language. Language teaching often stops at the instruction of form-function relationships. At best, it gives     80 clues as to the social parameters involved. Only rarely are students given information about the underlying values of a speech act. Part of the reason this is not taught is because teaching materials are not organized in this manner and because the details of a value system are more difficult to discern[20] than either form-function relations or the social parameters of the speech act. However, if students are to properly use a language, it is essential that we provide them with this sort of information.

This paper will exemplify[21] what the three levels of understanding a speech act look like for one kind of speech act, namely, negation. It will     90 illustrate how all three are needed in the interpretation of the message of negation.

[14]**annoyed:** Bothered; irritated.
[15]**cues:** Hints, suggestions, or clues.
[16]**dubious:** Doubtful; uncertain.
[17]**inherent:** Existing as a natural or basic part.

[18]**parameters:** Variables; factors.
[19]**comprises:** Makes up; forms.
[20]**discern:** Discover; understand.
[21]**exemplify:** Describe by examples.

It's not hard to find examples of similar ways of expressing "no" relations across several cultures. These are worth listing:

(1) Be silent, hesitate, show a lack of enthusiasm. In many cultures in the world, being silent is a way of refusing an offer or an invitation or of giving an answer.

- When asked whether you liked a movie or a dress, be silent.
- If you receive a written invitation, don't answer.

100 The big problem for a foreigner is that silence may mean many other things. Among the Western Apache,[22] as Basso (1972) has shown, silence is used in "social situations in which participants perceive their relationship vis-à-vis[23] one another to be ambiguous and/or unpredictable." Basso argues that "silence is defined as appropriate with respect to a specific individual or individuals."

(2) Offer an alternative. In some cases in order not to offend or to direct the conversation away from the request, the addressee[24] may divert attention[25] by suggesting an alternative.

- How do you like this book?
  It's good but I prefer—
110
- What time should we meet? Around 5?
  How about 4:30?
  Let's make it 5.
- Mary can you help with the cooking?
  Susan can do it better.
- Sylvia, can you do this?
  Mañana (note that *mañana* is translated as tomorrow, but it's real meaning in this situation is a subtle[26] negation).

(3) Postponement (delaying answers). Often in response to a request to perform something or to an invitation "no" is indicated by
120 postponement.

- Can you come over this evening?
  Not today, next time, I'll let you know.
- I think it's a great idea, but I don't have time at the moment.

---

[22]**Western Apache:** American Indian tribe.
[23]**vis-à-vis:** In relation to.
[24]**addressee:** Person being spoken to.

[25]**divert attention:** Draw or take away attention.
[26]**subtle:** Not obvious; not easy to see or understand.

- Say "yes" late (i.e., let the host know so late, it's impossible for them to act).
- We're very busy now, but we'll get someone on it as soon as possible.
- We'll take the matter under advisement.

(4)  Put the blame on a third party or something over which you have no control.

130

- My husband doesn't want me to, or I'll have to ask my husband.
- We'll put it up to the committee, but I can't promise anything.
- I can't drink because I have a bad liver.
- My budget doesn't permit me to go.
- It's too expensive.
- Tell Arthur Murray dance studio salespersons while talking on the telephone: "I'm sorry I only have one leg" (even when the speaker has two legs but wants to avoid a sales pitch).[27]

(5)  Avoidance. One way to answer a question or an offer is to avoid responding directly.

140

- If a boy comes to visit a girl, don't be at home to him.
- If offered food you don't like, say "I like X more."
- How do you like my dress?
  It's interesting (i.e., the addressee doesn't like it; interesting is a nondescript word with no real meaning here).

(6)  General acceptance of an offer but giving no details.

- In the United States, "drop in any time" is not an invitation.
- In Arabic speaking countries, the following is a negation:
  Let's have a picnic next Saturday?
  Imshaallah (God willing) (equivalent to "no").
  But Imshaallah plus time and details (equivalent to "yes").

150

- In Taiwan: I'll come but . . . (equal to "no").

(7)  Divert and distract[28] the addressee.

- In Hawaiian culture when a leader at a meeting begins to be too bossy,[29] he may find two kinds of refusal of his orders:
  —silence and a lack of enthusiasm (a hostile response)
  —playful questions and misbehavior (breaks up tension)

---

[27]**a sales pitch:** A planned speech by someone trying to sell something.

[28]**distract:** Draw or take attention away; divert.
[29]**bossy:** To act like a boss or one in charge.

- In the U.S., diverting a question is done by questioning the question.
160
- How old are you?
  Why do you ask? How old do you think? (Weiser, 1975).
- Address the speech act but not the content.
  —Please close the door.
  —Why?

Many of the above-mentioned seven approaches to saying 'no' are found in every culture. A foreigner has trouble when the relation between form and meaning are not the same in two different cultures. For example,

170    (1) Silence may mean "no" in one culture but "maybe" in another. In the U.S. if you don't receive an answer to an inquiry, it means "no." However, in Britain it means "maybe" or "I'll write later when I have something to say." Among the Western Apache, silence is used when meeting strangers, during the initial stages of courting,[30] when children come home, when being cussed out,[31] and when one is with people who are sad. Basso (1972) notes that "keeping silent among the Western Apache is a response to uncertainty and unpredictability in social relations" (p. 83).

(2) Verbal cues may give one message but nonverbal cues another. An example is that of a Toradjan in Indonesia who worked as a
180    laborer in a school headed by a British principal. The laborer always said "yes" but let her know by his body position that he didn't intend to do it.

(3) Societies differ in how food is offered and accepted and rejected:

- In the U.S., a hostess will offer more food usually only once.
  —Have some more.
  —No, thanks I'm really full.
  —O.K.
- In parts of the Arab world and many other parts of the world one
190    mustn't accept food the first or second time it is offered; however, refusal the third time is definitive.[32]

---

[30]**courting:** Social contact directed at marriage.    [32]**definitive:** Final; conclusive.
[31]**cussed out:** Scolded.

| Host | Guest |
|------|-------|
| —Have some. | —I'm full. |
| —I know you're full but have some more for X's sake.[33] | —As much as I like X, I do have to refuse. |
| —For my sake, have some. I cooked the food. | —For your sake, I'll take some. (May then leave it on the plate.) |

- An anecdote[34] was recounted[35] by an Arab speaker's first    200
encounter with some Americans. On his first visit to an American
home, he was served some delicious sandwiches. When the
hostess came to offer seconds, he refused. Much to his chagrin,[36]
the hostess didn't repeat the offer. Thus, the Arab sat there,
confronted by[37] some lovely sandwiches which he couldn't eat.

(4)   In France, when offered something, the best refusal is
"merci." The translation of this word is "thanks" but it means "no,
thanks." In the U.S. "thanks" means "yes, thanks."

(5)   Jakobson (1972) showed that head movements for "yes" and
"no" differ from culture to culture.                                              210

One of the more interesting observations about "no" is that
sometimes "no" may mean "maybe" given the right time and
circumstances. This is a quite important function in boy-girl relations
and in politics. An example of this function is shown by the following
sex-biased[38] joke:

> What's the difference between a lady[39] and a diplomat?
> When a diplomat says "yes," he means maybe.
> When a diplomat says "maybe," he means no.
> When a diplomat says "no," he's no diplomat.
> When a lady says "no," she means "maybe."                                      220
> When a lady says "maybe," she means "yes."
> When a lady says "yes," she's no lady!!!

It becomes important to know when a "no" is negotiable. Members in

---

[33]**for X's sake:** For the benefit of someone; in this case, to please someone.
[34]**anecdote:** A short, usually funny story about something that happens.
[35]**recounted:** Told.
[36]**chagrin:** Feeling of disappointment, annoyance, or embarrassment.
[37]**confronted by:** Face to face with.
[38]**sex-biased:** In this case, prejudiced against women.
[39]**lady:** In this case, a high class woman with good manners.

their own society need to know when a "no" is negotiable. Children, employees, and diplomats most often need to learn this quickly.

## ∾ Social Parameters of Saying 'No' ∾

All of these examples lead us to be careful not to assume that similar forms have the same function cross-culturally. We also know that we shouldn't assume that the task is one of merely finding the proper form
230 to express a function. The form-function relationship is just the tip of the iceberg.[40] We also need to consider how the performance of the speech act is related to social structure (that is, how you should address superiors, equals, respected persons and how this relates to your own status).[41] In some cultures children can be more direct than in others. In addition, we need to consider how the speech act is related to a whole set of values attached to these behaviors.

Some of the social features that can be spelled out[42] are as follows. In many societies, it is more important how you say "no" than the answer itself. It is more important to maintain proper social relations than
240 to be definitive.

Some examples which are related to social structure features are listed below:

- In Korea, when old men offer younger men food, the younger one may not refuse.
- In the Marshall Islands, one is not permitted to say "no" to a chief's son.
- In Poland, the older a person is, the harder it is to refuse.
- In Taiwan, the closer a relative is, the easier it is to say "no."

Saying "no" is also related to the variety of language used by the
250 respondent:

In some Arab groups, when you are invited to a feast, if the addressee responds in colloquial Arabic[43] and says, "Yes, sure I'll come," the speaker knows that the person will come. However, if the speaker responds using some classical Arabic,[44] his response means "no."

In many societies a higher value is placed on maintaining social relations than in getting an answer. For example, in the Philippines, one tries to avoid the embarrassing situation where someone can say "no"

[40]**tip of the iceberg:** The small tip or top of a huge block or mountain of ice that can be seen on the surface of the ocean; in this case, Rubin means that only the beginning of the subject is being considered.

[41]**status:** Position.
[42]**spelled out:** Described.
[43]**colloquial Arabic:** Conversational Arabic.
[44]**classical Arabic:** Formal Arabic used for special occasions and in literature.

directly to you. Instead you send out "feelers."[45] For example, if you
want to be invited to a party you might say to a person whom you know
is giving a party: I hear that you are a good cook/have a nice place. The       260
addresseé may refuse by saying: "It's only for extended family." Or, if
you want to get a job for some relative, you may send out a feeler (so as
not to be faced with a refusal). An example of this kind of transaction is:

- By the way, I hear you have a job to fill. I have a nephew who is
  hard-working and who lives not too far away.
  If yes, discuss his merits for the job.
  If no, shift responsibility to a third party by saying, "There's a
  committee deciding it."
- If employees want raises in salaries, they may send out a feeler
  telling a sob story,[46] telling how much in need of money they are.       270
  Boss can refuse by saying how bad sales are going or how tight
  the budget is this year.

In Taiwan, where there seems to be a similar effort to maintain
social relations and to avoid embarrassing situations, to get a job one
would go through an intermediary. Likewise to find a marriage partner,
Taiwanese would go through a broker. The broker (usually a friend),
would arrange a gathering of the three sides by going to a show or pre-
paring a meal. The girl can indicate her interest or lack thereof by whether
she will sit by the boy or not.

In the Arab world, it is common to use a go-between to get a job,       280
arrange a marriage, or get into a private school so that a direct refusal is
prevented. However, unlike the Philippines, in arranging a job for a
relative, one may tell the employer that there is a candidate who is
worthless but who will shine under the tutelage[47] of the employer.

On occasion in maintaining good social relations, one may not say
no, yet if one cannot fully comply,[48] one should do something to indicate good will. For example, in Taiwan and the Trust Territory,[49] invitees
to a party, funeral, or wedding must show they are a part of the community by attending. However, if this is impossible, they should either
show up, if only for a few minutes, or send a representative, friend, or       290
child.

In some cases, social relations may be such that people only understand the interchange if they know both the question and the answer.

[45]**feelers:** Sense organs, as on the head of an
insect; in this case, a remark or suggestion to find
out how other people feel about something.
[46]**sob story:** A story so sad that it would make the
listener cry (sob).
[47]**tutelage:** Teaching; direction.
[48]**comply:** Meet the requirements.

[49]**Trust Territory:** In this case, dependencies of
Taiwan.

For example, in Taiwan if food is offered and the guest refuses, and if food is not offered again, he/she may feel that the host/hostess is stingy.[50] The whole speech act consists of a series of questions and answers. In India, if people are offered food once and refuse, and if no second offer is made, they may recognize that the first offer was just a formality. In Indonesia, if people ask a wrong question (i.e., one that shouldn't be asked), then they may get a strange answer. For example, if a girl is asked by her sister-in-law whether she has a boyfriend, she will deny it because she is embarrassed to admit having one.

Recognizing a "no" not only depends on finding the proper form-function relationship, it depends as well on the setting and social structure which dictate[51] how and when "no" may be said. Interpretation of a negative is also related to underlying values in a society. In many cases, the problem is not one of truth and forthrightness;[52] rather it is one of how people like to be treated and talked to.

## ✎ Values ✎

The following is an example of two clashing value systems:

One time, when looking for a research assistant, I checked with the chairman of one of the departments to find some likely candidates. I interviewed several students and, after a month and a half, decided to offer the job to an international student studying in the United States. Since it was in the midst of a school year, I suggested she could work less time until the summer when she could make up the time. She indicated her willingness to take the job. A week later I called her to tell her the job was hers. She called me back the next night and said that she was afraid she wouldn't be able to take it because her husband and child were planning to go to another town and she planned to follow them. I sympathized with her but was a little bothered by having her refuse the offer once having accepted it. The next day I called the chairman of the department to tell him of her refusal of the position. It turned out that she had been in to see him the day before and reported that she couldn't take my job because I had insisted on her working full time during the semester. She asked the chairman whether she might have a fellowship for the next year. Both the chairman and I were annoyed. In sharp contrast, the student appeared quite at ease with seemingly no recognition of having done anything wrong.

---

[50]**stingy:** Does not like to give away possessions or spend money.

[51]**dictates:** Determines.
[52]**forthrightness:** Frankness; openness.

When we look at what happened, we can see that the form she took to say "no" is a common one in the U.S., namely, use a third party as an excuse, which is a good technique. The message was clear but still we were annoyed. The chairman was annoyed because she had tried to manipulate him and because after all his efforts to get her a job, she had refused to take a good one. I was annoyed because I had spent so much time finding the right person. Each of us interpreted the transaction differently, even though the form, function, and the social setting were shared. That is, it was clear she had refused. It was clear that she was using third party blaming to someone superior in status. However, the    340 chairman was annoyed because he felt he was manipulated and I was annoyed because time is money and mine had been wasted. She wasn't uncomfortable at all because she had done her job well vis-à-vis social relations.

## ∾ Conclusions ✍

Sending and receiving "no" messages requires three levels of knowledge. Visitors to unfamiliar countries who hope to develop communicative competence in sending and receiving messages must, first of all, find the appropriate form-function relationship. Next, they must learn which social parameters enter into the speech act. Finally, they    350 need to understand the underlying values of a society. Saying "no" is not, as many people suppose, simply finding the proper form-function relationship. That is only the tip of the iceberg. Visitors to another country need to probe more deeply if they are to express themselves adequately and to interpret messages sent by native speakers correctly.

## ∾ References ✍

Basso, K. H. 1972. "To Give Up on Words' Silence in Western Apache Culture," in *Language at Social Context* ed. by P. P. Giglioli. Baltimore, Penguin.

Jakobson, Roman. 1972. "Motor Signs for 'Yes' and 'No'," *Language in Society,* 1:1:91–96.

Ueda, Keiko. 1974. "Sixteen Ways to Avoid Saying 'no' in Japan," in *Intercultural Encounters with Japan. Communication Contact and Conflict* ed. by John C. Condon and Mitsuko Saito. Tokyo: The Simul Press.

Weiser, Ann. 1975. "How to Answer a Question: Purposive Devices in a Conversational Strategies," unpublished paper given at the Chicago Linguistic Meetings (April).

**1.** In "How to Tell When Someone Is Saying 'No'," Joan Rubin uses the terms *form-function relationship, social parameters,* and *underlying values.* Test your understanding of these terms by matching the term in column A with the statement in column B that best illustrates it. Write the appropriate number (1, 2, 3) before the term.

| *A* | *B* |
|---|---|
| _____ form-function relationship | 1. In country X, use a sharp, hissing noise (*sssss*) to attract the attention of clerks in markets and stores only. Hotel clerks, bank tellers, and government employees will be insulted if you use (*ssss*) to get their attention. |
| _____ social parameters | |
| _____ underlying values | |
| | 2. To get the attention of a store clerk or salesperson in country X, say "Here" followed by a sharp, hissing noise (*ssss*). |
| | 3. People in country X are never in a hurry, so you should not feel that you are being ignored if clerks or salespersons do not immediately respond to your attempt to attract their attention. |

Give examples of your own which show that you understand how Rubin is using these terms.

**2.** To show that form-function relationships do not always extend across cultures, Rubin uses examples of a Turk moving his head backward and his eyes upward to express negation, an Indian rolling his head from side to side to convey or get across the idea "go on, I'm listening," and a

Frenchman answering "merci" to refuse something offered him.

1. How would the responses of the Turk, the Indian, and the Frenchman most likely be interpreted by a native speaker of English?
2. How would these responses be interpreted by people of other cultures?
3. Can you think of other gestures or verbal expressions to signal "no" that might cause cross-cultural misunderstanding?

3. To illustrate an idiosyncratic or highly individualistic way of sending and receiving messages, Rubin gives an example of a student who knew how to avoid getting "no" answers from her father. In this instance, Rubin is contrasting individual or idiosyncratic behavior patterns with group or societal patterns.

1. Can you think of ways you or other people have of saying "no" that illustrate individual rather than group behavior patterns?
2. Write a short composition in which you describe the way you or someone you know manipulates or handles a particular person to avoid getting "no" answers. In your composition (a) identify the relationship between the two people; (b) describe the kinds of situations or requests that would ordinarily produce "no" answers; (c) describe the techniques the "manipulator" uses to be certain of getting a "yes" answer.

4. Rubin says that we can all give examples of misunderstanding a negative message while living in a foreign culture. Describe her experiences and any experiences that you or others have had with this problem.

5. Although Rubin presents all three of the ideas below, only one is the main point of the paper. Check the main point.

_____ 1. Language teaching places too much emphasis on the form-function relationship.

_____ 2. One must interpret a speech act on three levels in order to understand it.

_____ 3. Foreigners misunderstand speech acts because they are not aware of underlying cultural values.

Do you agree with *1*? What are the three levels of knowledge she speaks of in *2*? Explain *3*.

6. Rubin says that the seven approaches to saying "no" she discusses in her paper are found in many cultures but that foreigners have problems when form and meaning in their culture and the target culture do not match (see lines 169-222). Discuss each example in relation to your own experience, adding whatever comments and examples you may have.

7. What do you think would be the appropriate ways to say "no" in the following situations in the United States or in another English-speaking culture?

    1. You are invited to dinner by a close friend.
    2. Your employer invites you to a party.
    3. The father of a friend of yours offers you a job.
    4. A clerk in a store tries to sell you something you don't want.
    5. An acquaintance of yours phones and asks whether he (or she) can come to your house to see you.
    6. A classmate asks you to go to a disco.
    7. At dinner, your host offers you some food you don't like.
    8. Your teacher gives you an assignment you don't like.

    If these same situations occurred in another country, how would you handle them?

8. How people like to be treated and talked to is often related to their underlying values. Do you think Rubin's example of the clash of two value systems within the same culture (the values held by the prospective research assistant and the values shared by Rubin and the department chairman) illustrates this point? How do you think you would have reacted in this situation or a similar one? How do you generally like to be treated and addressed when someone refuses an invitation you have extended or an offer you have made?

9. Describe an experience of your own in saying "no" that clearly illustrates a clash in value systems. How did you feel about the situation? How did the other person or persons feel? What was the final outcome?

10. Assume that the following situations have occurred in the United States or another English-speaking culture. Decide when and how you might bring up the subject and what you might say.

    1. You have heard some of your classmates talking about a picnic next weekend. You haven't been told about it, but you would like to be included.
    2. Your professor has returned a paper to you with a B+ grade. You feel that you deserve at least an A − and want to talk to the professor about raising your grade.
    3. You hear that your history professor needs a student assistant to help correct papers. You want your sister, who is a history major, to get the job.

11. Choose one of the three situations in question 10 and write a composition based on class discussion or your own ideas. Here are some suggestions:

    1. First, identify the function: how to get an invitation to a social gathering; how to get a grade raised; or how to help someone get a job.
    2. Then, suggest the forms (sentences, expressions, etc.) that might be used in carrying out the functions.
    3. Next, explain the social parameters (setting and social features) that will determine when and how the forms you have identified can be used.
    4. Finally, discuss the underlying cultural values that explain how people in the United States expect to be treated or spoken to in this situation.

12. Write a composition in which you compare how the function you selected in question 11 is handled in your native language and culture. In your discussion, clarify the ways in which points 2, 3, and 4 in question 11 are the same as or different from the situation in an English-speaking culture.

# A LOOK AT THE LANGUAGE

1. In the Rubin essay, the same word frequently appears in a different form—for example, *appropriate* (adjective), *appropriately* (adverb); *interpret* (verb), *interpretation* (noun). Fill in the blanks in these sentences with the appropriate form of the *italicized* words.

    1. A "no" answer can be *ambiguous.* _____ is fairly common, in fact.

    2. A *competent* speaker of a language knows how to receive and send "no" messages. A person learning a language should try to develop this _____.

    3. One must be aware of the *appropriate* conditions for saying "no." In other words, one must consider the _____ of the response.

    4. Individuals are often *idiosyncratic* in sending "no" messages. One must, therefore, consider _____ as well as cultural patterning.

    5. It is relatively easy to *discern* the form-function relationship of a speech act, but _____ of details of a value system is another matter.

    6. For most of us, getting an answer may be more important than *maintaining* social relations, but in the Philippines higher value is placed on _____ of the latter.

    7. When one is expected to *comply* with social customs, one should try to show goodwill if full _____ is impossible.

2. Complete the sentences to the right with a phrase containing the noun form of the word in *italics*.

    1. He *denied* her request.
       His _____ was expected.

    2. We were surprised that he *refused* the invitation.
       We were surprised by his _____.

    3. They *affirmed* the policy.
       _____ was necessary.

4. It is unfortunate that      _____ is unfortunate.
   the lecture has been
   *postponed*.

5. His action *exemplified*     His action was an
   tact.                        _____ of tact.

6. They *recognized* the        The first step is _____.
   problem.

Do the sentences in the right column seem more formal
than those in the left column? In what kind of writing would
you be more likely to find sentences of this kind?

3. The focus of this exercise is on the use of *linking*—one of the
   four devices writers use to relate parts of a passage. (For
   further explanation of these devices, see Steinbeck, "A
   Look at the Language," question 4, page 12.) Linking or
   sequence signals like *however, for example,* or *conversely* tell
   us what is to follow. When you see "for example," you
   expect an illustration of a preceding point or statement.
   When you see "however," you expect a contrasting statement. When you see "conversely," you expect an opposite
   example, and so on.

   Look at the two paragraphs below: (a) Explain the purpose
   of each *italicized* word or phrase. What can we expect to
   follow—an explanation, an example, a contrasting statement, an equivalent point or statement, and so on? (b) For
   each *italicized* word or phrase, list as many synonyms
   (words with the same meaning) or related words as you
   can. (c) Decide whether substitution of any of the synonyms
   or related words requires a change in the structure of the
   sentence.

   1. One of the more important communicative tasks that
      confronts a traveler is the recognition of when a speaker
      has said "no." *That is,* one needs to be able to recognize
      that a respondent has refused or denied that which the
      speaker has demanded, solicited, or offered. *Equally,* one
      needs to acquire the appropriate manner in which to
      respond in the negative when offered, solicited, or de-
      manded something. *Granted that* it is sometimes difficult
      to recognize a refusal in one's mother tongue where the
      answer might be ambiguous or deliberately obscure.

*Nonetheless,* in many encounters the meaning is clear if one knows how to read the appropriate signals.

The first phrase—*that is*—is done for you:

(a) Purpose: explanatory; we can expect restatement of the idea to follow

(b) Synonyms or related words for *that is*: that is to say; in other words; I mean

(c) Necessary changes in the structure: a change is required only for "I mean," which requires a *that* clause—"I mean (that) . . ."

2. . . . If we compare form and function across cultures, it soon becomes clear that one form may be used to mean different things in another culture than in one's own. *For example,* in Turkish "no" is signaled by moving one's head backwards while rolling one's eyes upwards. *However,* to an American this movement is close to the signal used for saying "yes." *Further,* in still other cultures, head shaking may have nothing to do with affirmation or negation. In parts of India, rolling the head slowly from side to side means something like "Yes, go on. I'm listening." *Thus,* as one goes from culture to culture, form and function may not match.

4. The organization of this article is quite typical of papers written for science and social sciences journals. Typically, papers of this kind have three main parts: *introduction, body or discussion,* and *conclusion.* Examine the organization of the Rubin paper and answer the following questions:

   1. Does this essay have three main parts? If so, tell where each part begins and ends. Where does Rubin mention the purpose of the essay? What is her thesis or main idea?

   2. Does each main part have a heading? Which main part is divided into subparts (smaller parts)? How many subparts are there? Are all the subjects equally developed?

   3. Does the last main part present new information? What is its purpose?

5. Based on your examination of the content and organization of the Rubin essay (question 4 above), write a brief summary of the article. You might begin: *In the essay "How to Tell When Someone Is Saying 'No,'"* Joan Rubin says that . . .

## Ernest Hemingway (1899-1961)

*Ernest Hemingway was born in Oak Park, near Chicago. After leaving high school, he worked on the* Kansas City Star—*a newspaper known for its high standards—and there learned a great deal about exactness and style in reporting. Later, his experiences in World War I gave him material for many of his short stories and some of his novels, including* The Sun Also Rises *(1926) and* A Farewell to Arms *(1929). During the Spanish Civil War, he went to Spain to write newspaper articles and there gained background for the novel* For Whom the Bell Tolls *(1940). In 1954 he was awarded the Nobel Prize for Literature.*

*In this story from* Winner Take Nothing *(1933), Hemingway shows the feelings of a boy who, through a misunderstanding, undergoes a shattering experience. This very short story on the surface may seem to be only a simple anecdote. On another level, though, it has a serious theme.*

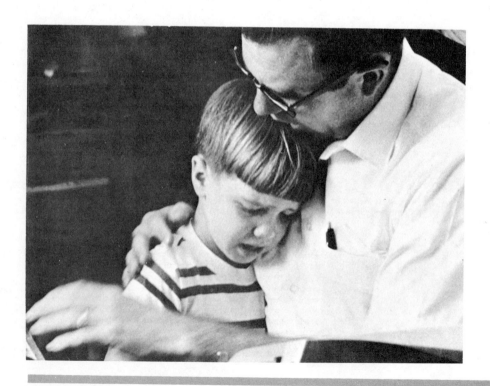

# 12

# A Day's Wait

He came into the room to shut the windows while we were still in bed and I saw he looked ill. He was shivering,[1] his face was white,[2] and he walked slowly as though it ached to move.

"What's the matter, Schatz?"[3]

"I've got a headache."

"You better go back to bed."

"No. I'm all right."

"You go to bed. I'll see you when I'm dressed."

But when I came downstairs he was dressed, sitting by the fire, looking a very sick and miserable boy of nine years. When I put my hand on his forehead[4] I knew he had a fever.[5]    10

"You go up to bed," I said, "you're sick."

"I'm all right," he said.

When the doctor came he took the boy's temperature.[6]

---

[1]**shivering:** Shaking as if cold.
[2]**white:** Pale, lacking in color.
[3]**Schatz:** A German term of endearment roughly equivalent to "darling." (The use of this term indicates that the family in the story has some acquaintance with European customs and culture.)
[4]**forehead:** Part of the face from the hairline to the eyebrows.

[5]**fever:** Degree of temperature over the normal of 98.6 Fahrenheit.
[6]**took the boy's temperature:** Put a thermometer in the boy's mouth to determine the degree of temperature.

"What is it?" I asked him.

"One hundred and two."[7]

Downstairs, the doctor left three different medicines in different colored capsules with instructions for giving them. One was to bring down the fever, another a purgative,[8] the third to overcome an acid condition. The germs of influenza can only exist in an acid condition, he explained. He seemed to know all about influenza[9] and said there was nothing to worry about if the fever did not go above one hundred and four degrees. This was a light epidemic of flu[10] and there was no danger if you avoided pneumonia.[11]

Back in the room I wrote the boy's temperature down and made a note of the time to give the various capsules.

"Do you want me to read to you?"

"All right. If you want to," said the boy. His face was very white and there were dark areas under his eyes. He lay still in the bed and seemed very detached[12] from what was going on.[13]

I read aloud from Howard Pyle's *Book of Pirates*; but I could see he was not following what I was reading.

"How do you feel, Schatz?" I asked him.

"Just the same, so far," he said.

I sat at the foot of the bed and read to myself while I waited for it to be time to give another capsule. It would have been natural for him to go to sleep, but when I looked up he was looking at the foot of the bed, looking very strangely.

"Why don't you try to sleep? I'll wake you up for the medicine."

"I'd rather stay awake."

After a while he said to me, "You don't have to stay in here with me, Papa, if it bothers you."[14]

"It doesn't bother me."

"No, I mean you don't have to stay if it's going to bother you."

I thought perhaps he was a little lightheaded[15] and after giving him the prescribed capsules at eleven o'clock I went out for a while. It was a bright, cold day, the ground covered with a sleet[16] that had frozen so that it seemed as if all the bare trees, the bushes, the cut brush[17] and all the grass and the bare ground had been varnished[18] with ice. I took the

---

[7]**one hundred and two:** 102 degrees Fahrenheit, almost 39 degrees Celsius.

[8]**purgative:** Laxative (a medicine to produce bowel movements).

[9]**influenza** (later referred to as "flu"): A disease usually accompanied by upset stomach, muscular pain, and inflammation—redness and swelling—of the nose and throat.

[10]**a light epidemic of flu:** Flu had spread to several people in the community but not many.

[11]**pneumonia:** Inflammation of the lungs, a serious illness.

[12]**detached:** Removed; far away.

[13]**going on:** Taking place.

[14]**bothers you:** Disturbs you; makes you uncomfortable.

[15]**lightheaded:** Dizzy and faint.

[16]**sleet:** Combination of rain and snow.

[17]**brush:** Low bushes and weeds.

[18]**varnished:** Covered as with a polish.

young Irish setter[19] for a walk up the road and along a frozen creek,[20]  50
but it was difficult to stand or walk on the glassy surface and the red dog
slipped and slithered[21] and I fell twice, hard, once dropping my gun and
having it slide away over the ice.

We flushed a covey of quail[22] under a high clay bank with overhanging brush[23] and I killed two as they went out of sight over the top of
the bank. Some of the covey lit[24] in trees, but most of them scattered[25]
into brush piles and it was necessary to jump on the ice-coated mounds
of brush[26] several times before they would flush.[27] Coming out while
you were poised[28] unsteadily on the icy, springy[29] brush they made
difficult shooting and I killed two, missed five, and started back pleased  60
to have found a covey close to the house and happy there were so many
left to find on another day.

At the house they said the boy had refused to let any one come into
the room.

"You can't come in," he said. "You mustn't get what I have."[30]

I went up to him and found him in exactly the position I had left
him, white-faced, but with the tops of his cheeks flushed[31] by the fever,
staring still, as he had stared, at the foot of the bed.

I took his temperature.

"What is it?"                                                                          70

"Something like a hundred," I said. It was one hundred and two
and four tenths.

"It was a hundred and two," he said.

"Who said so?"

"The doctor."

"Your temperature is all right," I said, "It's nothing to worry
about."

"I don't worry," he said, "but I can't keep from thinking."[32]

"Don't think," I said. "Just take it easy."

"I'm taking it easy," he said and looked straight ahead. He was  80
evidently holding tight onto himself[33] about something.

"Take this with water."

---

[19]**Irish setter:** Type of dog with red hair; a hunting dog.

[20]**creek:** Small stream.

[21]**slithered:** Slid unsteadily.

[22]**flushed a covey of quail:** Drove or forced out a group of small birds (quail). Note: *quail* is both singular and plural—a quail, *three* quail, etc.

[23]**clay bank with overhanging brush:** A small clay (a type of soil) cliff with bushes, weeds, and branches hanging over the edge.

[24]**lit:** Landed or settled.

[25]**scattered:** Went off in all directions.

[26]**mounds of brush:** Piles of little hills of brush.

[27]**flush:** Come out.

[28]**poised:** Balanced.

[29]**springy:** Quality of flexibility (as a spring moving up and down).

[30]**mustn't get what I have:** Mustn't catch the illness I have.

[31]**cheeks flushed:** Sides of the face rosy or reddened by flow of blood to the face.

[32]**I can't keep from thinking:** I can't stop thinking.

[33]**holding tight onto himself:** Keeping firm control over himself.

"Do you think it will do any good?"

"Of course it will."

I sat down and opened the *Pirate* book and commenced to read, but I could see he was not following, so I stopped.

"About what time do you think I'm going to die?" he asked.

"What?"

"About how long will it be before I die?"

90 "You aren't going to die. What's the matter with you?"

"Oh, yes, I am. I heard him say a hundred and two."

"People don't die with a fever of one hundred and two. That's a silly way to talk."

"I know they do. At school in France the boys told me you can't live with forty-four degrees. I've got a hundred and two."

He had been waiting to die all day, ever since nine o'clock in the morning.

"You poor Schatz," I said. "Poor old Schatz. It's like miles and kilometers. You aren't going to die. That's a different thermometer. On

100 that thermometer thirty-seven is normal. On this kind it's ninety-eight."

"Are you sure?"

"Absolutely," I said. "It's like miles and kilometers. You know, like how many kilometers we make when we do seventy miles in the car?"

"Oh," he said.

But his gaze at the foot of the bed relaxed slowly. The hold over himself relaxed too, finally, and the next day it was very slack[34] and he cried very easily at little things that were of no importance.

[34]**slack:** Loose; no longer tense; relaxed.

---
## A LOOK AT THE IDEAS
---

1. Summarize the situation at the beginning of the story. Comment on (a) what time of day it was; (b) how the boy acted and what his symptoms were; (c) what the father's response was; (d) what the doctor said and did; (e) what the boy's temperature actually was, and what he thought it was and why.

2. How did the boy respond when his father was reading to him? What do you believe he was thinking about? Why didn't he want to go to sleep? How did he feel when his

father left the room? If you were in the boy's situation, how do you think you would react at this point?

**3.** Which words would you use to describe the boy and his father? Write *B* for the boy and *F* for the father next to the appropriate words. (This exercise can be done individually or in groups.)

| | | |
|---|---|---|
| 1. ___ patient | 8. ___ happy | 15. ___ rigid |
| 2. ___ tense | 9. ___ pleased | 16. ___ casual |
| 3. ___ fearful | 10. ___ controlled | 17. ___ spoiled |
| 4. ___ slack | 11. ___ concerned | 18. ___ loving |
| 5. ___ cruel | 12. ___ brave | 19. ___ miserable |
| 6. ___ considerate | 13. ___ relaxed | 20. ___ silly |
| 7. ___ manly | 14. ___ thoughtless | 21. ___ passive |

What other words or phrases would you use to describe the two characters?

**4.** Although this is a very short, tightly constructed story that progresses almost entirely through dialogue, the author devotes two long paragraphs to the father's walk through the woods with his hunting dog. At first glance, the hunting scene seems to have little to do with the main plot. Check the statement or statements that you think most likely represent Hemingway's reasons for the description.

___ 1. It shows that the father was essentially thoughtless since he went out to enjoy himself.

___ 2. It creates a sense of time passing so that we know it is close to evening by the time he gets home.

___ 3. It suggests a contrast between the robust activities outside and the terrible tension of the boy inside.

___ 4. It diverts the reader so that the boy's real thoughts will be a greater surprise when they are revealed.

___ 5. It shows that the father didn't realize what the boy was thinking or he wouldn't have gone out.

___ 6. Since killing small birds and animals seems to be a frequent activity for the father, and perhaps for the boy too, it suggests that the boy is familiar with death.

_____ 7. It shows that the father is financially comfortable or well off since he apparently didn't have to go to work.

_____ 8. It gives Hemingway an opportunity to show that he can write very complex, interesting sentences.

What other reasons can you think of for including the hunting scene?

5. Although the story is told from the father's point of view, there are many hints about what Schatz is thinking and feeling. Read each of the statements below, and tell what the father thinks is going on and what Schatz is really thinking and feeling.

1. It would have been natural for him to go to sleep, but when I looked up he was looking at the foot of the bed, looking very strangely. (lines 36-38)

2. I went up to him and found him in exactly the same position I had left him, . . . staring still, as he had stared, at the foot of the bed. (lines 66-68)

3. He was evidently holding tight onto himself about something. (lines 80-81)

4. But his gaze at the foot of the bed relaxed slowly. (line 106)

Find other statements which suggest what the boy is really thinking and feeling, or which show problems of communication between father and son.

6. The very last sentence of the story describes how the boy reacted when he realized he wasn't going to die: "The hold over himself relaxed too, finally, and the next day it was very slack and he cried very easily at little things that were of no importance." What does this mean?

_____ 1. He had been so tense that he couldn't control his emotions when he finally relaxed.

_____ 2. He was usually a relaxed boy who often complained about unimportant things.

_____ 3. He had waited so long to die that in a sense he was disappointed.

Does his behavior the next morning seem natural to you? Explain.

7. Although we know that it was a misunderstanding of the expression "one hundred and two" that made the nine-year-old boy think he was going to die, the experience nonetheless was a real crisis for him. Do you think he showed courage in meeting this crisis? If so, what instances in the story show his courage? If you think he did not show courage, explain.

8. On the basis of ideas suggested in "A Day's Wait," do you think Hemingway would agree or disagree with the following statements? What is your opinion about each statement? Circle the correct letter for Hemingway and for yourself after each statement.

A – Strongly agree     C – Somewhat disagree
B – Somewhat agree     D – Strongly disagree

|  | Hemingway | You |
|---|---|---|
| 1. Since there is nothing frightening about death, the boy cannot be considered brave. | A B C D | A B C D |
| 2. Since many adults fear death, it must be even more frightening to children. | A B C D | A B C D |
| 3. Since children know nothing about death, they can't possibly be frightened by it. | A B C D | A B C D |
| 4. Since after death one can expect to have a happy existence of another kind, one should look forward to dying without fear. | A B C D | A B C D |

9. In this story, Hemingway gives us a limited amount of information about the boy and his father. He doesn't tell us, for example, exactly where the boy and his father were when the boy became ill, whether the boy had brothers and sisters, where his mother was when he became ill, or what his father's occupation was. He apparently gives us only those details that he considers essential to an understanding of the story.

   1. First, list the details that give us some information about (a) the nature of the boy's illness; (b) the doctor's visit;

(c) the boy's relationship with his father; (d) the boy's contact with European culture; (e) the boy's courage; (f) the kind of person the boy's father was; (g) the general setting of the story—the type of place.

2. Then, tell why this information is important to an understanding of the story. For example, why is the doctor's visit important? What is the significance of the boy's contact with European culture? What does the setting contribute to your understanding of the story?

3. What other details do you think Hemingway might have included in the story? How would the addition of those details change the story? Explain.

10. The theme of a short story is a general statement of the main point or message the writer wants to convey. Authors frequently use the same theme in different stories, changing the characters, details, and events or plot. The theme of "A Day's Wait," for example, is found in several of Hemingway's stories and gives us some understanding of his philosophy of life.

What is the theme of "A Day's Wait"?

_____ 1. One should communicate one's fears to others to avoid misunderstanding.

_____ 2. To control one's emotions and fears when facing death is a mark of courage.

_____ 3. Children cannot be expected to understand something as complex as death.

_____ 4. Misunderstandings can occur even though a relationship is a close one.

_____ 5. None of the above.

If you choose number 5, tell what you think the theme is.

Very often a title, a sentence, or a phrase tells the reader what the theme is. Find the phrases of sentences in the story that you believe are important clues to or illustrations of the theme.

11. Hemingway often thought of courage as a person's ability to be calm and controlled in the face of death. Do you agree or disagree with that kind of definition of courage? Are

there other ways that you think courage can be defined? Write a composition in which you define courage. Here are some suggestions:

1. Begin your essay with an introductory paragraph that ends with a statement of your own definition of courage. This statement is your *thesis* statement—or statement of your main idea.

2. Then, open your next paragraph with a transitional phrase or sentence that allows you to move from your thesis to an explanation of what you mean. For example, you could open your second paragraph with such statements as these:

   *By this definition of courage, I mean . . .*
   *One example of the behavior I see as courageous is . . .*
   *Many kinds of behavior fit my definition. For example . . .*

   It would be a good idea to include one or two illustrations or examples to clarify what courage means to you. You may want to use a separate paragraph for each illustration. If you do, connect these paragraphs with appropriate transitions. For instance, you can use such phrases or sentences as:

   *Here is another example . . .*
   *But (or However) this is not the only kind of courage . . .*
   *Although my first example of courage illustrates my definition, still another pattern of behavior can be called courageous.*

   Words like *but, however, nevertheless, therefore, indeed,* and *of course* are useful for transitions.

3. Finally, conclude your composition by briefly summing up your most important ideas. A conclusion is for emphasis and summary of *main ideas.* If you include too many ideas and details, the conclusion will be too repetitious to be effective. The transitional words you want for your conclusion should carry a sense of finality or summary: *Then, Thus, Finally, So, Therefore, In conclusion.* Your very last sentence can be a restatement of your original thesis.

1. Below are four sets of sentences. The first sentence in each set is from the Hemingway selection; the other four are not. (a) What does the *italicized* word or phrase in the first sentence mean? (b) Does the *italicized* word or phrase have the same meaning in the other sentences? (c) Are the last four sentences in each set idiomatic? Would a native speaker of English be likely to use the word or phrase in this way?

1. "It doesn't *bother* me."

   He didn't *bother* to call us.

   He is a *bother*.

   Don't *bother* me.

   It is too much *bother* to make fresh coffee.

2. He lay still in bed and seemed very *detached* from what was going on.

   The trailer was *detached* from the truck.

   He was *detached* from his responsibilities.

   I feel very *detached* from my classwork.

   His house was *detached* from the city.

3. One was to *bring down* the fever...

   He plans to *bring down* some friends next weekend.

   The porter will *bring down* your bags in a minute.

   He wants to *bring down* his weight to 150 pounds.

   Is there anything that will *bring down* the price of oil?

4. Coming out while you were *poised* unsteadily on the icy, springy brush they made difficult shooting...

   She was *poised* and charming.

   The cat was *poised* on the fence ready to jump.

   She *poised* her checkbook.

   He *poised* one idea against the other.

2. The *italicized* words and phrases indicate devices that link and relate parts of the passage. Explain what is omitted, referred to, linked, or replaced, and tell how these devices function in relating ideas in the passage. (For further information on this type of exercise, see Steinbeck, "A Look at the Language," question 4, page 12.)

I took his temperature
"What is *it*?"
"*Something* like a hundred," I said. *It* was one hundred and two and four tenths.
"*It* was a hundred and two," he said.
"Who said *so*?"
"*The doctor.*"

3. The misunderstanding between father and son is reflected in their conversation. Look at the *italicized* words in each quotation below. What is each character referring to? What is the misunderstanding?

    1. "You don't have to *stay* in *here* with me, Papa, if *it* bothers you."
       "*It* doesn't bother me."
       "No, I mean you don't have to *stay* if *it's* going to bother you." (lines 41-44)
    2. "Your temperature is all right," I said. "*It's* nothing to *worry* about."
       "I don't *worry*," he said, "but I can't keep from *thinking*." (lines 76-78)
    3. "Take *this* with water."
       "Do you think *it* will do *any good*?"
       "Of course *it will*." (lines 82-84)

    Find other examples where the father and son are each thinking of different things when they talk to one another.

4. The following sentences are from the Hemingway story. (a) First, make short sentences out of each sentence. (b) Then, write one or more sentences of your own, including all the information (but not necessarily all the words) in the short sentences. (c) Finally, compare your own sentences with Hemingway's, and tell how yours and Hemingway's differ in style and effect. The first is done as an example:

    1. He was shivering, his face was white, and he walked slowly as though it ached to move.
       a) Possible short sentences: *He was shivering. His face was white. He walked slowly. He moved. It seemed to hurt him.*
       b) Possible new sentences: *He was shivering and his face was white. It seemed to hurt him to move, so he walked slowly.*

   c) Comments on style and effect: For one thing, the second
      sentence establishes a *direct* cause-effect relationship: *It hurt
      him to move* (cause); *so he walked slowly* (result or effect). The
      cause-effect relationship in Hemingway's sentence is much
      more subtle. This sentence would perhaps be closer to the
      idea conveyed by Hemingway: *He walked slowly, apparently
      because it hurt him to move.*

      Do you agree with these observations? What else can you say
      about the difference in style and effect?

2. But when I came downstairs he was dressed, sitting by
   the fire, looking a very sick and miserable boy of nine
   years.

3. Downstairs, the doctor left three different medicines in
   different colored capsules with instructions for giving
   them.

4. I went up to him and found him in exactly the position I
   had left him, white-faced, but with the tops of his cheeks
   flushed by the fever, staring still, as he had stared, at the
   foot of the bed.

5. Do you think Hemingway's dialogue is realistic—that is,
   does it sound like a real conversation to you? Test your
   impression by reading lines 87-104 aloud with another person, preferably a native speaker of English. Is this the way
   people actually speak? If so, what makes it realistic? What, if
   anything, is not realistic about the conversation?

6. List the main events or happenings in the story and then
   consider the following questions:

   1. Is the story told entirely from the point of view of the
      boy's father? Does Hemingway give us any information
      about people, places, and events that does not come
      through the father?

   2. How does the story progress? Does the father relate the
      events in the order in which they take place? Are there
      any flashbacks to events that happened before the main
      action of the story?

   3. Review your list and write a short summary of the plot or
      main events in chronological order. Compare your

summary with those of other students to see if you have included the same information in the same order. Would someone who read your summary be able to recognize the theme of the story and understand the character of the boy and his father? Why or why not?

# William Carlos Williams (1883-1963)

William Carlos Williams is known primarily as a poet, but he also wrote short stories, novels, and essays. At the same time, he practiced medicine for over forty years in his home town, Rutherford, New Jersey.

In "The Use of Force," first published in Make Light of It in 1950, the main character is a doctor, and the story is told from the doctor's point of view. Williams undoubtedly drew upon his experiences as a physician in the telling of this story; but it is well to remember that it is a piece of fiction, not a case history. This brief story centers around the conflict that arises during the doctor's visit to a sick child. Out of this conflict emerges the theme of "the use of force."

## The Act

There were the roses, in the rain.
Don't cut them, I pleaded.
    They won't last, she said
But they're so beautiful
    where they are.
Agh, we were all beautiful once, she
    said,
and cut them and gave them to me
    in my hand.

—William Carlos Williams

# 13

# The Use

# of

# Force

They were new patients to me, all I had was the name, Olson.[1] "Please come down as soon as you can, my daughter is very sick."

When I arrived I was met by the mother, a big startled[2] looking woman, very clean and apologetic who merely said, "Is this the doctor?" and let me in. "In the back," she added. "You must excuse us, doctor, we have her in the kitchen where it is warm. It is very damp here sometimes."

The child was fully dressed and sitting on her father's lap near the kitchen table. He tried to get up, but I motioned for him not to bother, took off my overcoat and started to look things over. I could see that   10 they were all very nervous, eyeing me up and down distrustfully. As often, in such cases, they weren't telling me more than they had to, it was up to me to tell them;[3] that's why they were spending three dollars on me.

The child was fairly eating me up with her cold, steady eyes, and no expression to her face whatever. She did not move and seemed,

---

[1]**all I had was the name, Olson:** The only information I had was the name of the family, Olson.

[2]**startled:** Alarmed.
[3]**It was up to me to tell them:** It was my responsibility to tell them.

inwardly, quiet;[4] an unusually attractive little thing, and as strong as a heifer[5] in appearance. But her face was flushed,[6] she was breathing rapidly, and I realized that she had a high fever. She had magnificent
20    blonde hair, in profusion.[7] One of those picture children[8] often reproduced in advertising leaflets[9] and the photogravure sections of the Sunday papers.[10]

"She's had a fever for three days," began the father, "and we don't know what it comes from. My wife has given her things,[11] you know, like people do, but it don't do no good.[12] And there's been a lot of sickness around. So we tho't[13] you'd better look her over[14] and tell us what is the matter."

As doctors often do I took a trial shot at it as a point of departure.[15] "Has she had a sore throat?"
30    Both parents answered me together, "No... No, she says her throat don't hurt her."

"Does your throat hurt you?" added the mother to the child. But the little girl's expression didn't change nor did she move her eyes from my face.

"Have you looked?"

"I tried to," said the mother, "but I couldn't see."

As it happens we had been having a number of cases of diphtheria[16] in the school to which this child went during that month and we were all, quite apparently, thinking of that, though no one had
40    as yet spoken of the thing.[17]

"Well," I said, "suppose we take a look at the throat first." I smiled in my best professional manner and asking for the child's first name I said, "Come on, Mathilda, open your mouth and let's take a look at your throat."

Nothing doing.

"Aw, come on," I coaxed,[18] "just open your mouth wide and let

---

[4]**inwardly, quiet:** Calm inside.
[5]**heifer:** A young female cow.
[6]**flushed:** Red because of fever.
[7]**profusion:** Abundance; a large amount.
[8]**picture children:** Appealing children who photograph very well.
[9]**leaflet:** Small section with few pages.
[10]**photogravure sections of the Sunday papers:** A special part of some Sunday newspapers that includes photographs reproduced by a process known as *photogravure* or *gravure* (the pages usually have a brownish or greenish tint).
[11]**has given her things:** Has given her various types of medicine.
[12]**It don't do no good:** It doesn't do any good. ("It don't do no good" is nonstandard speech. You will notice other appearances of *don't* for *doesn't* in

this story. Note that the Olsons use the form, but that the doctor doesn't.)
[13]**tho't** (a variant spelling of *thought*): Thought.
[14]**look her over:** Examine her.
[15]**took a trial shot at it as a point of departure:** Made a guess as a start in determining the type of illness.
[16]**cases of diphtheria:** Occurrences of a contagious disease, characterized by the formation of a false membrane in the throat, produced by a specific bacillus.
[17]**no one had yet spoken of the thing:** No one had mentioned the possibility that the child might have diphtheria.
[18]**coaxed:** Attempted to persuade her (with the words "Aw, come on").

me take a look. Look," I said opening both hands wide,[19] "I haven't anything in my hands. Just open up and let me see."

"Such a nice man," put in the mother. "Look how kind he is to you. Come on, do what he tells you to. He won't hurt you." 50

At that I ground my teeth in disgust. If only they wouldn't use the word "hurt" I might be able to get somewhere. But I did not allow myself to be hurried or disturbed but speaking quietly and slowly I approached the child again.

As I moved my chair a little nearer suddenly with one catlike movement both her hands clawed[20] instinctively for my eyes and she almost reached them too. In fact she knocked my glasses flying and they fell, though unbroken, several feet away from me on the kitchen floor.

Both the mother and father almost turned themselves inside out in embarrassment and apology.[21] "You bad girl," said the mother, taking 60 her and shaking her by one arm. "Look what you've done. The nice man . . ."

"For heaven's sake," I broke in. "Don't call me a nice man to her. I'm here to look at her throat on the chance that she might have diphtheria and possibly die of it. But that's nothing to her. Look here," I said to the child, "we're going to look at your throat. You're old enough to understand what I'm saying. Will you open it now by yourself or shall we have to open it for you?"

Not a move. Even her expression hadn't changed. Her breaths however were coming faster and faster. Then the battle began. I had to 70 do it. I had to have a throat culture[22] for her own protection. But first I told the parents that it was entirely up to them. I explained the danger but said that I would not insist on a throat examination so long as they would take the responsibility.

"If you don't do what the doctor says you'll have to go to the hospital," the mother admonished[23] her severely.

Oh yeah? I had to smile to myself. After all, I had already fallen in love with the savage brat,[24] the parents were contemptible[25] to me. In the ensuing[26] struggle they grew more and more abject,[27] crushed,

---

[19]**opening both hands wide:** Opening both hands with palms up (so that the child could see that there was nothing in them).
[20]**clawed:** Scratched or reached (in the manner of an animal or bird).
[21]**turned themselves inside and out in embarrassment and apology:** Were completely embarrassed and apologized in every possible way.
[22]**throat culture:** A specimen of bacteria from the throat area.

[23]**admonished:** Reprimanded; warned; cautioned.
[24]**savage brat:** Wild, untamed child. ("Brat" generally refers to an unruly child. The term is used either jokingly or scornfully; it is not a synonym for "young child.")
[25]**contemptible:** Deserving of scorn or extreme dislike; despicable.
[26]**ensuing:** Following.
[27]**abject:** Miserable; wretched.

80  exhausted while she surely rose to magnificent heights of insane fury[28]
of effort bred of[29] her terror of me.

The father tried his best, and he was a big man but the fact that she
was his daughter, his shame at her behavior and his dread[30] of hurting
her made him release her just at the critical moment several times when I
had almost achieved success, till I wanted to kill him. But his dread also
that she might have diphtheria made him tell me to go on, go on though
he himself was almost fainting, while the mother moved back and forth
behind us raising and lowering her hands in an agony of apprehension.[31]

"Put her in front of you on your lap," I ordered, "and hold both
90  her wrists."

But as soon as he did the child let out a scream. "Don't, you're
hurting me. Let go of my hands. Let them go I tell you." Then she
shrieked[32] terrifyingly, hysterically.[33] "Stop it! Stop it! You're killing
me!"

"Do you think she can stand it,[34] doctor!" said the mother.

"You get out," said the husband to his wife. "Do you want her to
die of diphtheria?"

"Come on now, hold her," I said.

Then I grasped[35] the child's head with my left hand and tried to get
100  the wooden tongue depressor[36] between her teeth. She fought, with
clenched teeth,[37] desperately![38] But now I also had grown furious—at a
child. I tried to hold myself down[39] but I couldn't. I know how to expose
a throat for inspection. And I did my best. When finally I got the
wooden spatula behind the last teeth and just the point of it into the
mouth cavity, she opened up for an instant but before I could see anything she came down again and gripping the wooden blade between her
molars she reduced it to splinters[40] before I could get it out again.

"Aren't you ashamed," the mother yelled at her. "Aren't you
ashamed to act like that in front of the doctor?"

110  "Get me a smooth-handled spoon of some sort," I told the mother.
"We're going through with this."[41] The child's mouth was already
bleeding. Her tongue was cut and she was screaming in wild hysterical

---

[28]**Insane fury:** Uncontrollable anger.
[29]**bred of:** Produced by; caused by.
[30]**dread:** Fear.
[31]**agony of apprehension:** Great pain or suffering because of fear.
[32]**shrieked:** Screamed loudly and piercingly.
[33]**hysterically:** With uncontrollable emotion.
[34]**Do you think she can stand it:** Do you think she can endure or bear the pain?
[35]**grasped:** Seized.
[36]**wooden tongue depressor:** A narrow, flat wood

instrument used by a doctor to hold down the tongue for a throat examination.
[37]**with clenched teeth:** With teeth held tightly together.
[38]**desperately:** Violently (as a result of her despair and fear that she would lose the struggle).
[39]**hold myself down:** Control myself.
[40]**reduced it to splinters:** Broke the wooden tongue depressor into many small pieces.
[41]**going through with this:** Going to finish this (the examination).

shrieks. Perhaps I should have desisted[42] and come back in an hour or more. No doubt it would have been better. But I have seen at least two children lying dead in bed of neglect in such cases, and feeling that I must get a diagnosis[43] now or never I went at it again. But the worst of it was that I too had got beyond reason.[44] I could have torn the child apart in my own fury and enjoyed it. It was a pleasure to attack her. My face was burning with it.

The damned little brat must be protected against her own idiocy,[45] one says to one's self at such times. Others must be protected against her. It is a social necessity. And all these things are true. But a blind fury, a feeling of adult shame, bred of a longing for muscular release[46] are the operatives.[47] One goes on to the end. 120

In a final unreasoning assault[48] I overpowered the child's neck and jaws. I forced the heavy silver spoon back of her teeth and down her throat till she gagged.[49] And there it was—both tonsils covered with membrane.[50] She had fought valiantly[51] to keep me from knowing her secret. She had been hiding that sore throat for three days at least and lying to her parents in order to escape just such an outcome as this. 130

Now truly she *was* furious. She had been on the defensive before but now she attacked. Tried to get off her father's lap and fly at me while tears of defeat blinded her eyes.

[42]**desisted:** Stopped; ceased.
[43]**diagnosis:** Determination of the type of illness.
[44]**had got beyond reason:** Had lost control of myself.
[45]**idiocy:** Excessive stupidity.
[46]**muscular release:** Release from tension or nervous strain through great physical activity.

[47]**operatives:** Influencing or controlling forces; the causes.
[48]**assault:** Attack.
[49]**gagged:** Choked.
[50]**covered with membrane:** Had the sure sign of diphtheria.
[51]**valiantly:** Bravely; courageously.

## A LOOK AT THE IDEAS

1. Describe the situation when the doctor arrived at the Olson house. Comment briefly on (a) how long the doctor had known the family; (b) what the house was like; (c) where the child was and what was wrong with her; (d) how the parents behaved toward the doctor and why they behaved that way; (e) how the child looked and acted when the doctor came in; (f) how old you think the child was.

2. There are early clues in the story that tell you something about the economic and educational level of the Olson family. For example, the father says, "My wife has given her

things, you know, like people do, but it don't do no good."
What assumptions can you make about him from the way
he speaks? Do you think they are country or city people?
Find other clues in the story that tell you something about
the economic and educational level of the family. In what
way, if any, does knowledge of their economic, social, and
educational background help you interpret their behavior?

3. Since Mathilda's parents knew there were diphtheria cases
   at school, why did they wait three days before they called
   the doctor for Mathilda? Why didn't they discuss the
   diphtheria epidemic with the doctor as soon as he arrived?
   Do your answers to these questions help you to understand Mathilda's behavior and that of her parents? Explain.

4. Mathilda wouldn't tell her parents about her sore throat.
   Why?

   _____ 1. She knew that a sore throat meant she might have
   diphtheria and was too afraid to tell anyone.

   _____ 2. Like her parents, she thought, "What you don't
   know won't hurt you."

   _____ 3. She was afraid of the doctor and thought he
   would hurt her or take her to the hospital.

   _____ 4. All of the above reasons.

   _____ 5. None of the above reasons.

   Give reasons for your choice.

5. Describe what happened when the doctor first approached
   Mathilda. Comment on (a) what his attitude was and how
   he behaved; (b) how the child reacted to him; (c) why the
   mother's remark made the doctor angry; and (d) how you
   think the remark affected the child.

   Does the doctor control his anger at this point? What does
   he do?

6. Which words would you use to describe the doctor, the
   child, the mother, and the father in "The Use of Force"?
   Write *D* for the doctor, *C* for the child, *M* for the mother,
   and *F* for the father next to the appropriate words. (This
   exercise can be done individually or in groups.)

1. ___ abject       8. ___ valiant       15. ___ ignorant
2. ___ savage       9. ___ apprehensive  16. ___ uncontrolled
3. ___ magnificent  10. ___ agonized     17. ___ stubborn
4. ___ terrified    11. ___ reasonable   18. ___ spoiled
5. ___ brutal       12. ___ helpful      19. ___ self-critical
6. ___ furious      13. ___ worried      20. ___ defensive
7. ___ unreasoning  14. ___ calm         21. ___ sadistic

What other words or phrases would you use to describe the characters?

7. In this story, we see many examples of actions or remarks that produce surprising reactions. For instance, how does the doctor react when he approaches the child the second time? What is the reaction of the child to the doctor's approach this time? How do the parents respond to Mathilda's behavior? What is the reaction of the doctor to the parents?

8. The doctor says, "Look here . . . we're going to look at your throat. . . . Will you open it now by yourself or shall we have to open it for you?" (lines 65-68) How do you interpret the doctor's statement? Why does he say "we" instead of "I" here? How did the child react at this point? Find other statements in the story that sound like threats. Describe the effect these threats produce.

   The doctor also uses "we" in line 41 and "let's" in line 42. In these earlier examples, is he threatening Mathilda or does he have a different reason for speaking this way?

9. The doctor says: "Then the battle began." (line 70) The word *battle* here suggests a contest between two people of more or less equal strength. In what ways are the doctor and Mathilda equals?

10. The doctor says ". . . I had already fallen in love with the savage brat, the parents were contemptible to me." (lines 77-78) What does he mean?

    ___ 1. He admires the child's courage but hates the parents' lack of will power.

    ___ 2. He is physically attracted to Mathilda but finds the parents ugly.

_____ 3. He thinks the child is crazy, and he is furious about the parents' behavior.

Give reasons for your choice.

11. The doctor's feelings about Mathilda are complex, but there are statements in the story which show that he admires Mathilda and understands her situation. For example, he says: "Don't call me a nice man to her. I'm here to look at her throat on the chance that she might have diphtheria and possibly die of it. But that's nothing to her." (lines 63-65) What does he mean by this? How do the following quotations show that he understands Mathilda's situation and/or admires her?

   1. . . . she surely rose to magnificent heights of insane fury of effort bred of her terror of me. (lines 80-81)

   2. She fought, with clenched teeth, desperately! (lines 100-101)

   3. The child's mouth was already bleeding. Her tongue was cut and she was screaming in wild hysterical shrieks. (lines 111-113)

   4. She had fought valiantly to keep me from knowing her secret. (lines 128-129)

   5. She had been on the defensive before but now she attacked. Tried to get off her father's lap and fly at me while tears of defeat blinded her eyes. (lines 131-133)

Point out other quotations above or elsewhere in the story that help explain Mathilda's motivations and her behavior.

12. Describe what happened as the battle progressed. Tell (a) how the father behaved and how successful he was in helping; (b) what the mother did and whether she was helpful or not; (c) when force was first used on the child and what her reaction was; and (d) what happened to the doctor as he continued to use force on Mathilda.

13. Near the end of the battle, the doctor says: "But a blind fury, a feeling of adult shame, bred of a longing for muscular release are the operatives. One goes on to the end." (lines 122-124) What does he mean?

   _____ 1. The child's behavior is shameful, and he has to use force because she may need an operation.

_____ 2. He is angry at the uncooperative parents and must use force to save the child's life.

_____ 3. He feels ashamed because he enjoys using force, but he can't stop himself until he has won.

**14.** What clues in the story tell you that _now_ the doctor realizes that (a) he enjoyed using force, (b) he rationalized* about using force, and (c) he is ashamed of using force? Check the appropriate column for each quotation.

|  | He enjoyed using force | He rationalized using force | He is ashamed of using force |
|---|---|---|---|
| 1. I had to have a throat culture for her own protection. (line 71) | _____ | _____ | _____ |
| 2. But now I also had grown furious—at a child. (lines 101-102) | _____ | _____ | _____ |
| 3. I tried to hold myself down but I couldn't. (line 102) | _____ | _____ | _____ |
| 4. But I have seen at least two children lying dead in bed of neglect in such cases . . . (lines 114-115) | _____ | _____ | _____ |
| 5. But the worst of it was that I too had got beyond reason. (lines 116-117) | _____ | _____ | _____ |
| 6. It was a pleasure to attack her. My face was burning with it. (lines 118-119) | _____ | _____ | _____ |

*He explained his behavior in a way that sounded reasonable but hid his real motives or reasons.

|  | *He enjoyed using force* | *He rationalized using force* | *He is ashamed of using force* |
|---|---|---|---|
| 7. . . . a feeling of adult shame . . . (line 123) | _____ | _____ | _____ |
| 8. I could have torn the child apart in my own fury and enjoyed it. (lines 117-118) | _____ | _____ | _____ |
| 9. The damned little brat must be protected against her own idiocy . . . (line 120) | _____ | _____ | _____ |

Point out other quotations above or elsewhere in the story that tell you the doctor lost his self-control and his ability to reason.

Point out quotations above or elsewhere in the story that reveal how Williams feels about the use of force.

15. In "The Use of Force," Williams places the doctor in a difficult situation. Because he thinks that Mathilda may have diphtheria, the doctor seems to have no choice but to use force to examine her. The child's misunderstandings make her determined not to be examined, and a conflict develops. The main point of the story, however, has to do with what Williams, the writer, actually believes about using physical aggression as a means of exerting one's will and overcoming the resistance of other people.

Write a composition discussing what Williams believes about using force. Here are some suggestions for organizing your composition:

1. In your opening paragraph, identify the main idea or theme of "The Use of Force." Three or four sentences should be enough for this introduction. If you wish, you can begin by saying: *The main idea of "The Use of Force," by William Carlos Williams, is . . .*

2. Next, follow with a very brief summary of the plot itself, for you cannot assume your reader has necessarily read

the story. You can include a short explanation of Mathilda's misunderstandings.

3. Now, identify the evidence in the story that reveals what Williams thinks about using force to overcome the resistance of other people. How does he feel about the effect on both the victor and his opponent?

   In this section, you will not want to discuss whether or not the doctor should have used force. Instead, focus on evidence that shows what Williams believes about using physical aggression as a means of exerting one's will. Identify details in the story that reveal the author's views about (a) why people use force; (b) how people rationalize their behavior when they use force; and (c) what the negative consequences are when force is used.

   For example, does the doctor perceive the situation as a conflict of wills between himself and the child? What is the evidence that the doctor enjoys using force? How does he justify his behavior? How does he feel about losing his ability to reason? What is the effect of the situation on the child? What does the story tell you about Williams' views about using physical force to bend people to your will? (If you use short quotations from the story to illustrate the main points you are developing, try to incorporate them into your own sentences. Remember, too, that quotations must be accurate and properly punctuated.)

4. Finally, discuss the extent to which you agree or disagree with the writer's views about using force. Don't discuss the characters in the story here. This is your chance to explain why you think people use force and what the possible effects of using force are. Support your opinion with concrete examples from your own experience and observation.

16. Both this story and Hemingway's story "A Day's Wait" involve the misunderstandings of children and their reactions during a crisis. Write a composition in which you compare Schatz and Mathilda. Would you say that either, both, or neither of the children showed courage in their situations? Here are some suggestions:

    1. In your introduction, identify the characters you are going to compare; tell in what stories they are found, who wrote the stories, and what particular characteris-

tics you are going to discuss. When you first mention each story, use the author's full name and enclose the title of the story in quotation marks.

2. Then, you can explain Schatz's misunderstanding and briefly describe his reaction to the situation. If you think he was courageous, discuss the kind of courage he showed. If not, explain why not.

3. Next, briefly explain Mathilda's misunderstandings and describe her behavior. Indicate the extent to which you feel she was or wasn't brave. If you think she was courageous, discuss the kind of courage she showed. If not, explain why not.

4. Finally, conclude by summarizing your main reasons for considering either, both, or neither of the children brave or courageous. You might also comment briefly on what bravery means to you.

## A LOOK AT THE LANGUAGE

1. Circle the word or phrase closest in meaning to the *italicized* word or phrase from the story.

1. The father *dreaded* (was very afraid of, avoided, was blamed for) hurting the child.
2. Their behavior was *contemptible* (understandable, unexpected, inexcusable).
3. The girl *shrieked* (struck out, screamed, shut her mouth) as the doctor approached.
4. She *gagged* (bit, spit, choked) on the spoon.
5. A *profusion of* (a few, many, some) diphtheria cases were reported.
6. As time went on, they became more *abject* (tired and unhappy, miserable and wretched, angry and helpless).
7. The doctor felt he should have *desisted* (stopped, persisted, helped) when he realized how frightened the child was.
8. Her mother *admonished* (slapped, threatened, scolded) her for not obeying the doctor.
9. The child put up a *valiant* (courageous, stubborn, terrible) fight.

2. Fill in the blanks in these sentences with the appropriate form of the *italicized* words.

   1. She was filled with *apprehension.* Is she usually that

      _____ ?

   2. He had great *contempt* for them. Later he found his own actions _____ .

   3. You couldn't say the father was *valiant,* but his daughter certainly fought _____ .

   4. *Abject* behavior always angered him, and they were behaving more _____ every minute.

   5. They looked at her *distrustfully,* and he couldn't help reacting to such obvious _____ .

3. The *italicized* words and phrases indicate devices that relate parts of the passage. Explain what is omitted, referred to, linked, or replaced, and tell how these devices function in relating ideas in the passage. (For further information on this type of exercise, see Steinbeck, "A Look at the Language," question 4, page 12.)

> "Does your throat hurt you?" added the mother to the child. *But* the little girl's expression didn't change nor did she move her eyes from my face.
>
> "Have you *looked*?"
>
> "I tried *to*," said the mother, "but I couldn't *see*."
>
> "As it happens, *we* had been having a number of cases of diphtheria in the school to which this child went during that month and *we* were all, quite apparently, thinking of *that*, though no one had as yet spoke of *the thing*.

4. Williams uses some nonstandard verb forms and irregular spelling to reflect the speech of Mathilda's parents. In the sentences below, change the *italicized* words and phrases to a style that would be acceptable in a formal composition.

> "... but it *don't* do *no* good."
>
> "... No... No, she says her throat *don't* hurt her."
>
> "So we *tho't* you'd better look her over. ..."

5. The following paragraph is from the Williams story. (a) First, make short sentences out of the long sentences. (b) Then, rewrite the paragraph, combining the short sen-

tences in whatever way you think best. Use all the information (but not necessarily all the words) in the short
sentences. (c) Finally, compare your paragraph with Williams's, and tell how yours and Williams's differ in style and
effect.

> The father tried his best, and he was a big man but the fact
> that she was his daughter, his shame at her behavior and
> his dread of hurting her made him release her just at the
> critical moment several times when I had almost achieved
> success, till I wanted to kill him. But his dread also that
> she might have diphtheria made him tell me to go on, go
> on though he himself was almost fainting, while the
> mother moved back and forth behind us raising and low-
> ering her hands in an agony of apprehension.

Why do you think Williams repeats "go on" in the second
sentence? Did you repeat "go on" in your paragraph? Does
"go on" here have the same meaning as "goes on" in line
124? What is the effect of this repetition?

6. Why does Williams change from the "I" and "we" he has
   been using in the story to "one" in the paragraph below?

> The damned little brat must be protected against her own
> idiocy, *one* says to one's self at such times. Others must be
> protected against her. It is a social necessity. And all these
> things are true. But a blind fury, a feeling of adult shame,
> bred of a longing for muscular release are the operatives.
> *One* goes on to the end.

Is what follows an accurate paraphrase of Williams's paragraph? Point out how the paraphrase differs in style and
effect from Williams's paragraph.

> *At such times you say to yourself that it is a social necessity to*
> *protect the child from herself and to protect others from her.*
> *These are valid reasons, but you are not being guided by reason.*
> *You are being driven by an instinctive desire to attack the child*
> *physically and break her will; and this feeling creates in you such*
> *an insane fury and a deep sense of shame that you cannot control*
> *your impulse to strike her.*

Write your own paraphrase of Williams's paragraph above
or the paragraph that follows it (lines 125-130). Your paragraph should be written in your own words but be as close
in meaning to Williams's paragraph as possible.

7. Mathilda's mother is very apologetic and seems very anxious to make a good impression on the doctor. For exam-

ple, when she says, "In the back, . . . You must excuse us, doctor, we have her in the kitchen where it is warm. It is very damp here sometimes," she is apologizing for asking him to go back to the kitchen to see the child. What impression is she trying to make or what is she apologizing for when she says the following things to Mathilda?

> "Such a nice man . . . Look how kind he is to you. Come on, do what he tells you to. He won't hurt you." (lines 49-50)
>
> "You bad girl . . . Look what you've done. The nice man . . ." (lines 60-62)
>
> "Aren't you ashamed . . . Aren't you ashamed to act like that in front of the doctor?" (lines 108-109)

The doctor was obviously annoyed and even angered by her behavior. In fact, many Americans seem to react negatively to overly apologetic people, considering them unsure of themselves. What is your reaction? Do you know of other cultures where this type of behavior is regarded more positively?

8. Compare the language in the poem "The Act" (page 182) and the first three paragraphs of "The Use of Force." Could you imagine the narrator (the doctor) in "The Use of Force" as the narrator of the poem? Read the poem and the first two or three paragraphs of the story aloud. Do you find the rhythm of the sentences similar? Do you find the same matter-of-fact tone in both the poem and the story?

9. Rewrite the poem in the form of a short anecdote, keeping as close to Williams's meaning as possible. For example, you might begin: *It was raining yesterday afternoon, so I was somewhat surprised to see my neighbor cutting roses in her garden.*

10. List the main events in "The Use of Force" in the order in which they occur. You might compare your list with the lists of other students to see if your lists are similar. Using your list, write a brief summary of the plot or main events. Would someone who has not read the story know what it is about after reading your summary? What would the person miss?

# Lewis Thomas (b. 1913)

*Lewis Thomas, president of the Sloan-Kettering Cancer Center in New York, is a doctor, administrator, biologist, researcher, professor, and published poet and essayist. Although he had had an impressive career in medicine, had begun publishing poetry in his student days at Princeton University and at the Harvard Medical School, and had been writing essays for the* New England Medical Journal *since 1971, he did not come to wide public attention until publication of two collections of essays,* The Lives of a Cell *(1974) and* The Medusa and the Snail *(1979). Critics praised his insights, vision, and style, and enthusiastic readers made his books bestsellers.*

*Through years of observation of nature, Thomas has become optimistic about the future of the human race in the sense that he sees in nature a tendency toward union and harmony rather than a murderous struggle for life. In the following article from* The Wall Street Journal *(July 3, 1978), although concerned about decreasing funds for medical research, he is optimistic about future developments in medicine.*

# 14

## The Medical Lessons of History

$A$fter a two-decade period of spectacular[1] expansion of a very broad range of scientific programs, mainly under National Institutes of Health sponsorship, the federal sources of funds have begun to level off on a flat line,[2] and it is now the almost certain prospect that future funding will be held at about its present level, even decreasing somewhat each year due to inflation. Meanwhile, the proportion of the total cost of scientific programs supported by funds from private sources has steadily decreased in recent years.

There is an increasing tendency, understandable enough at a time of so much competition for a diminishing[3] pool of federal funds, favor-  10 ing the award of grant support to "safe and sound" research programs. This means that it will henceforth be much more difficult to obtain support for scientific "gambles." It is a particularly dismaying[4] prospect, since a backward look at the record of biomedical science in this century should convince anyone that the major advances have been made, almost without exception, by what seemed at the time to be gambling on an unlikely hypothesis.

[1]**spectacular:** Impressive and large-scale.
[2]**level off on a flat line:** Referring to a curve that stops going up and flattens out.
[3]**diminishing:** Decreasing.
[4]**dismaying:** Discouraging.

For century after century, all the way into the remote millennia[5] of its origins, medicine got along by sheer[6] guesswork and the crudest[7] sort
20 of empiricism.[8]

Bleeding, purging, cupping, the administration of infusions of every known plant, solutions of every known metal,[9] every conceivable diet including total fasting,[10] most of these based on the weirdest[11] imaginings about the cause of disease, concocted[12] out of nothing but thin air—this was the heritage of medicine up until a little over a century ago. It is astounding that the profession survived so long, and got away with[13] so much with so little outcry.[14]

Then, sometime in the early 19th Century, it was realized by a few of the leading figures in medicine that almost all of the complicated
30 treatments then available for disease did not really work, and the suggestion was made by several courageous physicians that most of them actually did more harm than good.

Gradually, over the succeeding decades, the traditional therapeutic[15] ritual[16] of medicine was given up, and what came to be called the "art of medicine" emerged to take its place.

Accurate diagnosis[17] became the central purpose and justification for medicine, and as the methods for diagnosis improved, accurate prognosis[18] also became possible, so that patients and their families could be told not only the name of the illness but also, with some
40 reliability, how it was most likely to turn out. By the time this century had begun, these were becoming generally accepted as the principal responsibilities of the physician.

### ∾ The Role of Bacteria Discerned ∾

Meanwhile, the basic science needed for a future science of medicine got under way.[19] The role of bacteria and viruses in illness was discerned,[20] and research on the details of this connection began in earnest. The major pathogenic organisms,[21] most notably the tubercle

[5]**millennia:** Thousands of years (millennium = 1,000 years).
[6]**sheer:** Complete, absolute.
[7]**crudest:** Rough, not finished properly, not refined; in this case, without skill.
[8]**empiricism:** Reliance on observation and experimentation rather than theory or intuition.
[9]**Bleeding ... metal:** Different kinds of cures used by physicians before the twentieth century, often viewed later either as not beneficial or as harmful.
[10]**fasting:** Deliberately not eating.
[11]**weirdest:** Strangest.
[12]**concocted:** Put together; invented.
[13]**got away with:** Succeeded without receiving punishment or blame.

[14]**outcry:** Public protest.
[15]**therapeutic:** Healing or beneficial.
[16]**ritual:** Procedure regularly followed (often refers to religious worship).
[17]**diagnosis:** Determination of the kind of disease or sickness through observation and/or testing.
[18]**prognosis:** Prediction of the probable course or outcome of a sickness or disease.
[19]**got under way:** Started; began to advance.
[20]**discerned:** Seen clearly; in this case, understood or perceived.
[21]**pathogenic organisms:** Disease-producing forms of life.

bacillus and the syphilis spirochete were recognized for what they were and did. By the late 1930s this research had already begun to pay off;[22] the techniques of active and passive immunization had been worked out for diphtheria, tetanus, lobar pneumonia and a few other bacterial infections; the taxonomy[23] of infectious disease had become an orderly discipline; and the time was ready for sulfanilamide, penicillin, streptomycin and all the rest.

50

I was a medical student at the time of sulfanilamide and penicillin, and I remember the earliest reaction of flat disbelief concerning such things. We had given up on therapy a century earlier. With a few exceptions which we regarded as anomalies,[24] such as Vitamin B for pellagra, liver extract for pernicious anemia, and insulin for diabetes, we were educated to be skeptical[25] about the treatment of disease. Military tuberculosis and subacute bacterial endocarditis were fatal in 100% of cases, and we were convinced that the course of master diseases like these could never be changed, not in our lifetime or in any other.

60

Overnight, we became optimists, enthusiasts. The realization that disease could be turned around by treatment, provided that one knew enough about the underlying mechanism, was a totally new idea just 40 years ago.

What was not realized then and is not fully realized even now was how difficult it would be to accomplish the same end for the other diseases of man. We still have heart disease, cancer, stroke, schizophrenia, arthritis, kidney failure, cirrhosis and the degenerative diseases[26] associated with aging. All told there is a list of around 25 major afflictions[27] of man in this country, and a still more formidable[28] list of parasitic, viral and nutritional diseases in the less developed countries of the world, which make up the unfinished agenda[29] of modern biomedical science.

70

How does one make plans for science policy with such a list? The quick and easy way is to conclude that these diseases, not yet mastered, are simply beyond our grasp. The thing to do is to settle down with[30] today's versions[31] of science and technology, and make sure that our health care system is equipped to do the best it can in an imperfect world.

80

The trouble with this approach is that we cannot afford it. The costs are already too high, and they escalate higher each year. We cannot go

---

[22]**pay off:** Produce results.
[23]**taxonomy:** Science of identification and classification.
[24]**anomalies:** Irregularities; different from the normal.
[25]**skeptical:** Doubt the truth.
[26]**degenerative diseases:** Diseases that cause deterioration or worsening of the body.

[27]**afflictions:** Sickness or suffering.
[28]**formidable:** Frightening; in this case, very difficult to overcome.
[29]**agenda:** List of things to be done.
[30]**settle down with:** Relax; in this case, accept.
[31]**versions:** Forms.

on indefinitely trying to cope[32] with heart disease by open-heart surgery, carried out at formidable expense after the disease has run its destructive course.

Nor can we postpone[33] such issues by oversimplifying the problems, which is what we do, in my opinion, by attributing[34] so much of today's chronic[35] and disabling[36] disease to the environment, or to wrong ways of living. The plain fact of the matter is that we do not know enough about the facts of the matter, and we should be more open about our ignorance.

At the same time (and this will have a paradoxical[37] sound) there has never been a period in medicine when the future has looked so bright.

The scientists who do research on the cardiovascular system are entirely confident that they will soon be working close to the center of things, and they no longer regard the mechanisms of heart disease as impenetrable mysteries.[38] The cancer scientists, for all their public disagreements about how best to organize their research, are in possession of insights into the intimate functioning of normal and neoplastic cells[39] that were unimaginable a few years back. The neurobiologists can do all sorts of things in their investigation, and the brain is an organ different from what it seemed 25 years ago.

In short, I believe that the major diseases of human beings have become approachable biological puzzles, ultimately solvable. It follows from this that it is now possible to begin thinking about a human society relatively free of disease. This would surely have been an unthinkable notion a half century ago, and oddly enough it has a rather apocalyptic[40] sound today. What will we do about dying, and about all that population, if such things were to come about? What can we die of, if not disease?

My response is that it would not make all that much difference. We would still age away and wear out, on about the same schedule as today, with the terminal event being more like the sudden disintegration and collapse[41] all at once of Oliver Wendell Holmes'[42] famous metaphor[43] for natural death, the one-hoss shay.[44] The main effect, almost pure benefit

---

[32]**cope:** Manage.
[33]**postpone:** Put off until another time.
[34]**attributing:** To regard as the result of; caused by.
[35]**chronic:** Continual; lasting for a long time.
[36]**disabling:** To make unable; to weaken or destroy capability.
[37]**paradoxical:** Contradictory; seeming to say opposite things at the same time.
[38]**impenetrable mysteries:** Mysteries that cannot be understood.
[39]**neoplastic cells:** The growth of abnormal cells (such as tumors).

[40]**apocalyptic:** Predicting disaster and universal destruction; the reference is from the last book of the Bible, the Apocalypse or Revelations, in which disaster and destruction of the world are predicted.
[41]**disintegration and collapse:** falling apart.
[42]**Oliver Wendell Holmes:** United States poet, essayist, novelist, and physician, 1809–1894.
[43]**metaphor:** Word or phrase used to suggest that one thing is like something else.
[44]**one-hoss shay:** A reference to a poem by Oliver Wendell Holmes about a horse cart or carriage that ran on and on until it was very old and finally collapsed completely.

it seems to me, would be that we would not be beset[45] and riddled[46] by disease in the last decades of life, as most of us are today. Strokes, senile     120 dementia, cancer and arthritis are not natural aspects of the human condition, and we ought to rid ourselves of such impediments[47] as quickly as we can.

My argument about how to do this will come as no surprise. I say that we must continue doing biomedical research, on about the same scale and scope as in the past 20 years, with expansion and growth of the enterprise being dependent on where new leads seem to be taking us. It is an expensive undertaking, but still it is less than 3% of the total annual cost of today's health industry in the U.S., which at last count was over $140 billion, and it is nothing like as expensive as trying to live with the     130 halfway technologies we are obliged to depend on in medicine today; if we try to stay with these for the rest of the century the costs will go through the ionosphere.[48]

## ◆ Our Cultural Sadness ◆

These ought to be the best of times for the human mind, but it is not so. All sorts of things seem to be turning out wrong, and the century seems to be slipping through our fingers here at the end, with almost all promises unfilled. I cannot begin to guess at all the causes of our cultural sadness, not even the most important ones, but I can think of one thing that is wrong with us and eats away at us: We do not know enough     140 about ourselves.

We are ignorant about how we work, about where we fit in, and most of all about the enormous, imponderable[49] system of life in which we are embedded[50] as working parts. We do not really understand nature, at all. Not to downgrade us; we have come a long way indeed, but just to learn enough to become conscious of our ignorance.

Only two centuries ago we could explain everything about everything, out of pure reason, and now most of that elaborate and harmonious structure has come apart before our eyes. We are *dumb*.

This is, in a certain sense, a health problem after all. For as long as     150 we are bewildered[51] by the mystery of ourselves, and confused by the strangeness of our uncomfortable connection to all the rest of life, and dumbfounded[52] by the incomprehensibility of our own minds, we cannot be said to be healthy animals in today's world.

---

[45]**beset:** Surrounded by.
[46]**riddled:** Pierced through with many holes.
[47]**Impediments:** Physical defects; obstructions; obstacles.
[48]**Ionosphere:** The earth's atmosphere above the stratosphere; in this case, Thomas is saying that costs will get so high that they will be impossible to meet.

[49]**Imponderable:** Cannot be measured or evaluated.
[50]**embedded:** Fixed firmly.
[51]**bewildered:** Confused.
[52]**dumbfounded:** Amazed, astonished, made speechless.

*In response to Lewis Thomas's article, James V. McConnell, Professor of Psychology at the University of Michigan, wrote the following letter to the editor of* The Wall Street Journal. *This letter, which appeared in the July 17, 1978, issue of* The Wall Street Journal, *presents McConnell's view of what brings about important changes, or breakthroughs, in medicine.*

# The Breakthroughs

# in

# Medicine

I read with great delight Lewis Thomas's "The Medical Lessons of History" (July 3). It is good to know that such a wise and scholarly physician believes that we can learn from our past mistakes, and that he has some hope for the future of the medical sciences. It is a pity, however, that Dr. Thomas seems not to have learned the real lesson that history offers us—namely, that the "great breakthroughs" in any technology are always preceded[1] by a radical change[2] in how we view ourselves, and how we behave.

Take penicillin, for example. As Dr. Thomas points out, its benefits
10   were denied us for a decade after its discovery by Sir Alexander Fleming. Dr. Thomas holds that the medical doctors failed to put penicillin to use because they "disbelieved" it could do what plainly it did. Well, that's a nice way of explaining matters. But in truth Fleming's colleagues quite literally "sent him to Coventry"[3] for 10 years because they refused to accept scientific data showing that penicillin "worked." Just as a century earlier, the medical leaders in Vienna refused to accept Semmelweiss's studies showing that the death rate for childbed fever could

---

[1]**preceded:** Coming before; in this case, change comes before "breakthroughs."
[2]**radical change:** Extreme or complete change.
[3]**"sent him to Coventry":** Ignored him or refused to associate with him. The expression comes from English history. In the seventeenth century, supporters of Charles I of England were imprisoned in Coventry.

be cut from about 26% to about 2% if the attending physicians would
only wash their hands before delivering babies. In fact, medical doctors
(like most of us) are highly reluctant[4] to judge their actions solely in    20
terms of the objective consequences of what they do. Like most other
humans, MDs usually prefer that they be evaluated according to their
intentions and feelings. Any reader who doubts my contention[5] might
remember that, in malpractice[6] suits,[7] the physician's defense typically
is, "I followed standard medical procedure," rather than, "I did what
was necessary to cure the patient." Just ask your own family physician
some time what his or her own particular "cure rate" is for a given medical problem—and demand statistical evidence to back up the claim. My
guess is that you will shortly be dismissed as a patient.

As Dr. Thomas suggests in his article, medical technology is at an-    30
other of those difficult crossroads. For the medical profession has blos-
somed in the past 100 years by taking the viewpoint that most human
woes and miseries are biologically determined. In fact, man is not a
purely biological animal; we are social and psychological animals as
well. The long-term medical "cure rate" for obesity is less than 10%;
the behavioral cure rate is about 60%. Yet most physicians continue to
prescribe pills and fancy diets for weight loss, when what 90% of the
patients need is encouragement in learning how to eat sanely. These
"cure rate" data have been reported in dozens of scientific journals for
dozens of years. Yet just a month ago a man I know informed me that    40
his doctor had told him, "You are too damned fat. If you don't lose
weight, you're going to die, and it will serve you right." Needless to say,
the man became so depressed that he went on an eating jag.[8]

For almost a decade now, I have been sending behaviorally trained
undergraduates into hospitals to help physicians learn how to handle
their patients in more humane,[9] rewarding ways. We have demonstrated
time and again that we can take some of the most difficult patients
imaginable and, using both love and behavioral technology, increase
certain "cure rates" dramatically. Most of our techniques involve rewarding patients for following good medical regimens,[10] and teaching    50
patients how to handle their own emotional and behavioral problems.
Since we have ample objective proof that our techniques save lives,
you'd think that the medical profession would be beating down our
doors asking us to teach them our skills. Alas, what we get mostly is the
response, "This patient is a medical case, not a psychiatric problem, and

---

[4]**reluctant:** Unwilling.
[5]**contention:** Argument or idea, often
disagreement with another idea.
[6]**malpractice:** Improper practice of a professional
person.

[7]**suits:** Law claims against another person.
[8]**eating jag:** A period of uncontrollable eating.
[9]**humane:** Kind-hearted.
[10]**regimens:** Sets of rules or schedules to promote
good health.

only pills and surgery will help." So much for objectivity and the scientific method.

Despite what Dr. Thomas has said, the next great leap forward will come when medical students are routinely taught that the way they act toward the patient—and the way the patient is taught to think, feel, and behave—are as important in achieving a lasting "cure" as are drugs and surgical interventions.[11] That's the real "medical lesson of history." I do hope that Dr. Thomas and his colleagues learn that fact before it's too late.

[11]**interventions:** Things that happen to modify or interfere with events; in this case, the use of drugs or surgical procedures.

## ———————— A LOOK AT THE IDEAS ————————

**1.** What was most likely Lewis Thomas's primary purpose in writing "The Medical Lessons of History"?

  1. He wanted to justify government funding of biomedical research.
  2. He wanted to show how much medicine has progressed in recent centuries.
  3. He wanted to convince people that society can be disease free in the future.
  4. All of the above.
  5. None of the above.

  Give reasons for your choice.

**2.** What was most likely Professor McConnell's main purpose in responding to the Thomas article?

  1. He wanted to support Thomas's position that biomedical research must continue to be funded by the federal government.
  2. He thought it was a good opportunity to praise Thomas publicly for his wisdom and scholarship and his faith in the medical sciences.
  3. He wanted to express his view that there is more involved in the treatment of disease than biological factors.

4. All of the above.

5. None of the above.

Give reasons for your choice.

3. Why does Thomas feel that it is unfortunate that federal funds from now on will probably be given only to "safe and sound" research projects? Do you think McConnell would agree or disagree with him on this point? How do you feel about it?

4. Summarize the development of the medical sciences from early times to today, described by Thomas in paragraphs 3 through 8.

5. Thomas says that the medical profession was at first skeptical about treating disease with penicillin and sulfanilamide. What explanation does he give for this skepticism? What is McConnell's reaction to Thomas's explanation? What does McConnell say about the attitude of the medical profession toward Sir Alexander Fleming and Dr. Semmelweiss?

6. Explain what McConnell means when he says that medical doctors, like everyone else, prefer to be judged on the basis of their intentions and feelings rather than on the objective consequences of their work. What is your reaction to McConnell's statement? What experiences have you had with medical doctors (or other people) that make you inclined to agree or disagree with McConnell?

7. According to Thomas, the medical profession became very optimistic about the treatment of disease after the discovery of penicillin and sulfanilamide in the late 1930s. What progress has biomedical science made since then in discovering successful treatments for major diseases? What two solutions for dealing with the long list of diseases of man does Thomas discuss? Why does he reject the solutions?

8. Do you think Thomas and McConnell are equally optimistic about finding cures for all the major disease of man? Do they differ in the ways they believe progress toward a rela-

tively disease-free world can be made? What is your own reaction to their points of view?

9. Some people claim that a relatively disease-free society would result in overpopulation. What is Thomas's response to this fear? What is your view?

10. Read the statements below and indicate whether Thomas and McConnell would be likely to agree or disagree with them. Then indicate how you feel about the statements. Write *A* for *agree* and *D* for *disagree* in the appropriate columns.

|  | *Thomas* | *McConnell* | *You* |
|---|---|---|---|
| 1. The degenerative diseases of man, like cancer, arthritis, strokes, and senility, can best be eliminated by continued and extensive support of biomedical research. | _____ | _____ | _____ |
| 2. In the long run, treatment of disease based on present medical technology will cost more than the research that will enable us to get rid of these diseases. | _____ | _____ | _____ |
| 3. Physicians should be as objective as possible in discussions with their patients. | _____ | _____ | _____ |
| 4. The interpersonal relationship between patient and physician is of great importance in helping a patient get well. | _____ | _____ | _____ |
| 5. The job of a physician is primarily to diagnose an illness and then tell the patient what his chances are of getting well. | _____ | _____ | _____ |
| 6. A person who is dying should be prepared, along | | | |

|  | Thomas | McConnell | You |
|---|---|---|---|
| with his family, for what is going to happen. | ——— | ——— | ——— |
| 7. An overweight person suffering from high blood pressure deserves to die if he doesn't stop eating and drinking so much. | ——— | ——— | ——— |
| 8. Modern living is respon- sible for some of the major diseases. | ——— | ——— | ——— |
| 9. Medical and surgical treat- ments can be found for major diseases. | ——— | ——— | ——— |
| 10. Doctors should be eval- uated on the basis of the number of patients they are successful in curing. | ——— | ——— | ——— |

**11.** Thomas sees our cultural sadness as the result of ignorance about ourselves. Does McConnell agree or disagree with this idea? What kind of knowledge does Thomas think we need? What kind of knowledge does McConnell think we must have? What is your view?

**12.** McConnell distinguishes between behavioral and medical cures, suggesting that social and psychological factors are often more important than biological factors in curing dis- ease. Which of the following methods seem to be as- sociated with behavioral cures and which are more typical of medical cures?

|  | Behavioral | Medical |
|---|---|---|
| 1. Prescribing appropriate pills to lower blood pressure | ——— | ——— |
| 2. Learning about factors that contri- bute to the patient's anxieties | ——— | ——— |
| 3. Helping patients to recognize and control stress-producing situations | ——— | ——— |
| 4. Giving patients tranquilizers to reduce their anxiety | ——— | ——— |

*Behavioral*     *Medical*

5.  Treating patients with appropriate medicines but protecting them from knowledge of their illnesses.          _____     _____

6.  Helping patients become receptive to psychotherapy          _____     _____

7.  Maintaining good professional distance from a patient so as to remain objective          _____     _____

8.  Learning about the patient's family, job, and total environment          _____     _____

9.  Trying to understand the patient's value system          _____     _____

10.  Advising patients about what to do and then letting them take the responsibility for doing it          _____     _____

What other examples can you think of that are typical of behavioral and medical cures? Which approach do you think is most appropriate in what kinds of situations?

13. If you or someone in your family needed medical help, which type of doctor would you rather have? (a) Dr. Baker is efficient, polite, and impersonal; he focuses on the biological causes of illness and prescribes professionally acceptable cures. (b) Dr. Stanton is not quite as efficient, but he is interested in many personal dimensions of the patient's life. He does not necessarily confine himself to the biological factors and traditional cures in diagnosing and treating illness.

Write a composition in which you indicate which doctor you would choose and why that doctor's approach would appeal to you more. Be specific in describing the behavior and course of treatment you would expect from the doctor. You might want to include examples from your own experience and observation to illustrate the reason for your choice.

14. Write a composition in which you discuss the medical lessons of history from the point of view of both Thomas and McConnell, and then indicate which view is more acceptable to you. Here are some suggestions:

1. State Thomas's view of the medical lessons of history, or what these lessons teach or reveal to us.

2. State McConnell's view of these lessons, or what he says the "real" medical lessons of history are.

3. Make a list of the main points Thomas uses to support his view. Make a similar list for McConnell. Then decide which view is more acceptable to you.

4. Begin your composition with the statement you wrote for 1 above and follow with the statement you wrote for 2 above. You might want to use a transitional word or phrase between statements 1 and 2. If you think McConnell and Thomas hold the same views, you could begin the second sentence with a word like "Similarly." If you think their views are somewhat or largely different, you might use a phrase like "On the other hand."

5. In the next paragraph or paragraphs, present the supporting points for each author.

6. Conclude with a paragraph in which you explain which view is closer to your own or more acceptable to you. You might begin this paragraph with a sentence like this: *Thomas's (or McConnell's) argument is more convincing to me for several reasons.*

## _____ A LOOK AT THE LANGUAGE _____

**1.** Here are several common medical words that are useful in a conference with a doctor. Match the term on the left with the definition on the right.

| | |
|---|---|
| 1. ____ therapeutic | a. determination of the probable course or outcome of a sickness or disease |
| 2. ____ prognosis | |
| 3. ____ diagnosis | |
| 4. ____ chronic | b. set of rules or a schedule to be followed to promote good health |
| 5. ____ regimen | |
| | c. healing or curing |
| | d. determination of the kind of sickness or disease through observation |
| | e. continual, lasting for a long time |

2. The two-word verbs in this exercise appear in the Thomas article. Fill in the missing letters; the meaning of the two-word verb is given in parentheses. Notice that some of the two-word verbs are followed by a preposition.

   1. For hundreds of years medicine _g o_ _ _
      _a l_ _ _ _ _ _ (managed) by guesswork and primitive empiricism.
   2. In past history, physicians _g o_ _ _ _a w_ _ _ _
      _w i_ _ _ _ (used without being held responsible for) some strange remedies for disease.
   3. Diagnosis _g o_ _ _u n d_ _ _ _ _w a_ _ (became an established practice) during the nineteenth century.
   4. Thomas says that physicians in the nineteenth century _g a_ _ _ _ _u_ _ _o_ _ (abandoned) traditional therapeutic medicine.
   5. Thomas feels that we should not
      _s e t_ _ _ _ _ _ _ _d o_ _ _ _ _w i_ _ _ _ (establish) present medical technology as the best solution for our national health problem.
   6. Thomas is not greatly concerned about overpopulation in a disease-free society because people will still
      _w e_ _ _ _ _ _o u_ _ (deteriorate and die).
   7. We cannot _d e p_ _ _ _ _ _ _o_ _ (rely on) our present knowledge of ourselves to solve the health problems of our society.
   8. Thomas points out that most of the harmonious structure of the universe created through pure reason a couple of centuries ago has _c o_ _ _ _ _ _a p_ _ _ _ _ _ (fallen to pieces), leaving us ignorant of ourselves.

3. The *italicized* words and phrases indicate devices that relate parts of the passage below. Explain what is omitted, referred to, linked, or replaced, and tell how these devices function in relating ideas in the passage. (For further information on this type of exercise, see Steinbeck, "A Look at the Language" question 4, page 12.)

   . . . All told there is a list of around 25 major afflictions of man in this country, and a still more formidable list of parasitic, viral and nutritional diseases in the less de-

veloped countries of the world, *which* make up the unfinished agenda of modern biomedical science.

How does one make plans for science policy with *such a
list*? The quick and easy way is to conclude that these
diseases, not yet mastered, are simply beyond our grasp.
The thing to *do* is settle down with today's versions of
science and technology, and make sure that our health
care system is equipped to do the best *it* can in an imperfect world.

The trouble with *this approach* is that we cannot afford *it*.
The costs are already *too high*, and *they* escalate higher
each year. We cannot go on indefinitely trying to cope
with heart disease by open-heart surgery, carried out at
formidable expense after the disease has run *its* destructive course.

*Nor* can we postpone *such issues* by oversimplifying the
problems. . . .

4. For what kind of reader did Thomas write this article? How
   different do you think his approach would be if he were
   writing for his colleagues? For example, what would he
   probably assume that his colleagues already knew?

   What references and phrases indicate that he was writing
   for readers in the United States? What references and
   phrases would need to be changed or explained if he were
   writing for readers in another country?

5. Work through the following steps in order to see how
   Thomas organized his article. Make other observations on
   organization of the article as you go along.

   1. There are twenty-three paragraphs in the article; number
      each paragraph consecutively.

   2. Write a brief paraphrase of each paragraph. Here is a
      possible paraphrase of the first paragraph:

      *Scientific programs will not continue to expand as they have in
      the last twenty years because the proportion of funding from
      private sources has already declined and federal funding is ex-
      pected to remain at the present level but actually to decrease due
      to inflation.*

   3. Then identify the paragraphs that cover the same topic or
      idea and assign a common letter to identify each group of
      related paragraphs. For example, paragraphs 1 and 2
      cover the importance and justification for funding scien-
      tific programs. These two paragraphs can be marked *A*.

4. Locate the paragraph or point at which Thomas's main point or thesis first occurs. Then look for restatements of his main point.

5. In addition to restating his main point, Thomas also re-states some of his other important points. For example, in paragraph 14 he introduces the idea of our present ignorance of ourselves.

   Locate the points at which he brings up this idea again. Find other similar examples. Why do you think Thomas uses this kind of repetition in his essay?

6. Write a brief summary of the essay. Begin by stating the main point or thesis.

**6.** Refer to the McConnell letter to answer these questions:

1. Where does McConnell state his main point? Where does he bring it up again?

2. Before McConnell reveals his reaction to Thomas's ideas, he makes some polite remarks. What phrases does he use to compliment Thomas? Why do you think he is being so polite? How might he have written the opening paragraph if he had not begun so politely? What phrase does he introduce in the first paragraph to alert the reader to the fact that he may not completely agree with Thomas?

3. Write a brief summary of McConnell's letter. Begin by stating the main point at or near the beginning of the paragraph.

## William Faulkner (1897 - 1962)

*William Faulkner was born in Mississippi, and, except for occasional periods of work on films in Hollywood or travel abroad, he preferred to stay at his home in Oxford, Mississippi. He wrote numerous short stories and novels about a few southern families who lived in an imaginary county in Mississippi. For his work he received the 1949 Nobel Prize for Literature.*

*Faulkner's style of writing is complex—a style that reflects his intricate themes of good and evil and the social and psychological decay that he observed in the Deep South. "A Rose for Emily," from* These Thirteen *published in 1931, is about Miss Emily, the last of the Grierson family. Through Miss Emily, we see the final fading and deterioration of a once grand and noble southern family; through her, we find the old order in the South becoming, like her house, "an eyesore among eyesores" and "filled with dust and shadows," and like "Poor Emily" something to be pitied.*

# 15

# A Rose
# for
# Emily

When Miss Emily Grierson died, our whole town went to her funeral: the men through a sort of respectful affection for a fallen monument,[1] the women mostly out of curiosity to see the inside of her house, which no one save[2] an old manservant—a combined gardener and cook—had seen in at least ten years.

It was a big, squarish frame house that had once been white, decorated with cupolas and spires[3] and scrolled balconies[4] in the heavily lightsome style of the seventies,[5] set on what had once been our most select street. But garages and cotton gins[6] had encroached[7] and obliterated[8] even the august[9] names of that neighborhood; only Miss Emily's house was left, lifting its stubborn and coquettish[10] decay above the

[1]**monument:** A structure built to keep alive the memory of a person or an event (in this case, the word refers to the dead woman, indicating that her position in the town was like a "fallen monument").
[2]**save:** Except for.
[3]**cupolas and spires:** Small domes and towers or steeples on the roof of a building.
[4]**scrolled balconies:** Balconies or platforms on the sides of the house decorated with curving or spiral designs.
[5]**heavily lightsome style of the seventies:** The "light" style of architecture of the 1870s, which was considered heavy rather than light by later generations.
[6]**cotton gins:** Machines that separate cotton from seeds.
[7]**encroached:** Intrude upon; move in on.
[8]**obliterated:** Erased; blotted out.
[9]**august:** Imposing; high-ranking.
[10]**coquettish:** Flirtatious; lightheartedly rather than seriously romantic.

cotton wagons and the gasoline pumps—an eyesore[11] among eyesores. And now Miss Emily had gone to join the representatives of those august names where they lay in the cedar-bemused cemetery[12] among the ranked[13] and anonymous[14] graves of Union and Confederate soldiers who fell at the battle of Jefferson.

Alive, Miss Emily had been a tradition, a duty, and a care; a sort of hereditary obligation[15] upon the town, dating from that day in 1894 when Colonel Sartoris, the mayor—he who fathered the edict[16] that no
20   Negro woman should appear on the streets without an apron—remitted her taxes,[17] the dispensation[18] dating from the death of her father on into perpetuity.[19] Not that Miss Emily would have accepted charity. Colonel Sartoris invented an involved tale to the effect that Miss Emily's father had loaned money to the town, which the town, as a matter of business, preferred this way of repaying. Only a man of Colonel Sartoris' generation and thought could have invented it, and only a woman could have believed it.

When the next generation, with its more modern ideas, became mayors and aldermen,[20] this arrangement created some little dissatisfac-
30   tion. On the first of the year they mailed her a tax notice. February came, and there was no reply. They wrote her a formal letter, asking her to call at the sheriff's office at her convenience. A week later the mayor wrote her himself, offering to call or to send his car for her, and received in reply a note on paper of an archaic[21] shape, in a thin, flowing calligraphy[22] in faded ink, to the effect that she no longer went out at all. The tax notice was also enclosed, without comment.

They called a special meeting of the Board of Aldermen. A deputation[23] waited upon her, knocked at the door through which no visitor had passed since she ceased giving china-painting[24] lessons eight or ten
40   years earlier. They were admitted by the old Negro into a dim hall from which a stairway mounted into still more shadow. It smelled of dust and disuse—a close, dank[25] smell. The Negro led them into the parlor. It was furnished in heavy, leather-covered furniture. When the Negro opened the blinds of one window, they could see that the leather was cracked; and when they sat down, a faint dust rose sluggishly[26] about their thighs,[27] spinning with slow motes[28] in the single sun-ray. On a tar-

---

[11]**eyesore:** An unpleasant sight.
[12]**cedar-bemused cemetery:** Cemetery (burial place) with many cedar trees.
[13]**ranked:** Arranged in lines.
[14]**anonymous:** Unmarked.
[15]**hereditary obligation:** An obligation passed on from generation to generation.
[16]**edict:** Order; proclamation; decree.
[17]**remitted her taxes:** Exempted her from the payment of taxes.
[18]**dispensation:** Exemption.
[19]**perpetuity:** Eternity.

[20]**aldermen:** Town officials.
[21]**archaic:** Old-fashioned.
[22]**calligraphy:** Handwriting.
[23]**deputation:** Delegation (the members appointed for this mission).
[24]**china-painting:** Painting designs—usually flowers—on dishes (china).
[25]**dank:** Disagreeably damp.
[26]**sluggishly:** Moving slowly.
[27]**thigh(s):** The part of the leg between hip and knee.
[28]**motes:** Specks; small particles.

nished gilt easel[29] before the fireplace stood a crayon portrait of Miss Emily's father.

They rose when she entered—a small, fat woman in black, with a thin gold chain descending to her waist and vanishing into her belt, leaning on an ebony cane with a tarnished gold head. Her skeleton was small and spare;[30] perhaps that was why what would have been merely plumpness[31] in another was obesity[32] in her. She looked bloated,[33] like a body long submerged in motionless water, and of that pallid hue.[34] Her eyes, lost in the fatty ridges of her face, looked like two small pieces of coal pressed into a lump of dough[35] as they moved from one face to another while the visitors stated their errand.

She did not ask them to sit. She just stood in the door and listened quietly until the spokesman came to a stumbling halt. Then they could hear the invisible watch ticking at the end of the gold chain.

Her voice was dry and cold. "I have no taxes in Jefferson. Colonel Sartoris explained it to me. Perhaps one of you can gain access[36] to the city records and satisfy yourselves."

"But we have. We are the city authorities, Miss Emily. Didn't you get a notice from the sheriff, signed by him?"

"I received a paper, yes," Miss Emily said. "Perhaps he considers himself the sheriff... I have no taxes in Jefferson."

"But there is nothing on the books to show that, you see. We must go by the—"

"See Colonel Sartoris. I have no taxes in Jefferson."

"But, Miss Emily—"

"See Colonel Sartoris." (Colonel Sartoris had been dead almost ten years.) "I have no taxes in Jefferson. Tobe!" The Negro appeared. "Show these gentlemen out."

≪ II ≫

So she vanquished them,[37] horse and foot,[38] just as she had vanquished their fathers thirty years before about the smell. That was two years after her father's death and a short time after her sweetheart—the one we believed would marry her—had deserted her. After her father's death she went out very little; after her sweetheart went away, people hardly saw her at all. A few of the ladies had the temerity[39] to call, but

---

[29]**tarnished gilt easel:** Stand (easel) covered with a thin layer of discolored gold (tarnished gilt).
[30]**spare:** Small-boned (smaller in size than the ordinary woman of her build).
[31]**plumpness:** Fullness of figure; rather fat (but with a suggestion of attractiveness).
[32]**obesity:** Fat (with a suggestion of unattractiveness).
[33]**bloated:** Swollen.
[34]**pallid hue:** Very pale color.
[35]**lump of dough:** Shapeless piece of the flour-water mixture used to make bread.
[36]**access:** Entrance.
[37]**vanquished them:** Defeated them; forced them into submission.
[38]**horse and foot:** Horse soldiers and foot soldiers; that is, all of them.
[39]**temerity:** Boldness; rashness.

were not received, and the only sign of life about the place was the Negro man—a young man then—going in and out with a market basket.

"Just as if a man—any man—could keep a kitchen properly," the ladies said; so they were not surprised when the smell developed. It was another link between the gross,[40] teeming world[41] and the high and mighty Griersons.

A neighbor, a woman, complained to the mayor, Judge Stevens, eighty years old.

90  "But what will you have me do about it, madam?" he said.

"Why, send her word to stop it," the woman said. "Isn't there a law?"

"I'm sure that won't be necessary," Judge Stevens said. "It's probably just a snake or a rat that nigger[42] of hers killed in the yard. I'll speak to him about it."

The next day he received two more complaints, one from a man who came in diffident deprecation.[43] "We really must do something about it, Judge. I'd be the last one in the world to bother Miss Emily, but we've got to do something." That night the Board of Aldermen met—

100 three graybeards and one younger man, a member of the rising generation.

"It's simple enough," he said. "Send her word to have her place cleaned up. Give her a certain time to do it in, and if she don't. . . ."

"Dammit, sir," Judge Stevens said, "will you accuse a lady to her face of smelling bad?"

So the next night, after midnight, four men crossed Miss Emily's lawn and slunk[44] about the house like burglars, sniffing[45] along the base of the brickwork and at the cellar openings while one of them performed a regular sowing motion[46] with his hand out of a sack slung[47] from his

110 shoulder. They broke open the cellar door and sprinkled lime[48] there, and in all the outbuildings. As they recrossed the lawn, a window that had been dark was lighted and Miss Emily sat in it, the light behind her, and her upright torso[49] motionless as that of an idol.[50] They crept quietly across the lawn and into the shadow of the locusts that lined the street. After a week or two the smell went away.

That was when people had begun to feel really sorry for her. People in our town, remembering how old lady Wyatt, her great-aunt,

---

[40]**gross:** Vulgar; unrefined; uncultured.
[41]**teeming world:** World full of people.
[42]**nigger:** Negro (the term "nigger" is used mainly by people who look down upon Blacks).
[43]**diffident deprecation:** Shy protest (he was shy about his protest).
[44]**slunk:** Moved quietly; sneaked.
[45]**sniffing:** Smelling (in an attempt to detect where the bad smell was coming from).

[46]**sowing motion:** The motion used by someone planting (sowing) seeds by repeatedly taking seeds from a sack and throwing them on the ground.
[47]**slung:** Hanging; suspended.
[48]**lime:** A chemical (calcium oxide) sometimes used to purify or to remove bad smells.
[49]**torso:** Body.
[50]**idol:** Statue of a god.

had gone completely crazy at last, believed that the Griersons held themselves a little too high for what they really were. None of the young men were quite good enough for Miss Emily and such. We had long thought of them as a tableau,[51] Miss Emily a slender figure in white in the background, her father a spraddled silhouette[52] in the foreground, his back to her and clutching a horsewhip, the two of them framed by the back-flung front door.[53] So when she got to be thirty and was still single, we were not pleased exactly, but vindicated;[54] even with insanity[55] in the family she wouldn't have turned down all of her chances if they had really materialized.      120

When her father died, it got about that the house was all that was left to her; and in a way, people were glad. At last they could pity Miss Emily. Being left alone, and a pauper,[56] she had become humanized.[57] Now she too would know the old thrill and the old despair of a penny more or less.      130

The day after his death all the ladies prepared to call at the house and offer condolence[58] and aid, as is our custom. Miss Emily met them at the door, dressed as usual and with no trace of grief on her face. She told them that her father was not dead. She did that for three days, with the ministers calling on her, and the doctors, trying to persuade her to let them dispose of the body. Just as they were about to resort to law and force, she broke down, and they buried her father quickly.

We did not say she was crazy then. We believed she had to do that. We remembered all the young men her father had driven away, and we knew that with nothing left, she would have to cling to that which had robbed her, as people will.      140

### ⚞ III ⚟

She was sick for a long time. When we saw her again, her hair was cut short, making her look like a girl, with a vague resemblance to those angels in colored church windows—sort of tragic and serene.

The town had just let the contracts for paving the sidewalks, and in the summer after her father's death they began the work. The construction company came with niggers and mules and machinery, and a foreman[59] named Homer Barron, a Yankee[60]—a big, dark, ready man, with      150

[51]**tableau:** Picture.
[52]**spraddled silhouette:** A dark shape with legs spread apart (that is, the way the father appeared in contrast to Miss Emily's slim figure in white).
[53]**back-flung front door:** A door thrown open toward the inside of the house.
[54]**vindicated:** Justified (in our own belief that the Griersons held themselves too high).
[55]**insanity:** Madness; mental illness.

[56]**pauper:** Very poor person; person who lives on charity.
[57]**humanized:** Human; like other people.
[58]**condolence:** Expression of sympathy.
[59]**foreman:** Person in charge of a group of workers.
[60]**Yankee:** A Northerner—someone from one of the states on the Northern (or Union) side during the American Civil War (1861-1865).

a big voice and eyes lighter than his face. The little boys would follow in groups to hear him cuss[61] the niggers, and the niggers singing in time to the rise and fall of picks. Pretty soon he knew everybody in town. Whenever you heard a lot of laughing anywhere about the square, Homer Barron would be in the center of the group. Presently we began to see him and Miss Emily on Sunday afternoons driving in the yellow-wheeled buggy[62] and the matched team of bays[63] from the livery stable.

160     At first we were glad that Miss Emily would have an interest, because the ladies all said, "Of course a Grierson would not think seriously of a Northerner, a day laborer." But there were still others, older people, who said that even grief could not cause a real lady to forget *noblesse oblige*[64]—without calling it *noblesse oblige*. They just said, "Poor Emily. Her kinsfolk[65] should come to her." She had some kin in Alabama; but years ago her father had fallen out with them over the estate of old lady Wyatt, the crazy woman, and there was no communication between the two families. They had not even been represented at the funeral.

170     And as soon as the old people said, "Poor Emily," the whispering began. "Do you suppose it's really so?" they said to one another. "Of course it is. What else could..." This behind their hands; rustling of craned[66] silk and satin behind jalousies[67] closed upon the sun of Sunday afternoon as the thin, swift clop-clop-clop of the matched team passed: "Poor Emily."

She carried her head high enough—even when we believed that she was fallen. It was as if she demanded more than ever the recognition of her dignity as the last Grierson; as if it had wanted that touch of earthiness[68] to reaffirm[69] her imperviousness.[70] Like when she bought

180     the rat poison, the arsenic. That was over a year after they had begun to say "Poor Emily," and while the two female cousins were visiting her.

"I want some poison," she said to the druggist. She was over thirty then, still a slight woman, though thinner than usual, with cold, haughty[71] black eyes in a face the flesh of which was strained across the temples and about the eye-sockets as you imagine a lighthouse-keeper's face ought to look. "I want some poison," she said.

---

[61]**cuss:** Curse; swear at.
[62]**buggy:** Carriage.
[63]**bays:** Reddish-brown horses.
[64]**noblesse oblige (French):** The idea that people of high birth or position should behave nobly toward others.
[65]**kinsfolk** (more commonly, *kinfolk*): Relatives.
[66]**craned:** Stretched.
[67]**jalousies:** Window shades made of narrow horizontal strips of wood.

[68]**earthiness:** Crudeness; vulgarity.
[69]**reaffirm:** Again declare (or in this case, show) positively.
[70]**imperviousness:** Unmovable, unchangeable position (a position that prevented anyone from getting close to her).
[71]**haughty:** Proud; arrogant.

"Yes, Miss Emily. What kind? For rats and such? I'd recom—"

"I want the best you have. I don't care what kind."

The druggist named several. "They'll kill anything up to an elephant. But what you want is—" 190

"Arsenic," Miss Emily said. "Is that a good one?"

"Is . . . arsenic? Yes, ma'am. But what you want—"

"I want arsenic."

The druggist looked down at her. She looked back at him, erect, her face like a strained flag. "Why, of course," the druggist said. "If that's what you want. But the law requires you to tell what you are going to use it for."

Miss Emily just stared at him, her head tilted back in order to look him eye for eye, until he looked away and went and got the arsenic and wrapped it up. The Negro delivery boy brought her the package; the 200 druggist didn't come back. When she opened the package at home there was written on the box, under the skull and bones: "For rats."

## ⤳ IV ⤶

So the next day we all said, "She will kill herself,"; and we said it would be the best thing. When she had first begun to be seen with Homer Barron, we had said, "She will marry him." Then we said, "She will persuade him yet," because Homer himself had remarked—he liked men, and it was known that he drank with the younger men in the Elks' Club—that he was not a marrying man. Later we said, "Poor Emily" 210 behind the jalousies as they passed on Sunday afternoon in the glittering buggy. Miss Emily with her head high and Homer Barron with his hat cocked[72] and a cigar in his teeth, reins and whip in a yellow glove.

Then some of the ladies began to say that it was a disgrace to the town and a bad example to the young people. The men did not want to interfere, but at last the ladies forced the Baptist minister—Miss Emily's people were Episcopal—to call upon her. He would never divulge[73] what happened during the interview, but he refused to go back again. The next Sunday they again drove about the streets, and the following day the minister's wife wrote to Miss Emily's relations in Alabama.

So she had blood-kin under her roof again and we sat back to 220 watch developments. At first nothing happened. Then we were sure that they were to be married. We learned that Miss Emily had been to the jeweler's and ordered a man's toilet set in silver, with the letters H.B. on each piece. Two days later we learned that she had bought a complete outfit of men's clothing, including a nightshirt, and we said, "They

[72]**cocked:** Set on one side.          [73]**divulge:** Reveal; disclose.

are married." We were really glad. We were glad because the two female cousins were even more Grierson than Miss Emily had ever been.

230　　So we were not surprised when Homer Barron—the streets had been finished some time since—was gone. We were a little disappointed that there was not a public blowing-off, but we believed that he had gone on to prepare for Miss Emily's coming, or to give her a chance to get rid of the cousins. (By that time it was a cabal,[74] and we were all Miss Emily's allies[75] to help circumvent[76] the cousins.) Sure enough, after another week they departed. And, as we had expected all along, within three days Homer Barron was back in town. A neighbor saw the Negro man admit him at the kitchen door at dusk one evening.

　　And that was the last we saw of Homer Barron. And of Miss Emily for some time. The Negro man went in and out with the market basket, but the front door remained closed. Now and then we would see her at a
240　window for a moment, as the men did that night when they sprinkled the lime, but for almost six months she did not appear on the streets. Then we knew that this was to be expected too; as if that quality of her father which had thwarted[77] her woman's life so many times had been too virulent[78] and too furious to die.

　　When we next saw Miss Emily, she had grown fat and her hair was turning gray. During the next few years it grew grayer and grayer until it attained an even pepper-and-salt iron-gray, when it ceased turning. Up to the day of her death at seventy-four it was still that vigorous iron-gray, like the hair of an active man.

250　　From that time on her front door remained closed, save for a period of six or seven years, when she was about forty, during which she gave lessons in china-painting. She fitted up a studio in one of the downstairs rooms, where the daughters and granddaughters of Colonel Sartoris' contemporaries were sent to her with the same regularity and in the same spirit that they were sent to church on Sundays with a twenty-five-cent piece for the collection plate. Meanwhile her taxes had been remitted.

　　Then the newer generation became the backbone and the spirit of the town, and the painting pupils grew up and fell away and did not
260　send their children to her with boxes of color and tedious[79] brushes and pictures cut from the ladies' magazines. The front door closed upon the last one and remained closed for good. When the town got free postal delivery, Miss Emily alone refused to let them fasten the metal numbers above her door and attach a mailbox to it. She would not listen to them.

---

[74]**cabal:** A small group joined together in a plot or scheme.
[75]**allies** (*singular, ally*): Friendly nations or helpful people in time of war.

[76]**circumvent:** Get the better of; defeat.
[77]**thwarted:** Obstructed; blocked.
[78]**virulent:** Deadly; very harmful.
[79]**tedious:** Tiresome; boring.

Daily, monthly, yearly we watched the Negro grow grayer and more stooped, going in and out with the market basket. Each December we sent her a tax notice, which would be returned by the post office a week later, unclaimed. Now and then we would see her in one of the downstairs windows—she had evidently shut up the top floor of the house, like the carven[80] torso of an idol in a niche,[81] looking or not     270 looking at us, we could never tell which. Thus she passed from generation to generation—dear, inescapable, impervious, tranquil, and perverse.[82]

And so she died. Fell ill in the house filled with dust and shadows, with only a doddering[83] Negro man to wait on her. We did not even know she was sick; we had long since given up trying to get any information from the Negro. He talked to no one, probably not even to her, for his voice had grown harsh and rusty, as if from disuse.

She died in one of the downstairs rooms, in a heavy walnut bed with a curtain, her gray head propped on a pillow yellow and moldy[84]     280 with age and lack of sunlight.


≈ V ≈

The Negro met the first of the ladies at the front door and let them in, with their hushed, sibilant[85] voices and their quick, curious glances, and then he disappeared. He walked right through the house and out the back and was not seen again.

The two female cousins came at once. They held the funeral on the second day, with the town coming to look at Miss Emily beneath a mass of bought flowers, with the crayon face of her father musing[86] profoundly above the bier[87] and the ladies sibilant and macabre;[88] and the     290 very old men—some in their brushed Confederate uniforms—on the porch and the lawn, talking of Miss Emily as if she had been a contemporary of theirs, believing that they had danced with her and courted[89] her perhaps, confusing time with its mathematical progression, as the old do, to whom all the past is not a diminishing road but, instead, a huge meadow which no winter ever quite touches, divided from them now by the narrow bottle-neck of the most recent decade of years.

---

[80]**carven** (*poetic*): Carved; shaped out of wood or stone.
[81]**niche:** A hollow place in a wall (where a statue might be placed); a particularly fitting place for an object.
[82]**perverse:** Contrary; difficult to get along with or put up with.
[83]**doddering:** Shaky (as from old age).
[84]**moldy:** Covered with a growth caused by decay.

[85]**sibilant:** Hissing; speaking with frequent "s-like" sounds.
[86]**musing:** Meditating; considering at length.
[87]**bier:** Stand on which the coffin is placed.
[88]**macabre:** Grim; suggesting death.
[89]**courted:** Acted as if they were trying to get her to marry them.

300 Already we knew that there was one room in that region above stairs which no one had seen in forty years, and which would have to be forced. They waited until Miss Emily was decently in the ground before they opened it.

The violence of breaking down the door seemed to fill this room with pervading dust.[90] A thin, acrid pall[91] as of the tomb, seemed to lie everywhere upon this room decked and furnished as for a bridal: upon the valance curtains[92] of faded rose color, upon the rose-shaded lights, upon the dressing table, upon the delicate array of crystal and the man's toilet things backed with tarnished silver, silver so tarnished that the monogram[93] was obscured.[94] Among them lay a collar and tie, as if they had just been removed, which, lifted, left upon the surface a pale cres-
310 cent in the dust. Upon a chair hung the suit, carefully folded; beneath it the two mute[95] shoes and the discarded socks

The man himself lay in the bed.

For a long while we just stood there, looking down at the profound and fleshless grin. The body had apparently once lain in the attitude of an embrace, but now the long sleep that outlasts love, that conquers even the grimace[96] of love, had cuckolded him.[97] What was left of him, rotted[98] beneath what was left of the nightshirt, had become inextrica-ble[99] from the bed in which he lay; and upon him and upon the pillow beside him lay that even coating of the patient and biding[100] dust.
320 Then we noticed that in the second pillow was the indentation of a head.[101] One of us lifted something from it, and leaning forward, that faint and invisible dust dry and acrid in the nostrils, we saw a long strand of iron-gray hair.[102]

[90]**pervading dust:** Dust spread throughout.
[91]**acrid pall:** Sharp and bitter (to the taste or smell) dark covering.
[92]**valance curtains:** Short curtains across the top of a window.
[93]**monogram:** Initial (or initials); in this case, "H.B." for Homer Barron.
[94]**obscured:** Difficult to understand or, in this case, to read.
[95]**mute:** Silent.
[96]**grimace:** Ugly facial expression, frequently showing pain or disgust.

[97]**had cuckolded him:** Had made a cuckold of him (that is, a man whose wife has deceived him).
[98]**rotted:** Spoiled; fallen apart because of decay.
[99]**inextricable:** Not possible to separate or remove.
[100]**biding:** Patiently waiting; enduring.
[101]**indentation of a head:** A hollow space or mark left by a head.
[102]**a long strand of iron-gray hair:** One long single iron-gray hair.

―――――――――――― A LOOK AT THE IDEAS ――――――――――――

1. Describe the situation when Emily Grierson died. Com-ment on (a) when the house she lived in was built and how it had changed over the years; (b) what kind of neighbor-

hood she lived in and how it had changed over the years; (c) who went to her funeral and why; (d) where she was buried; and (e) who is telling the story.

2. Describe the situation when Miss Emily's father died. Explain (a) how she reacted to his death; (b) what the townspeople did; (c) what happened to Miss Emily after her father was buried; and (d) how she looked when the townspeople finally saw her again.

3. Colonel Sartoris exempted Miss Emily from paying taxes. Why did he do that?

    _____ 1. Her father had lent the town a lot of money, which the townspeople preferred to repay this way.

    _____ 2. She supported the Colonel's edict that no Negro woman should appear on the streets without an apron.

    _____ 3. After her father died, she couldn't afford to pay taxes and was too proud to accept charity from anyone.

    _____ 4. All of the above reasons.

    _____ 5. None of the above reasons.

    Give reasons for your choice.

    When the next generation sent Miss Emily a tax notice, what did she do? When a delegation called on her, how did she look and behave?

4. Describe Homer Barron. Explain (a) where he was from; (b) what he was doing in the town of Jefferson; (c) what kind of person he was; (d) what social class he represented in relation to Miss Emily; (e) why Miss Emily probably started going out with him and why he probably went out with her.

5. When Miss Emily was first seen with Homer Barron, how did the townspeople feel?

    _____ 1. They were glad that she finally would be going out with a man.

_____ 2. They were shocked that she would go out with a lower-class Yankee.

_____ 3. They were certain that she had gone crazy like her great-aunt Wyatt.

How else do you think the townspeople felt about their relationship? Discuss Miss Emily's attitude toward the townspeople. What was her reaction to their disapproval and gossip? Give examples of her behavior that clarify her attitude about herself and toward the people in the town.

6. The narrator says: "She carried her head high enough—even when we believed that she was fallen. It was as if she demanded more than ever the recognition of her dignity as the last Grierson; as if it had wanted that touch of earthiness to reaffirm her imperviousness." He means:

_____ 1. Miss Emily knew that when she was buried in the cemetery, she would be the last of the dignified and untouchable Griersons.

_____ 2. Since there were no more Griersons, she wanted to be able to carry on the family name so that it would be honored forever.

_____ 3. Even though she was having a shocking relationship with Homer Barron, she was more proud and untouchable than ever.

_____ 4. All of the above reasons.

_____ 5. None of the above reasons.

Give reasons for your choice.

7. Describe the situation before the townspeople sent for Miss Emily's relatives. What did they do first? Why did they finally send for her cousins?

The townspeople said "Poor Emily" when her cousins were visiting her. Why did they say that?

_____ 1. They knew she couldn't afford to entertain her relatives properly.

_____ 2. They believed her cousins would forbid her marriage to Homer Barron.

_____ 3. She was a disgrace to the town and a bad example to the young people.

Did the cousins succeed in carrying out the purpose of their visit? What kind of conversation do you think Miss Emily and her cousins had?

Do you think the townspeople really felt sorry for Miss Emily, or do you think they had other feelings about her too? Use examples from the story to support your view.

8. Describe the situation when Miss Emily bought the rat poison. Comment on (a) how she behaved and (b) what the druggist did.

   When she bought the poison, what did the townspeople think?

   \_\_\_\_ 1. She would kill the rats.

   \_\_\_\_ 2. She would kill Homer.

   \_\_\_\_ 3. She would kill herself.

   Why do you think she bought the poison? What else did Miss Emily buy about the same time she bought the poison? Why do you think she bought those things? What did she intend to do with them?

9. About two years after her father's death, the townspeople noticed a bad smell around Miss Emily's house. Explain (a) what the townspeople thought caused the smell; (b) what they attempted to do about it; and (c) why they said again that they had begun to feel sorry for her.

   Do you think the townspeople really felt sorry for her this time?

10. What made the townspeople believe that Miss Emily and Homer Barron were going to get married? Were they sympathetic to her at that time? When was the last time they saw Homer? How did they interpret his disappearance? When did they see Miss Emily again?

11. Describe Miss Emily's appearance and behavior in the years after Homer's disappearance. Tell (a) what kind of relationship she had with the townspeople; (b) when and why she gave china-painting lessons and why she stopped; (c) how she responded to the changing times; (d) who took care of her; (e) when she died and what happened after she died.

**12.** Which words would you use to describe how the townspeople felt about Emily Grierson: (a) when she was young, (b) when her father died, (c) when she went out with Homer Barron, (d) after Homer disappeared, (e) after she died. (This exercise can be done individually or in groups.)

| | | |
|---|---|---|
| 1. ___ concerned | 8. ___ affectionate | 15. ___ critical |
| 2. ___ horrified | 9. ___ sympathetic | 16. ___ afraid |
| 3. ___ responsible | 10. ___ proud | 17. ___ mystified |
| 4. ___ respectful | 11. ___ angry | 18. ___ embarrassed |
| 5. ___ indifferent | 12. ___ amused | 19. ___ jealous |
| 6. ___ envious | 13. ___ loyal | 20. ___ spiteful |
| 7. ___ contemptible | 14. ___ curious | 21. ___ astonished |

Which words describe how you feel about her? What other words and phrases would you use? How do you think Homer Barron felt about Miss Emily?

**13.** "A Rose for Emily" is told presumably by a person who lived in the town of Jefferson and knew Miss Emily. He begins the story with her funeral and ends with her death and what took place a few days after she was buried. In between, he relates a number of other events in Miss Emily's life. As would be true in real life, the storyteller is often vague or unclear about dates, and he does not relate the events in the exact order in which they occurred in Miss Emily's life. William Faulkner undoubtedly intended it to be this way, for Miss Emily's life, like her house, was "filled with dust and shadows."

It is important for the reader, however, to straighten out events. Fortunately, Faulkner is reported to have established Miss Emily's death at around 1924. With this date in mind, (a) number the list of events below in chronological order—the order in which they occurred in Miss Emily's life; (b) set as accurate a date as possible next to each event; and (c) identify Miss Emily's age at each event.

| Order | Date | Age | |
|---|---|---|---|
| 1. ___ | ___ | ___ | the birth of Emily Grierson |
| 2. ___ | ___ | ___ | the building of the Grierson house |

A Rose for Emily 231

| Order | Date | Age | |
|---|---|---|---|
| 3. ___ | ___ | ___ | the edict by Colonel Sartoris remitting Miss Emily's taxes |
| 4. ___ | ___ | ___ | the death of Miss Emily's father |
| 5. ___ | ___ | ___ | the deputation about the taxes |
| 6. ___ | ___ | ___ | the china-painting lessons |
| 7. ___ | ___ | ___ | the smell |
| 8. ___ | ___ | ___ | the arrival of Homer Barron |
| 9. ___ | ___ | ___ | the death of Colonel Sartoris |
| 10. ___ | ___ | ___ | the purchase of the arsenic |
| 11. ___ | ___ | ___ | the arrival of Miss Emily's cousins |
| 12. ___ | ___ | ___ | the purchase of gifts for Homer |
| 13. ___ | ___ | ___ | the death of Homer Barron |
| 14. ___ | ___ | ___ | the death of Emily Grierson |

Except for Miss Emily's birth, there are relevant details in the story connected with each of these events. List these details.

14. "A Rose for Emily" is a kind of mystery story, and, like most mysteries, you don't really understand everything that has happened until you get to the end of the story. Were you surprised when you discovered that Homer Barron was dead? Were you amazed, like the townspeople, when you discovered that Homer's body was in the bed in the room upstairs and you realized the significance of the "long strand of iron-gray hair" on the pillow? If you read the story a second time, however, you will find that Faulkner gives the reader clues as he goes along that suggest that Miss Emily was not psychologically normal and that forecast or prepare you for the events to come. For example, what do these clues suggest to you now?

1. She looked bloated, like a body long submerged in motionless water, and of that pallid hue. (lines 53-54)

2. We did not say she was crazy then. (line 140)

3. So she vanquished them, horse and foot, just as she had vanquished their fathers thirty years before about the smell. (lines 75-76)

Find other clues in the story that forecast Miss Emily's behavior. Explain the meaning of each clue.

Also, look for special clues that help you interpret the meaning of "the long strand of iron-gray hair" on the indented pillow. Where else does Faulkner mention the length and color of Miss Emily's hair? What do you think he wants you to understand in the last paragraph of the story? How do the earlier clues about Miss Emily's hair help you interpret that paragraph?

15. What kind of person was Miss Emily Grierson? Does Faulkner feel basically sympathetic toward her? Do you? Use details from the story to support your ideas.

    Think of situations for giving flowers, especially roses. Then, explain the significance of the title "A Rose for Emily." Does the title help you decide what Faulkner's attitude toward Miss Emily is?

16. The theme or main idea of a story usually gives us some understanding of the author's views about people and life. Write a paragraph in which you explain the theme of "A Rose for Emily." Discuss the sentences, phrases, and words in the story or in the title that you think reveal the theme or make it more obvious to the reader. You might begin your paragraph like this: *The theme of "A Rose for Emily" by William Faulkner is . . .*

17. Write a composition in which you discuss the psychological and social forces that explain the pattern of Miss Emily's life, her relationship with the townspeople and with Homer Barron, and her seclusion after his death. One way to organize your composition is as follows:

    1. In your opening sentence, identify the author and title of the story. Next, briefly describe the pattern of Miss Emily's life. Include a short comment on her position in the town of Jefferson, her relationship with Homer Barron, and the way she lived after Homer's death.

    2. Next, you can focus on some of the social forces that influenced her life. For example, how did the Griersons regard themselves and the townspeople, and how did the townspeople regard the Griersons? How did they view the fading and decay of the old aristocracy? In what ways does the deterioration of the "old order in the South" parallel Miss Emily's deterioration? To what extent is Miss Emily able to adjust to changing times?

What factors contribute to her isolation? How does she view herself as the last of the Griersons? Why does the narrator refer to her as "dear, inescapable, impervious, tranquil, and perverse"? (lines 272-273)

3. Now, identify some of the important psychological factors that influenced her attitudes and behavior. For instance, what was her relationship with her father like and how did his behavior toward Emily contribute to her isolation? To what extent was she deprived of normal human emotions and relationships as she was growing up? Is there any connection between her seclusion during her father's lifetime and her choice of Homer Barron as a lover after her father's death? What signs are there that she wants time to stand still? Why would she want to hold on to Homer forever?

4. You might now conclude with a brief summary of the main points you have developed in 2 and 3 above, stressing the ways in which the psychological and social forces in Miss Emily's life interact with or reinforce each other.

Another way to organize your composition would be start with a paragraph similar to the one described in 1 above, and then discuss *both* the psychological and sociological forces that interacted in Miss Emily's life to account for the way she lived and to explain her motivations, decisions, and behavior.

## _____ A LOOK AT THE LANGUAGE _____

1. Each sentence below has three words or phrases in parentheses. Circle the word or phrase that has a meaning opposite to the *italicized* word.

   1. Elizabeth is as *haughty* as Anne is (proud, beautiful, modest).

   2. One day Jim *vanished*. When he suddenly (reappeared, disappeared, recovered) two years later, everyone was greatly surprised.

   3. It is sometimes difficult to know how much information to *divulge* and how much information to (give out, keep to yourself, believe).

4. That silver bowl is *tarnished* and should be (used, polished, sold).

5. The first plan was received with strong *deprecation*, but the second met with unexpected (approval, opposition, silence).

6. Her *temerity* in speech and action was matched by her husband's extreme (aggressiveness, confidence, caution).

7. Their belief in the boy was *vindicated*. The community's belief in his guilt was (not justified, proved, never clear).

2. Faulkner's rich and varied vocabulary is part of his style. To see the effect of his vocabulary, read aloud the sentences below, substituting the words or phrases in parentheses for the *italicized* words and phrases. Compare the two versions. How do they differ in style and effect?

1. So she *vanquished* (defeated) them, *horse and foot* (every last one of them), just as she had *vanquished* (defeated) their fathers thirty years before.

2. But garages and cotton gins had *encroached* (moved in) and *obliterated* (wiped out) even the *august* (most prominent and important) names of that neighborhood.

3. A week later the mayor wrote her himself, offering to call or send his car for her, and received in reply a note on paper of *an archaic shape* (a size no longer in use), in a thin, flowing *calligraphy* (handwriting).

4. A *deputation* (delegation) *waited upon her* (came to see her), knocked at the door through which no visitor had *passed* (entered) since she *ceased* (stopped) giving china-painting lessons eight or ten years earlier.

5. Thus she passed from generation to generation—dear, *inescapable* (unforgettable), *impervious* (impossible to get close to), *tranquil* (quiet and peaceful), and *perverse* (difficult to get along with).

3. Faulkner's writing also contains rich sensory images. Describe what you see, hear, smell, or feel as you read each sentence from the story.

1. Her skeleton was small and spare; perhaps that was why what would have been merely plumpness in another was obesity in her.

2. Her voice was dry and cold.

3. "Poor Emily," the whispering began.... This behind their hands; rustling of craned silk and satin behind jalousies closed upon the sun of Sunday afternoon as the thin, swift clop-clop-clop of the matched team passed: "Poor Emily."

4. He [the Negro] talked to no one, probably not even to her, for his voice had grown harsh and rusty, as if from disuse.

5. She died in one of the downstairs rooms... her gray head propped on a pillow yellow and moldy with age and lack of sunlight.

6. ... and leaning forward, that faint and invisible dust dry and acrid in the nostrils, we saw a long strand of iron-gray hair.

4. Faulkner uses many comparisons in describing people and situations. For example, he compares Miss Emily to a monument that has toppled or fallen to the ground in these lines: "When Miss Emily Grierson died, our whole town went to her funeral: the men through a sort of respectful affection for a fallen monument..."

Explain the comparisons Faulkner makes in these statements about Miss Emily:

1. Her eyes, lost in the fatty ridges of her face, looked *like two small pieces of coal* pressed into a lump of dough...

2. ... her hair was cut short, making her look *like a girl,* with a vague resemblance to those angels in colored church windows—sort of tragic and serene.

3. She looked back at him [the druggist], erect, her face *like a strained flag.*

4. During the next few years it [her hair] grew grayer and grayer until it attained an even *pepper-and-salt* iron-gray...

5. ... at seventy-four it [her hair] was still that vigorous iron-gray, *like the hair of an active man.*

6. Now and then we would see her in one of the downstairs windows... *like the carven torso of an idol in a niche...*

Find other comparisons in the story. Tell what is being compared and describe the images or pictures these comparisons create for you.

5. The *italicized* words and phrases indicate devices that relate parts of the passage. Explain what is omitted, referred to, linked, or replaced, and tell how these devices function in relating ideas in the passage. (For further information on this type of exercise, see Steinbeck, "A Look at the Language," question 4, page 12.)

> The day after his death all the ladies prepared to call at the house and offer condolence and aid, as is our custom. Miss Emily met *them* at the door, dressed as usual and with no trace of grief on her face. *She* told them that her father was not dead. She *did that* for three days, with the ministers calling on her, and the doctors, trying to persuade her to let *them* dispose of *the body*. Just as *they* were about to resort to law and force, she broke down, and they buried her father quickly.
>
> We did not say she was crazy *then*. We believed *she* had to *do that*. We remembered all the young men her father had driven away, and we knew that with nothing left, she would have to cling to *that* which had robbed her, as people *will*.

Notice the pronoun *we* in the second paragraph. This paragraph comes at the end of section II, line 140. Is this the first time that *we* occurs? Who does *we* refer to?

6. Using the chronology you prepared in "A Look at the Ideas," question 13, write a short summary of Miss Emily's life. Compare your summary with those written by other students to see if you have included more or less the same material. Would someone who has not read the story know what it was about after reading your summary? What would the person miss?

# Index

# of

# Exercise Types

*The first number (in **boldface**) after an entry indicates the page number on which the type of exercise may be found; the second number (in parentheses) indicates the specific exercise on the page. The author's name that follows the numbers identifies the relevant story or essay. Although most major types of exercises are covered in this index, simple comprehension exercises are not included.*

## ————————— COMPOSITION AND WRITING —————————

*Note:* Under this heading, an asterisk (*) indicates composition assignments that include suggestions for organization.

Analysis:
   crosscultural, of family relationships, **19** (12)* Nin
   main character, behavior of, **232** (17)* Faulkner
   situation in an English-speaking country, **163** (11)* Rubin
   theme of story, with supporting evidence, **192** (15)* Williams

Classification, of a "tall" or "short" person, **55** (7) Hagopian

Comparison:
   of characters:
      for individual or universal characteristics, **133** (17) Tyler
      in Vonnegut and Hagopian stories, **56** (9)*
      in Williams and Hemingway stories, **193** (16)*
   crosscultural:
      of attitudes toward animals, **10** (14)* Steinbeck
      of family relationships, **19** (2)* Nin

_____ CROSSCULTURAL COMPARISONS _____

---

## INTERPRETATION

---

*Note:* Under this heading, types of exercises are indexed under the last name of the author; the names appear in alphabetical order. Some of the subentries include additional details following the exercise number.

Key phrases and sentences:
  meaning of, **187** (2, clues to social status
    of Olsons); **189** (9, use of word "bat-
    tle"); **189** (10, "in love with the sav-
    age brat"); **190** (13, "One goes on to
    the end")

significance of, **190** (11, the doctor's per-
    ceptions about Mathilda); **191** (14,
    the doctor's understanding of his
    behavior and the author's attitude
    toward use of force)

## ─────────────── ORGANIZATION AND MECHANICS ───────────────

Cohesive devices:
  omission, reference, linking, substitu-
    tion, **12** (4) Steinbeck (with explana-
    tion); **22** (6,7) Nin; **33** (3) Farb; **47** (2)
    Vonnegut; **58** (3) Hagopian; **81** (2)
    Sagan; **102** (4) Saroyan; **135** (3)
    Tyler; **145** (2) Mead; **165** (3) Rubin;
    **178** (2) Hemingway; **195** (3)
    Williams; **212** (3) Thomas/
    McConnell; **236** (5) Faulkner
  repetition, effect of, **44** (4), **45** (6) Von-
    negut; **59** (4) Hagopian; **69** (2,3)
    Mannes

Deduction/induction:
  development, order of, **84** (8,9) Sagan
  modes, description of, **72** (10) Mannes
  thesis/main point, identification of, **66** (6)
    Mannes; **84** (8) Sagan

Development:
  paragraph, **33** (4) Farb; **213** (5) Thomas/
    McConnell
  presentation, order of, **84** (4) Sagan; **146**
    (4) Mead

Main ideas:
  finding, **166** (4) Rubin; **213** (5) Thomas/
    McConnell
  paraphrasing, **213** (5) Thomas/McConnell
  identifying thesis/main point, **66** (6)
    Mannes; **84** (8) Sagan; **161** (5) Rubin;
    **213** (5) Thomas/McConnell

Paragraph:
  development, **33** (4) Farb
  model, **34** (5) Farb

Punctuation:
  dialogues, **103** (5) Saroyan
  quotations, use of and accuracy, **81** (4), **83**
    (5) Sagan

Quotations:
  accuracy, **83** (5) Sagan
  direct quotations and reporting quoted
    information, comparison of, **83** (7)
    Sagan
  punctuation of, **81** (4), **83** (5) Sagan

Thesis/main point, **66** (6) Mannes; **84** (8) Sa-
    gan; **161** (5) Rubin; **213** (5)
    Thomas/McConnell

## ───────────────────── STYLE ─────────────────────

Academic style:
  characteristics of, **70** (5) Mannes
  elimination of emotional tone, **70** (6)
    Mannes
  inclusion of subject and predicate, **69** (4)
    Mannes

Author's style:
  adaptation to readers, **213** (4) Thomas/
    McConnell
  comparison with paraphrases, **23** (8) Nin;
    **48** (4) Vonnegut; **59** (5) Hagopian;

    **179** (4) Hemingway; **195** (5), **196** (6)
    Williams; **234** (2) Faulkner
  in dialogue, written vs. spoken, **180** (5)
    Hemingway
  expansion of dialogue, **11** (3) Steinbeck

Deduction/induction:
  explanation of, **72** (10) Mannes, **84** (8)
    Sagan
  summaries of main points, **84** (9) Sagan

Imagery:
  comparison (similes and metaphors), ef-

Imagery (*cont.*)

    fect of, **61** (7) Hagopian; **235** (4)
       Faulkner

description, use of, **173** (4) Hemingway

dialogue, use of speaker identification
    tags, **103** (5) Saroyan

future events, clues to, **231** (14) Faulkner

narrator's viewpoint, **49** (5) Vonnegut;
    **105** (10) Saroyan

paradox, effect of, **58** (2) Hagopian; **104**
    (7) Saroyan

sensory images, effect of, **234** (3) Faulk-
    ner

special effects, words for, **189** (8,9), **196**
    (6) Williams

Paragraph length, **23** (9) Nin

Questions:
    effectiveness of, **70** (7) Mannes
    use of, **65** (3) Mannes

Rhythm, in prose and poetry, **197** (8)
    Williams

Sentence length, effect of, **104** (8) Saroyan

Translation:
    effect of, **30** (2) Farb
    into English speech, **103** (6) Saroyan

## VOCABULARY

Adaptation to readers, **213** (4) Thomas/
    McConnell

Abstract/concrete words and phrases, **60** (6)
    Hagopian

Adjectives, used in description, **7** (2) Stein-
    beck; **17** (4) Nin; **44** (3) Vonnegut; **54**
    (5) Hagopian; **98** (3) Saroyan; **129** (5)
    Tyler; **142** (4) Mead; **173** (3)
    Hemingway; **188** (6) Williams; **230**
    (12) Faulkner

Antonyms, **11** (2) Steinbeck; **21** (3) Nin; **102**
    (2) Saroyan; **134** (1) Tyler; **233** (1)
    Faulkner

Connotative meaning, **17** (2), **21** (5) Nin; **30**
    (1) Farb; **54** (5) Hagopian

Conversation, converted to reported
    speech, **48** (3) Vonnegut

Definition of terms, **141** (2) Mead; **160** (1)
    Rubin; **211** (1) Thomas/McConnell

Idioms/paraphrase, **102** (3) Saroyan

Meaning in context, **10** (1) Steinbeck; **20** (1)
    Nin; **178** (1) Hemingway

Paraphrase, **102** (3) Saroyan; **145** (3) Mead;
    **228** (6) Faulkner

Synonyms and substitutions, **21** (4) Nin; **31**
    (1) Farb; **47** (1) Vonnegut; **65** (2), **68**
    (1) Mannes; **134** (2) Tyler; **194** (1)
    Williams
    inappropriate word, **144** (1) Mead
    for special effect, **32** (2) Farb
    with two-word verbs, **212** (2) Thomas/
      McConnell

Translation:
    effect of, **30** (3) Farb
    problems, **30** (4,5,6,7) Farb

Word forms, **56** (1) Hagopian; **80** (1) Sagan;
    **101** (1) Saroyan; **195** (2) Williams
    nonstandard, **195** (4) Williams
    nouns (only), **20** (2) Nin; **164** (1,2) Rubin